IMAGES
of America

GRAND ENCAMPMENT

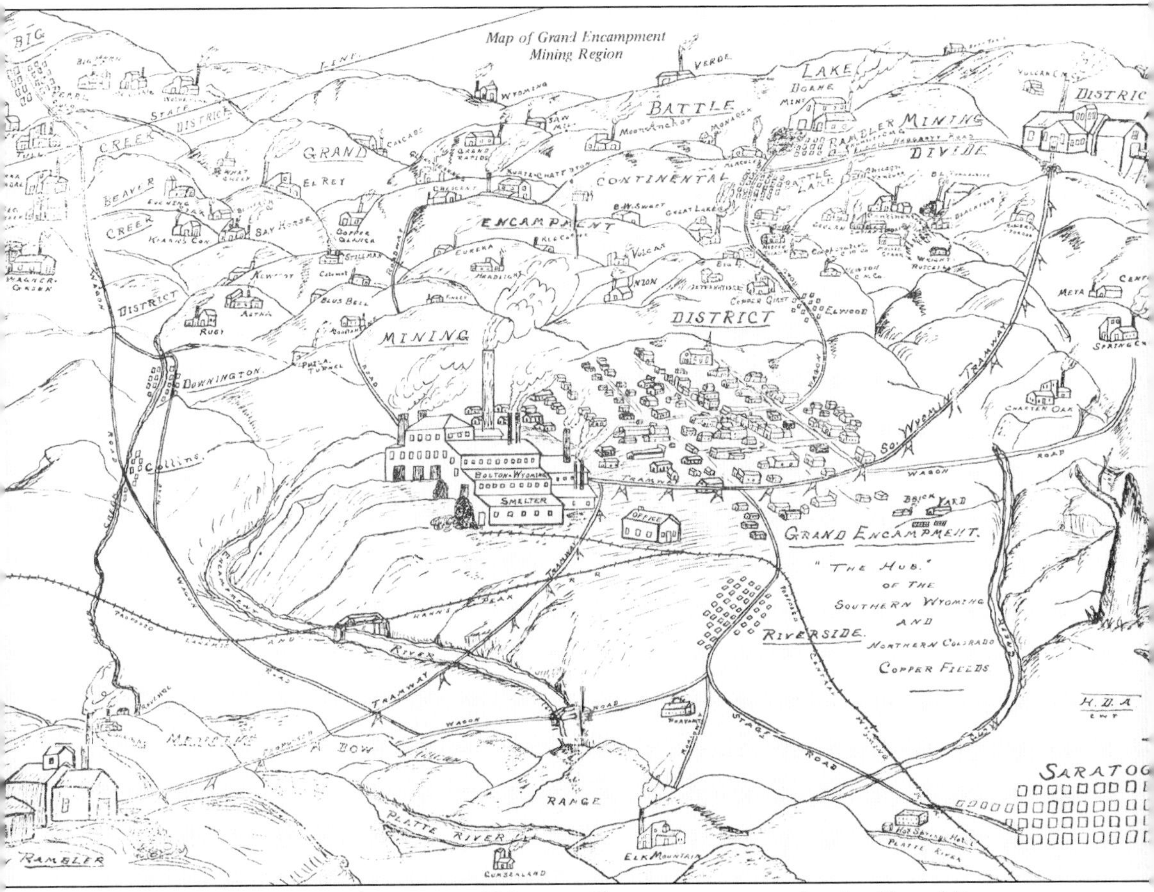

Created for the National Register of Historic Places nomination for the Grand Encampment Mining District, this map represents the district and general area, including Grand Encampment, the smelter, Southern Wyoming Tramway, Ferris-Haggarty (Rudefeha) Mine, Elwood, Battle Lake, Rambler, and Riverside (Doggett). The map depicts the Big Creek Mining District and the Beaver Creek Mining District and is not to scale. (Courtesy of GEM/Wyoming State Historic Preservation Office.)

On the Cover: Owned and operated by Mary Bohn, the Bohn Hotel advertised as the "Neatest and Best hotel in Southern Wyoming." Indeed, the establishment was elegantly furnished and could attract a crowd, such as this group of residents who may have been celebrating Independence Day. (Courtesy of GEM/Grace Kuntzman Healey.)

IMAGES
of America

GRAND ENCAMPMENT

Candy Moulton and Terry A. Del Bene

ARCADIA
PUBLISHING

ISBN 978-0-7385-8882-7

Published by Arcadia Publishing
Charleston, South Carolina

Printed in the United States of America

Library of Congress Control Number: 2011928029

For all general information, please contact Arcadia Publishing:
Telephone 843-853-2070
Fax 843-853-0044
E-mail sales@arcadiapublishing.com
For customer service and orders:
Toll-Free 1-888-313-2665

Visit us on the Internet at www.arcadiapublishing.com

This book is dedicated to the people who have called Grand Encampment home: Native Americans, fur trappers, ranchers, miners, loggers, and townspeople. We also wish to dedicate this book to Clifford Duncan, who reminds us that in the puzzle of life, eventually all the pieces tend to look alike.

Contents

Acknowledgments		6
Introduction		7
1.	Once Upon a Time	9
2.	Cowboy Up	17
3.	Industrial Revolutions	43
4.	The Good, the Bad, and the Friendly	73
5.	The Corners of Our World	109

Acknowledgments

We appreciate the Grand Encampment Museum for giving us permission to use their excellent collection of photographs for this volume. We have also selected photographs from the collections of the Wyoming State Archives and the Department of State Parks and Cultural Resources and appreciate permission from Nancy Anderson to use photographs from the Lora Nichols Collection. Betty Herring Vyvey provided photographs from her personal collection and gave us valuable research assistance. Candy Moulton also used her personal photographic collection, which includes both historic images and her own photographs. All images from the Grand Encampment Museum are credited GEM with the specific donor or collection identified when known.

We have researched this volume in the collections of the Grand Encampment Museum, Carbon County Museum, Saratoga Historical & Cultural Center, American Heritage Center at the University of Wyoming, and in the holdings of the Wyoming State Archives. We have used our own prior publications as sources, including *The Donner Party Cookbook* by Terry A. Del Bene; Candy Moulton's books *The Grand Encampment: Settling the High Country*, *Roadside History of Wyoming*, and *Forts, Fights & Frontier Sites: Wyoming's Historic Places*; as well as the project we recently coedited with James A. Crutchfield, *The Settlement of America: Encyclopedia of Westward Expansion from Jamestown to the Closing of the Frontier.*

Because we have benefitted from their efforts, we must recognize several individuals who have researched, written about, and therefore preserved the history of Grand Encampment: Vera and Bert Oldman, Hila Parkison, Nancy Anderson, James Ehrenberger, R. Richard Perue, Grace Kuntzman Healey, Carol Kuntzman Herring, Starley Talbott, Penny Walters, Kate Moon, Mary Martin, Rick Martin, Betty Merrill, Lillian Barnes, Harry Robert Herring, Mark Dunning, Justin Howe, Fred Lorenz, Linda Hammer, Gay Day Alcorn, Grace Vyvey Gregory, Mark Junge, Elva Evans, Lora Nichols, R.D. Martin, and the dozens of volunteers at the Grand Encampment Museum through the decades.

INTRODUCTION

The wind, the sun, and the water have worked their wills upon this land. They were here before the dinosaurs, the mammoth, the bison, the elk, and the people. These primal forces continue their artistic sculpting of the hills and valleys. It will always be so.

For millions of years, the story of Grand Encampment was a tale of nature. The environment evolved through time and the current ecosystem is a relative newcomer to this land. Roughly 11,000 years ago, humans became part of the equation. The earliest known inhabitants of the Grand Encampment area were nomadic hunters and gatherers skilled in survival. The hunting of Ice Age megafauna was but a part of the economic pursuits of these earliest inhabitants, the Paleo-Indians, who exploited small game, fish, and plants as well.

With the passing of the great herds of megafauna, the free-roaming inhabitants are thought to have focused more upon making maximum use of local resources. This pattern continued for thousands of years with little change, though horticulture and pottery were added to the technology of the area's occupants. It is thought that early Shoshonean speakers, ancestors of the Utes and Shoshones, migrated to the area.

Early native people traveled through the area following trade routes that connected the villages along the Missouri River with trading centers in the southwest of today's New Mexico and other areas in present southwest Wyoming.

For centuries, people have been coming to the Grand Encampment area during the summer to hunt, fish, and enjoy the cool weather in the mountains as they explored along the Continental Divide. Early people hunted, gathered, fished, camped, visited sacred places, and blazed the first trails through the area.

During the early 19th century, trappers took advantage of the cold waters and abundant wildlife as they gathered pelts for markets farther east. Initially, they came in small numbers mainly seeking furs. Those trappers and traders held a rendezvous every year somewhere in the intermountain West to trade furs for supplies. In 1838, the main mountain-man rendezvous was in what is now central Wyoming, but a smaller gathering later took place that year in the area that was called Camp le Grande by the French-Canadian trappers; the name for the area became the Grand Encampment.

The trickle turned into a steady stream of emigrants traveling upon the overland trail corridors farther north. With the start of the California gold rush in 1849, the stream became a torrent. A new route was blazed through the area in 1850 by a California-bound Cherokee wagon company. The Cherokee Trail opened the countryside for more permanent settlement. Thousands followed the narrow ribbon navigating through a sea of grasses, sage, and trees on a path that served as a communications artery for years.

Not until the late 1870s did the emigrants come to the area to stay. The first were cattlemen who recognized the value of this area to raise livestock. Soon, other ranchers and homesteaders moved in and began the first major cash industry in the Grand Encampment Valley: agriculture.

From the first ranches established in 1879 until the present, this country has produced cattle. Because of the high elevation, over 7,300 feet, ranchers realized the need to raise hay to feed the livestock during the long winters. Homesteaders grubbed sagebrush and planted alfalfa, hay, and grains that they could use for winter fodder for their herds. A great livestock industry and the traditions associated with it flourished. This industry remains a mainstay of the local economy.

Already, men (and a few women) were building cabins in the mountains and establishing camps where all winter they cut trees, hewing them into railroad ties. These were transported down the streams and rivers for use in construction of railroads. Timbering became the second major industry of the area, and it continues to the present.

In 1896, Edward Haggarty found a copper ore deposit in the Sierra Madre mountain range. The following year, he established the first major copper mine in the Grand Encampment Copper District. This brought a new flood of people to the area and spawned the town of Grand Encampment, formally organized in 1897. (The town is incorporated as Grand Encampment, although the post office and modern maps use only the name *Encampment.*)

The mining operations spawned other significant communities (most of which are ghost towns) and were an economic bonanza for a 10-year period from 1897 to 1908. Although shorter lived, mining became the third major industry. From the beginning, transportation was a critical issue. The mines in the mountains required extensive freighting operations to haul goods and supplies to mine sites. Towns that developed to support mining included Elwood, Battle, Rambler, Copperton, and Dillon, which are now virtually ghosts. Riverside (formerly called Doggett) remains a vital community. The freight wagons were never empty, for when they returned to Grand Encampment, they were filled with ore, which had to be freighted another 40 miles to the railroad at Walcott Junction.

The transportation hurdle of moving ore from the most productive mine in the district—the Ferris-Haggarty—was solved in 1902 with construction of the 16-mile-long Southern Wyoming Tramway. Simultaneous with the tramway came construction of smelting works at Grand Encampment. This made it possible to refine the ore for market, producing blister copper that was 99 percent pure. There remained the obstacle of getting the copper to markets, which required that 40-mile, one-way haul to Walcott.

Promoters and mining company owners began discussing rail service to Grand Encampment shortly after the first load of ore was recovered. It took until 1908 to build a line that served the area, and by then, falling copper prices, untimely fires, and other business issues had burst the Grand Encampment copper bubble.

The people and the places that make up the community are integral to the culture, and certainly, Grand Encampment had some interesting characters and unique places. The hardy folk who live and work in the Grand Encampment area—from its earliest development to the present—are captured in photographs from all eras and in places throughout the valley.

Although people learned to live in the high-altitude valley year round, the place has always been most attractive during summer and fall when visitors from around the world come to experience the recreational opportunities in the Medicine Bow–Routt National Forest with its four wilderness areas (Huston Park, Encampment River, Savage Run, and Platte River). The Continental Divide National Scenic Trail attracts hikers and horseback explorers. The mountain streams, lakes, and rivers tempt anglers, and the abundant wildlife was a draw for hunters in the 19th century and remains so today. Many visitors come for the snow, exploring trails and mountain areas on cross-country skis, snowshoes, and snow machines.

Visitors can learn about the customs and culture of this area by taking part in annual festivals, including the Sierra Madre Winter Carnival in February, Woodchoppers Jamboree and Rodeo in June, the Ranchers Family Camp Meeting and Grand Encampment Cowboy Gathering (both in July), the Chug and Tug Tractor Club Copper Days Festival in September, and the Grand Encampment Opera Company melodramas that are periodically presented at the Historic Grand Encampment Opera House. All can learn more about the history of the region by visiting the Grand Encampment Museum.

One

Once Upon a Time

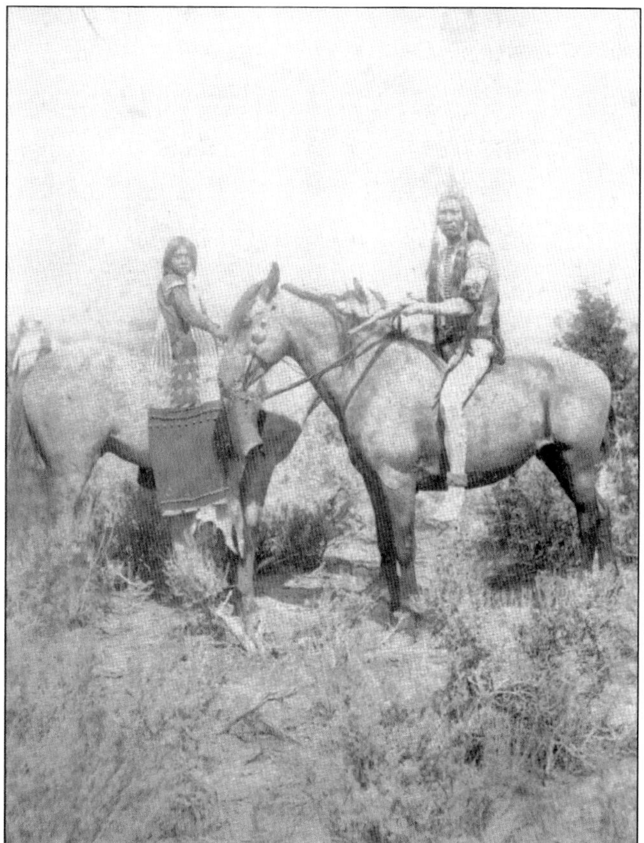

For thousands of years, the Grand Encampment area was inhabited by Indian groups. Coming first on foot and by the 18th century on horseback, nomadic bands of hunters and gatherers harvested the abundant game, fish, and plants. This Ute warrior and his bride have a horse collar similar to one on display in the Grand Encampment Museum. This photograph is by John K. Hillers. (Courtesy of US Library of Congress/ National Archives, 43-0797a.)

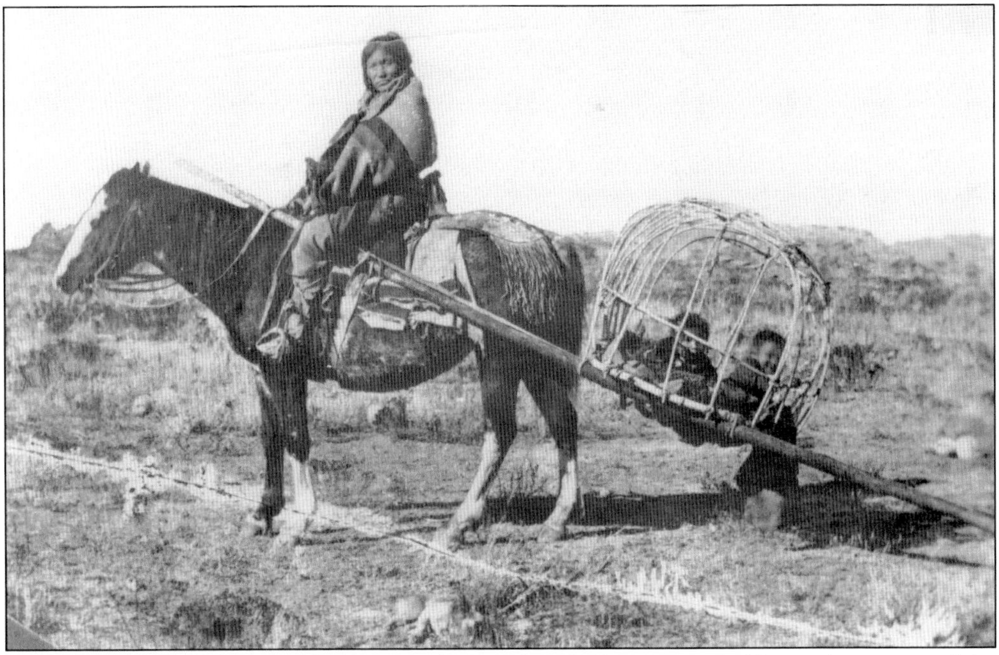

The introduction of the horse from Europe had profound effects upon the Native Americans of the Great Plains. Mobility increased efficiency and allowed for increases in population. This woman is using a travois for hauling children, but it could be used to carry possessions and supplies as well. (Courtesy of Wyoming State Archives, Department of State Parks and Cultural Resources.)

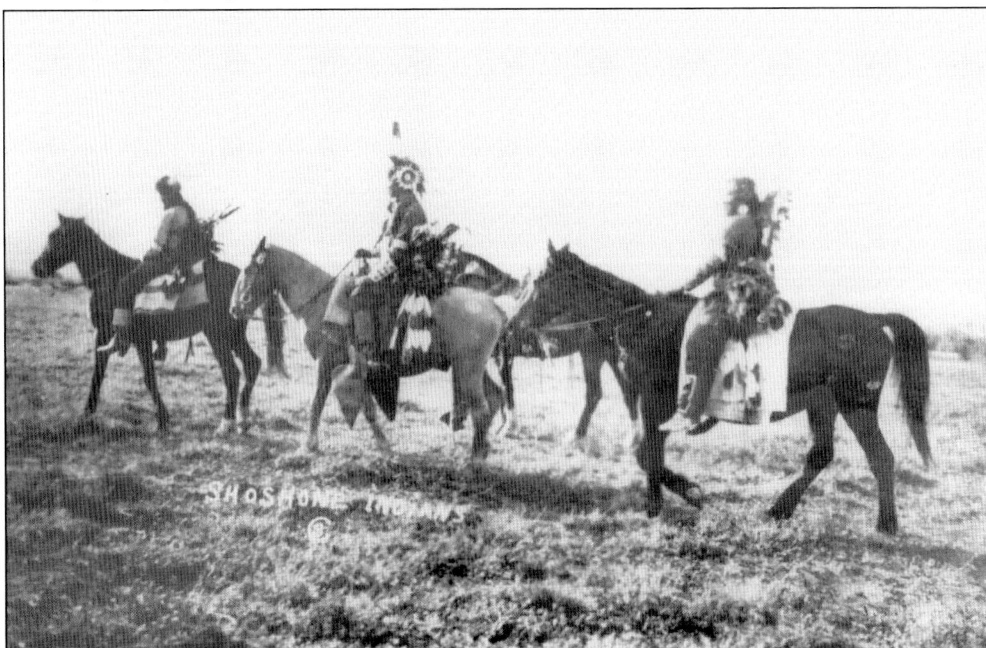

The Encampment Valley was within the overlapping territory of several powerful Indian nations. The area was used mainly in the summer by Shoshones, Utes, and Arapahos. This image is of Shoshones. (Courtesy of Wyoming State Archives, Department of State Parks and Cultural Resources.)

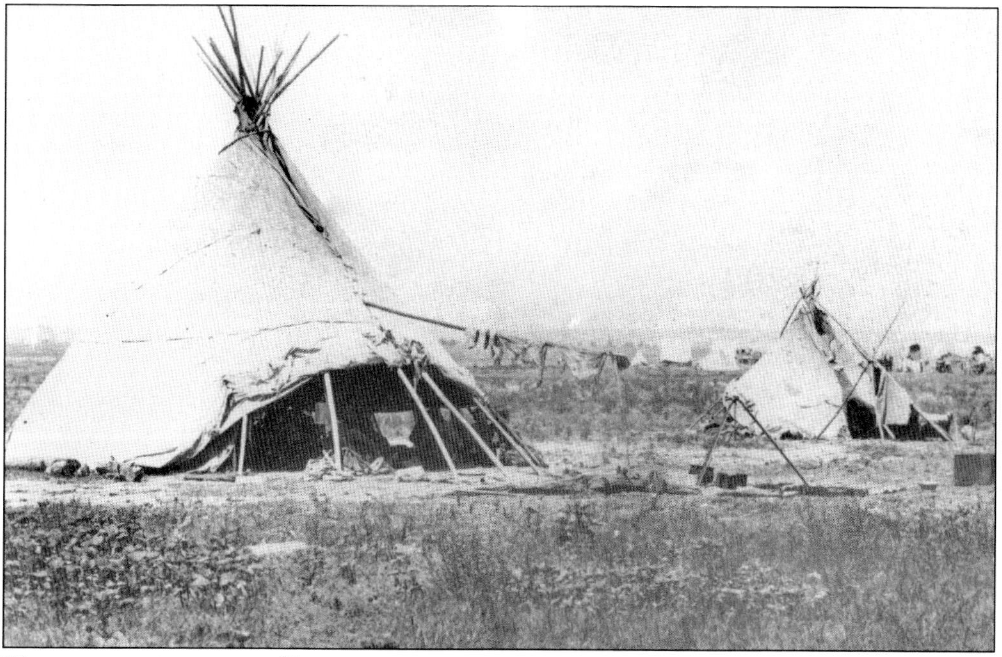

The tepee, or tipi, was used by numerous Plains Indian nations and is one of the most successful tent designs ever conceived. Sturdy tepees could be rapidly erected or taken down in a short period of time, giving the owners great flexibility. Here, the base of a tipi has been lifted to provide better ventilation. Stones once placed around tepees are still visible in the Encampment area. (Courtesy of Wyoming State Archives, Department of State Parks and Cultural Resources.)

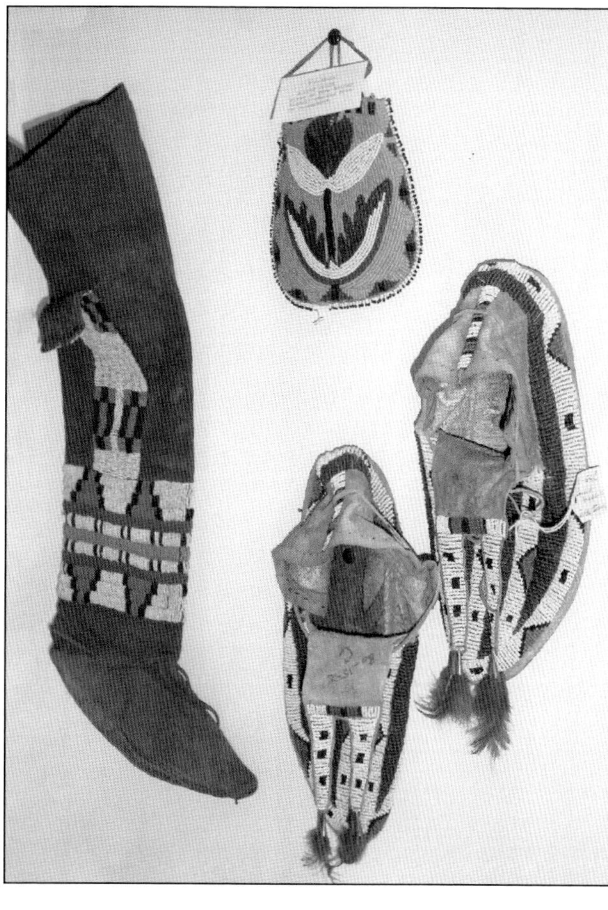

These moccasins are of Ute manufacture. The thread is commercial, not sinew. The bag's beading pattern is Shoshone, a tribe that uses flower designs in beadwork, especially roses. The beading is laid out five or six at a time, then tied down. French trappers were in the Encampment area in the 1880s and married into the local tribes. Indian women traveled with their husbands and continued making traditional items. (Courtesy of Candy Moulton.)

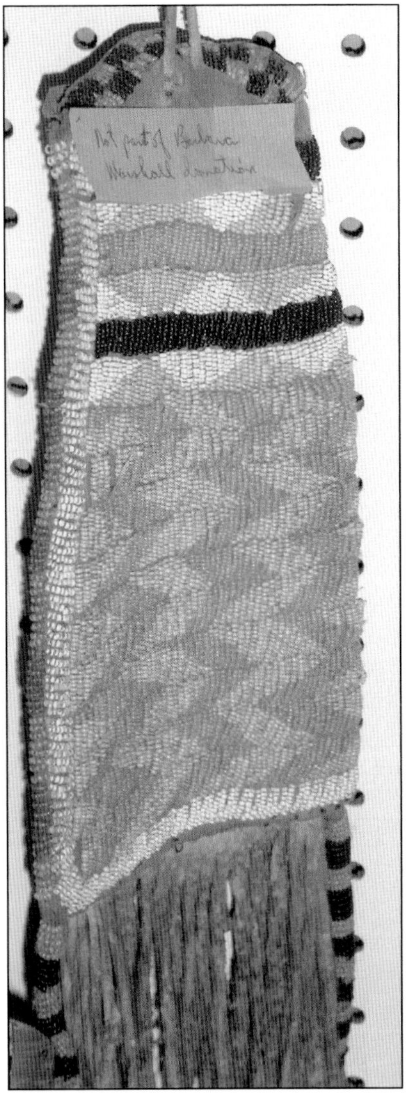

Even simple items can tell a story. This style of bag was used for carrying important ceremonial items, such as tobacco, red ochre, antelope horn, or rabbit fur. It has brass tinklers and wood-dyed thread. The cross design in the beadwork is the style seen in Ute items. The Ute pattern is different on the front and back sides of the bag. (Courtesy of Candy Moulton.)

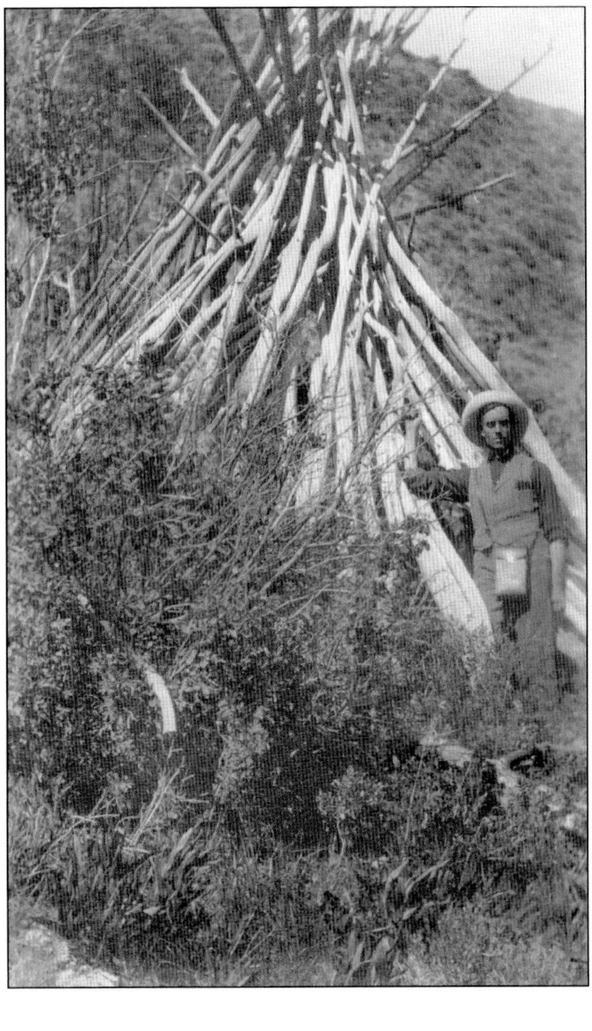

Ira Casteel, co-owner of the Big Creek Ranch, stands beside an abandoned eagle-trapping lodge. Such structures often are mistaken for tepees. Eagle-trapping lodges were used in the seasonal rituals related to the capturing of these revered birds. Eagles represent spiritually powerful elements, and their capture by American Indians requires careful preparation of the participants, who usually pray and take sweat baths. (Courtesy of GEM/Big Creek Ranch Album.)

Explorer John C. Fremont "the Pathfinder" skirted north of the Encampment Valley in 1842 while traveling west but passed through the area again in June 1844. On June 14, 1844, he camped about eight miles southeast of the site that became Encampment on a stream he named Beaver Dam Creek. Fremont rode his political connections and fame as an explorer to become a general and presidential candidate. (Courtesy of Wyoming State Archives, Department of State Parks and Cultural Resources.)

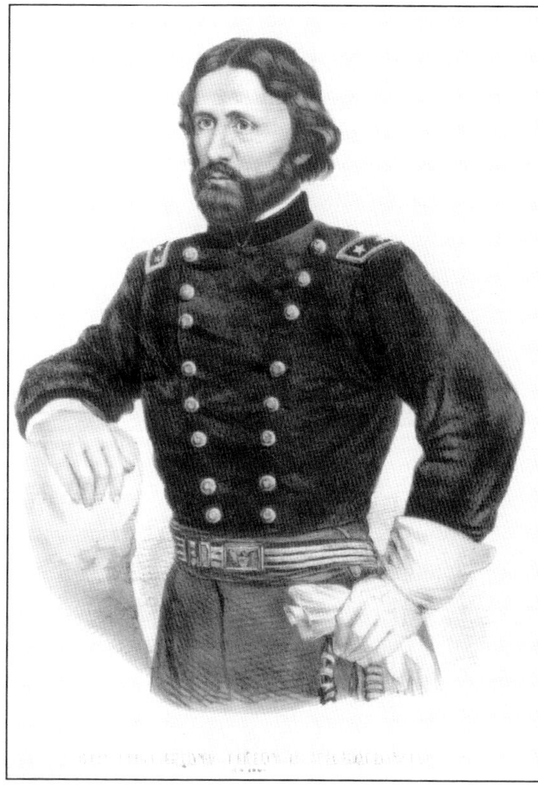

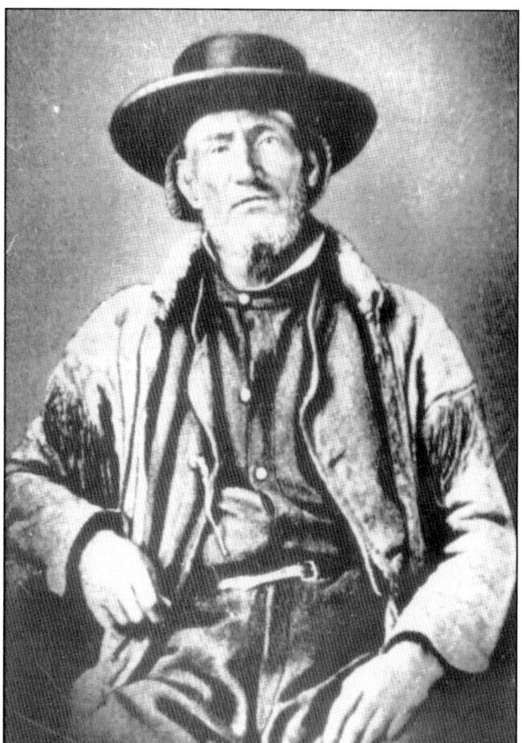

Jim Bridger, traveler and mountaineer, did his share of exploration near the Encampment Valley. Working with Jim Baker, the young Bridger learned much about the area and its resources. Fellow mountain men occasionally gathered at Camp le Grande (Grand Encampment). These men paved the way for others to follow. (Courtesy of Wyoming State Archives, Department of State Parks and Cultural Resources.)

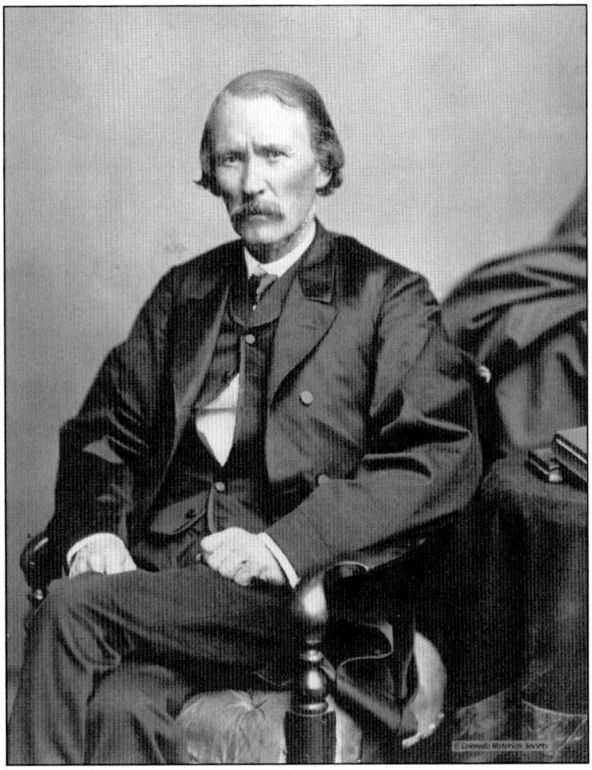

Famous mountaineer and infamous gunman Christopher "Kit" Carson guided John C. Fremont through the Encampment Valley in 1844. Their party traveled east, crossing the Continental Divide on June 13, 1844, and traversing the east flank of the Sierra Madre range. Fremont wrote that they had their noon meal "on Potter's fork—a clear and swift stream, forty yards wide, and in many plases deep enough to swim our animals." (Courtesy of Library of Congress Prints and Photographs Division.)

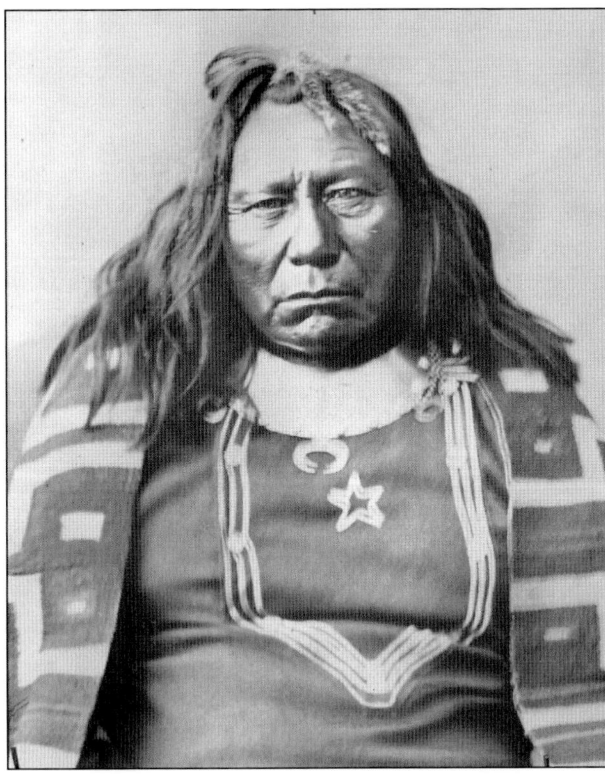

A Comanche by birth, Colorow was one of the Northern Ute chiefs who regularly spent time in the area around Grand Encampment. In the 1879 war, Colorow led an attack on the homestead of Robert "Bud" Ellsworth at Big Creek. Bud hid under floorboards in a dugout but almost suffocated as the Indians set fire to the structure. In 1888, Colorow's men defeated a posse on the White River near Rangley, Colorado. (Courtesy of GEM.)

This marker comes from a site five miles southeast of Encampment where it was placed after miners Frank Marrion, Joe Brun, and John Scott were killed along the Cherokee Trail. Following their burial by John H. Mullison and Tom Castle, the hand-carved stone was placed at the site. Although the original stone was removed and donated to the Grand Encampment Museum, a replacement was set at the gravesite, which is on private land. (Courtesy of Candy Moulton.)

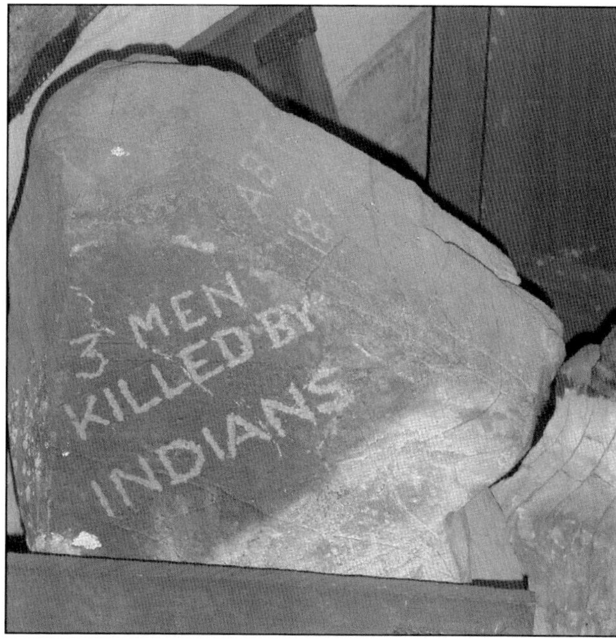

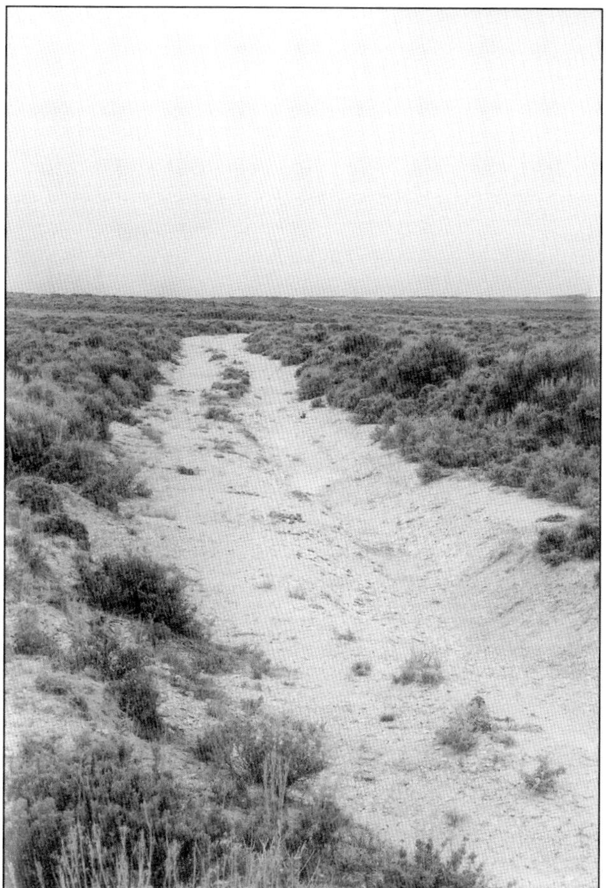

In 1850, mixed parties of Cherokee Indians and non-Indians living in Indian Territory (Oklahoma) joined the flood of gold-seekers bound for the California goldfields. These Argonauts avoided the cholera-infested wagon trails by blazing a series of southerly routes linking the Santa Fe Trail with Fort Bridger. Collectively, these routes became known as the Cherokee Trail and served as vital routes for commerce and settlement. One of these routes goes through the Encampment Valley. (Courtesy of Candy Moulton.)

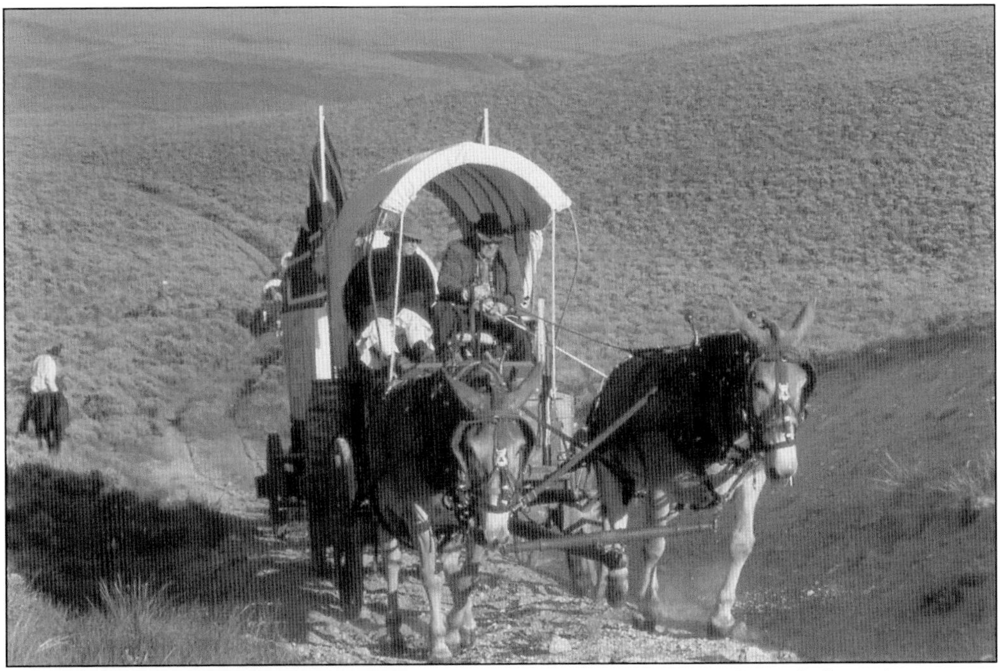

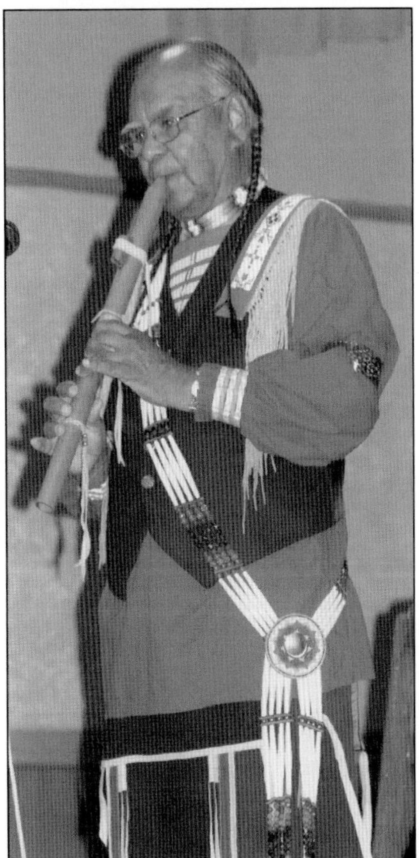

This is a 2003 re-creation of travel along the Cherokee Trail through the Encampment Valley. Many wagons during the 1850 journey were pulled by teams of oxen, although some companies had mules, which enabled more rapid hauling. Intact trail ruts left by the passage of thousands of wagons, people, and animals still can be visited today. (Courtesy of Candy Moulton.)

Native American music and voices are still heard in the Encampment Valley. Here, Northern Ute tribal elder and recognized tribal history expert Clifford Duncan recalls the not-so-distant past. Tribal members honor their ancestors' memories and educate the public through participation in the many cultural events held in the valley. According to Duncan, "We are still here. It's good to be back." (Courtesy of Candy Vyvey Moulton Collection.)

Two

Cowboy Up

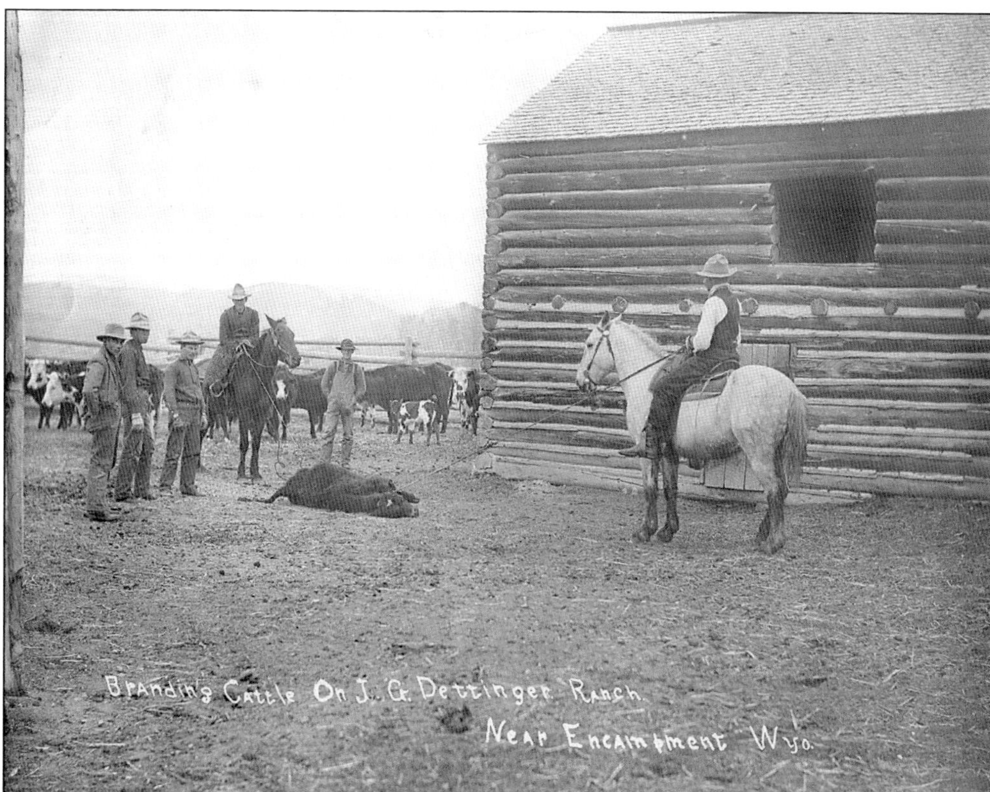

James G. Dettinger (on white horse) holds a calf rope tight during a branding on his ranch. Roy Dettinger is on the bay horse. The third man from the left is Andy Wagoner, a neighbor. It still is common practice for neighbors to assist with ranch work when a crew is needed. In 2011, Randy Boykin owned what had been the Dettinger Ranch. (Courtesy of GEM.)

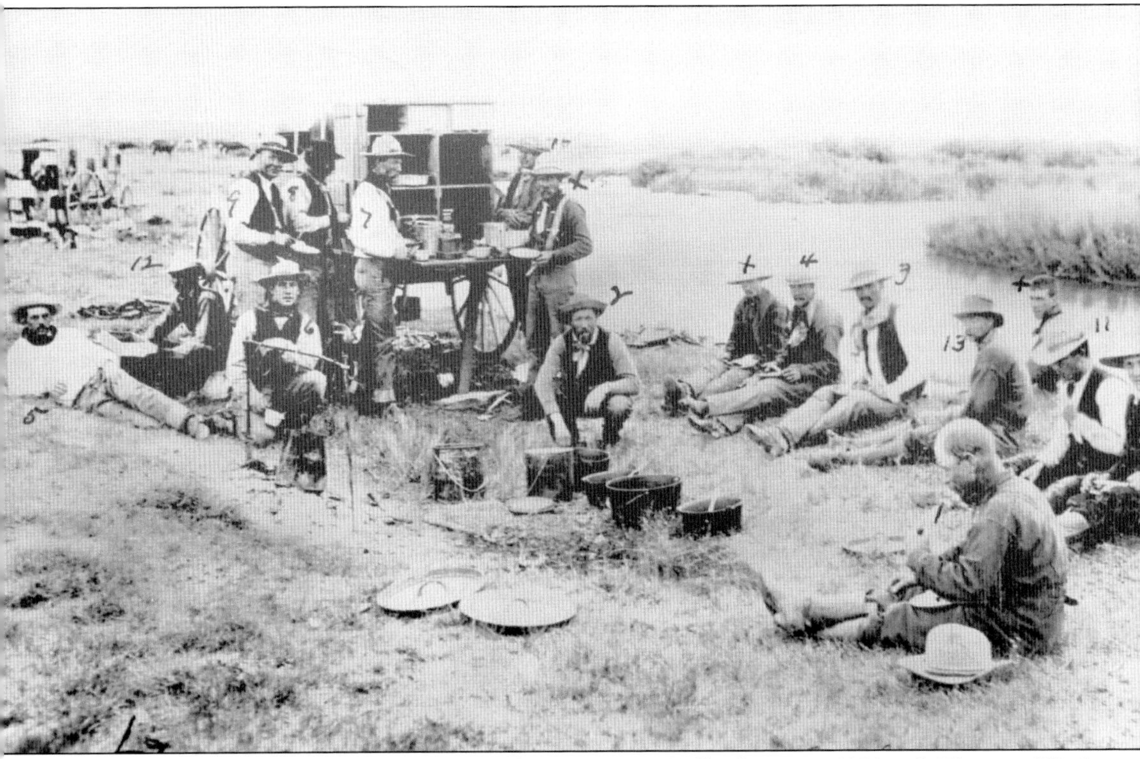

The earliest cattle ranching in the Grand Encampment Valley began in 1881 with Thomas ("Red Tom"), Lewis, William, and Obadiah Swan. This 1884 image shows the Hash Knife Chuckwagon and the L7 Cattle Company outfit (owned by cousins of the Encampment Swans). The image lists the ranch the men worked for if known and the number on the image. From left to right are (5) Frank Cunningham—L7, (12) Billy Monroe—Hash Knife, (9) Edd Rice (standing), (6) George Meason (kneeling)—Saratoga, (8) Vicente Ortega (standing), (7) John Bicktold—Texas, (10) Pete Wilson—L7, (X, standing at wagon) unidentified, (2) Mike Quealey—Elk Mountain, (X, left of No. 4) John Kuykendall, (4) Al Watkins—Hash Knife, (3) Henry "Rooster" Wilson—L7, (13) Edd Mathison—L7, (X, no hat) unidentified, (11) John Wilcox—foreman of the L7, (X, right of No. 11) Rubie Rivera, and (1) Charles Wilcox—L7. (Courtesy of GEM/Mamie Brown Marshall.)

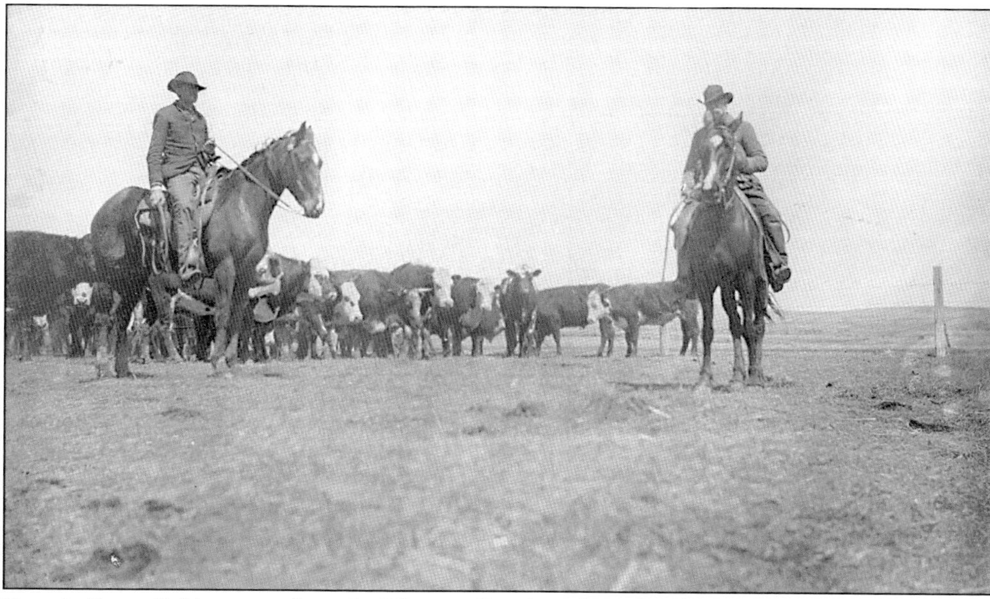

Dennie Stout (left) was working for Thomas Stanley when the above photograph was taken of them moving cattle in 1905. Johnny Calley was the foreman for the Bar H Ranch and may be the man standing behind the cow with hands on his hips (below) watching as one cowboy does the branding on an animal that has been roped and tied. While the cowboys could throw and hold a smaller calf by hand, with a large animal, such as this one, it was necessary to rope and tie the legs together. (Both, courtesy of GEM/Florence Ellis.)

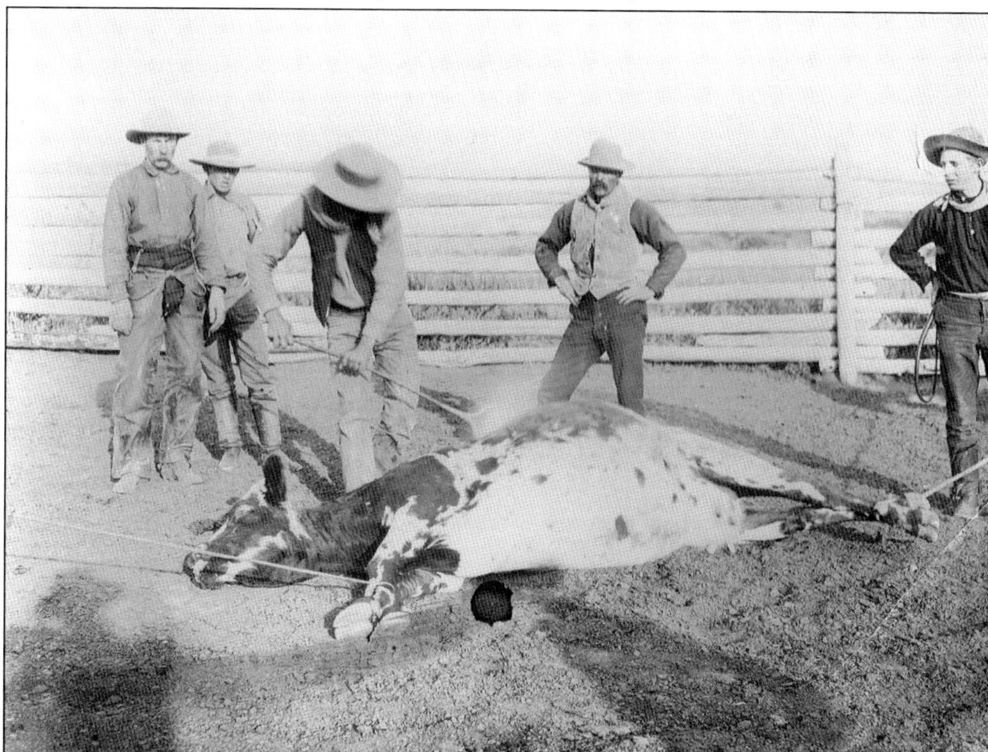

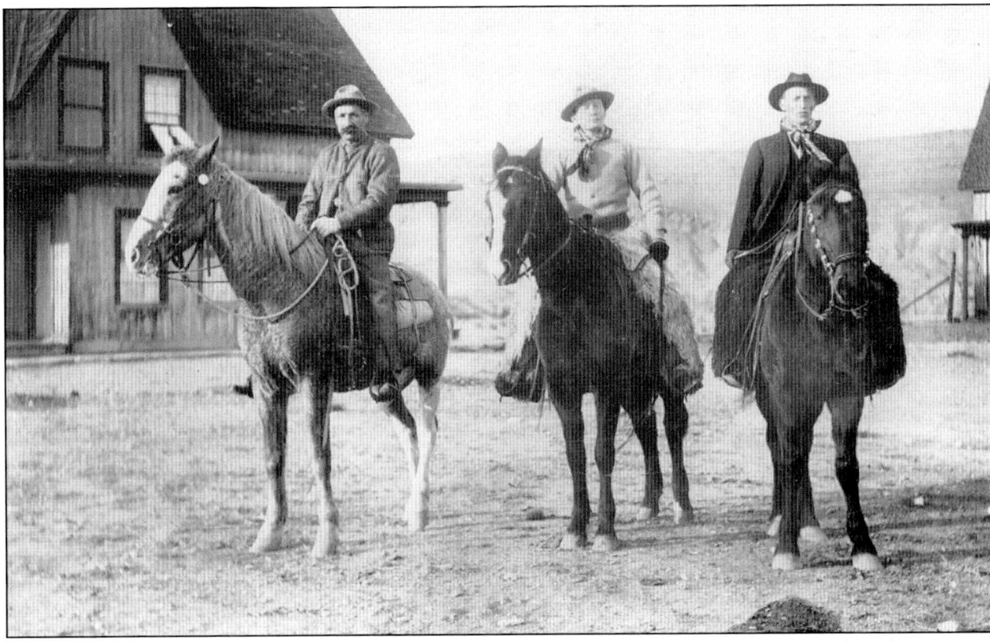

Malcolm Carlson (left) was straw boss for Cosgriff Sheep Company of Rawlins. When he was not teaching at Fort Steele, J.B. Owens (middle) worked for Cosgriff, and Ernest Bogren (right) was a blacksmith for Cosgriff. Mrs. Carlson wrote on the postcard photograph, "This is the bunch I cook for 3 times a day. . . . note the curtain blowing out the window Ernest left his window open Darn him." (Courtesy of GEM/John Marshall.)

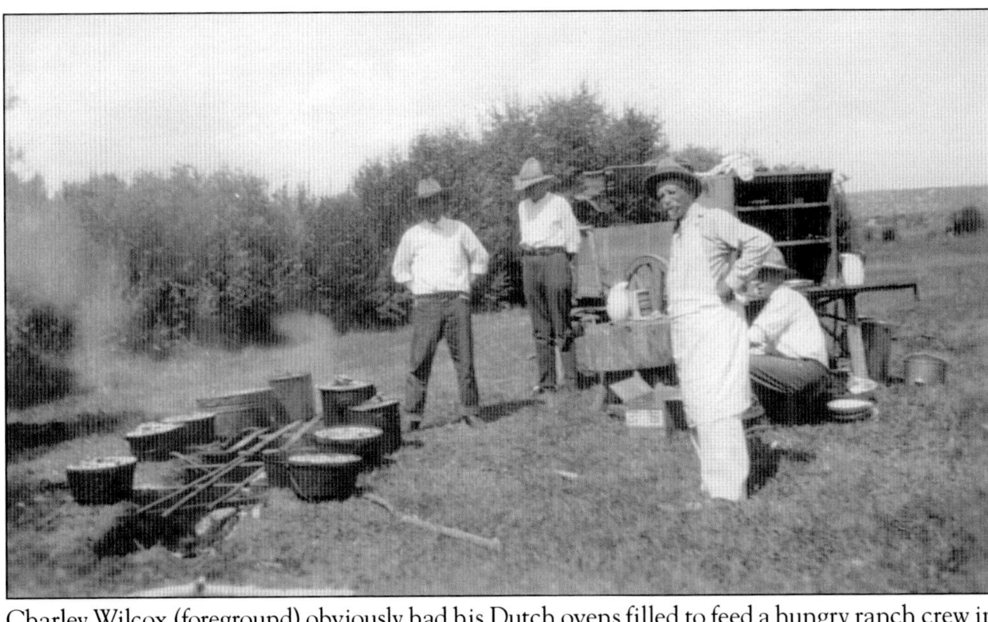

Charley Wilcox (foreground) obviously had his Dutch ovens filled to feed a hungry ranch crew in August 1926. Wilcox made a reputation for himself driving the stagecoach from Walcott Junction to Grand Encampment. As often occurred, when men were older and no longer as actively driving freight or stage teams, they took to assisting ranches by driving the chuckwagon on roundups and then doing the cooking. (Courtesy of GEM.)

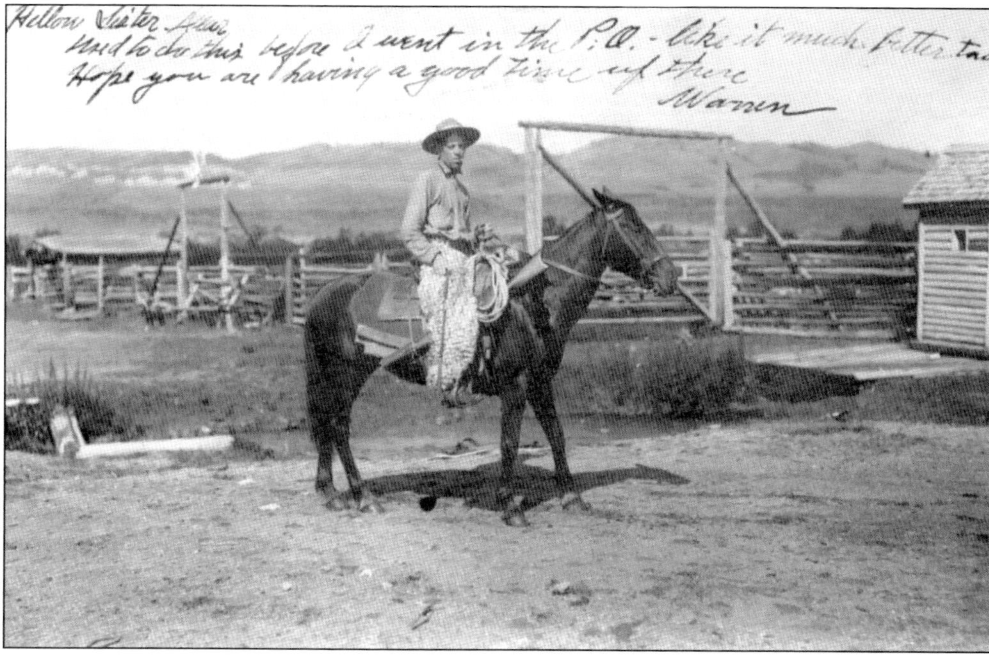

Sent to Miss Julia Campbell in Saratoga, Wyoming, the postcard above showing a cowboy on horseback is apparently of Campbell's brother Warren. He wrote on the card, "Hellow Sister Dear. Used to do this before I went in the P.O.—like it much better. Hope you are having a good time up there Warren." The cowboys below appear to be on a break at a mountain cabin. Because one cowboy is not wearing a shirt, there must have been no problem that day with deerflies, horseflies, or mosquitoes—or possibly, he had not take a bath in some time, and the pests avoided him as a result of his natural aroma. (Both, courtesy of GEM.)

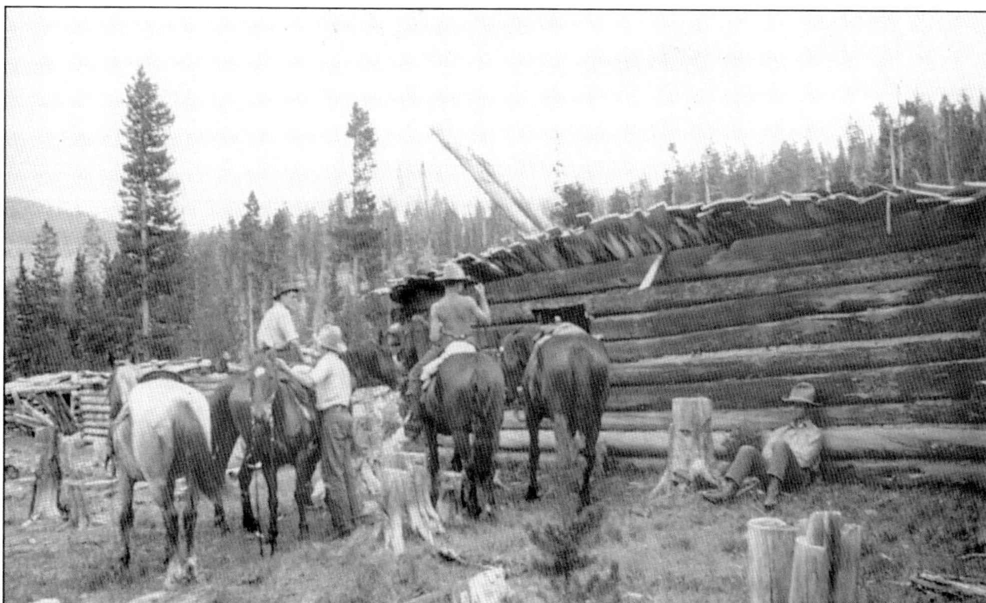

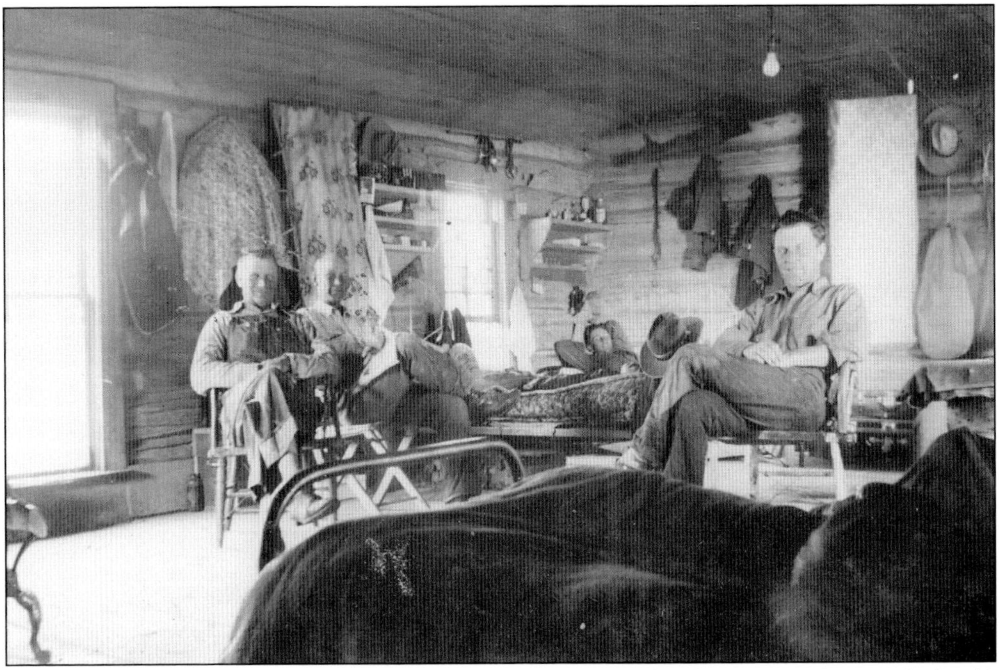

From left to right, Ernest Hubenka, Tex Reams, Larry Reeves, and Melvin "Greg" Gregory (in bunk) relax in the bunkhouse at Big Creek Ranch. The person in the foreground bunk is unidentified. Because it was (and is) a large cattle operation, Big Creek always had a number of single cowboys who needed a place to stay, and it was not practical for those men to have individual houses. (Courtesy of GEM/Grace Vyvey Gregory.)

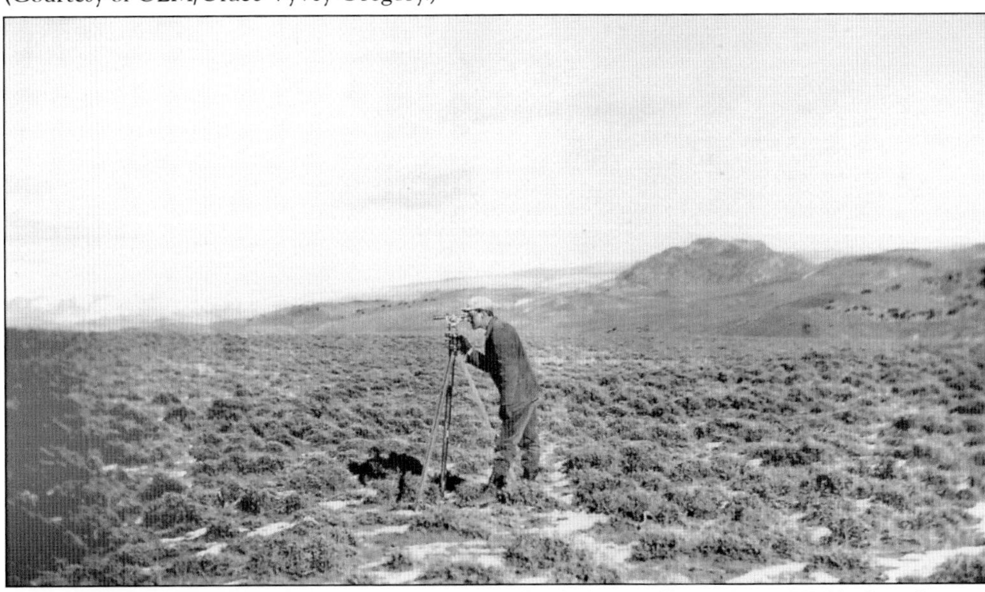

Noah Wolfard received his primary education from his father, William Henry Wolfard, in the one-room Wolfard School just west of Encampment and then studied civil engineering at Valparaiso University in Indiana. After an engineering career elsewhere, Noah returned to Encampment in the 1950s and worked as a land surveyor and irrigation consultant. The Wolfard School building is now at the Grand Encampment Museum. (Courtesy of GEM.)

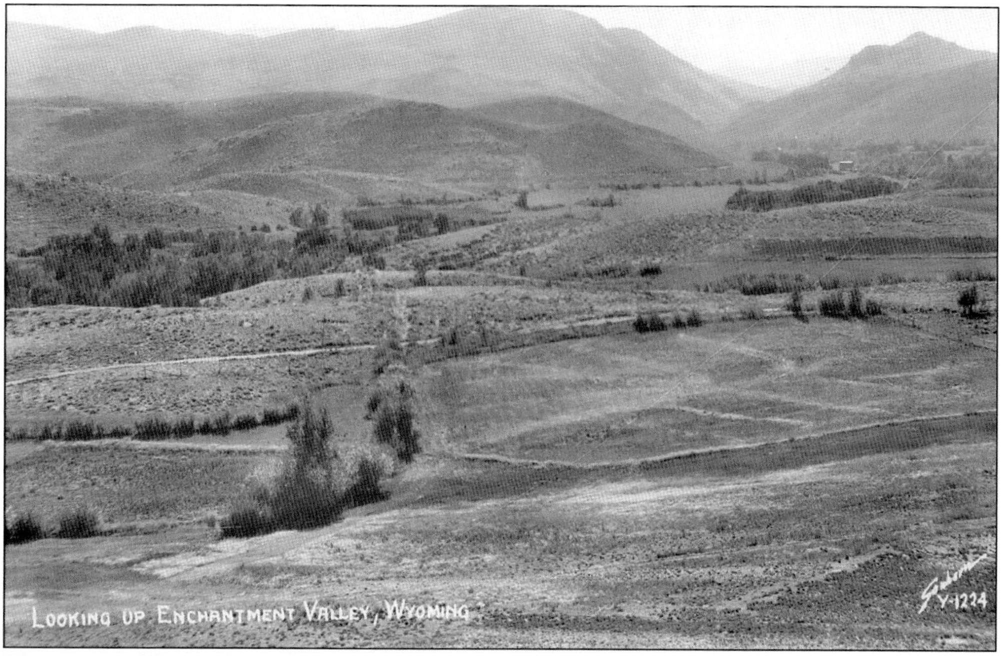

This postcard by Sanborn shows the early agricultural development in the Encampment Valley. Primary crops included native and alfalfa hay, all produced to provide fodder for livestock during the long, cold winters. Some ranchers also raised oats, and the Anderson family began raising dryland wheat in the 1930s. (Courtesy of GEM.)

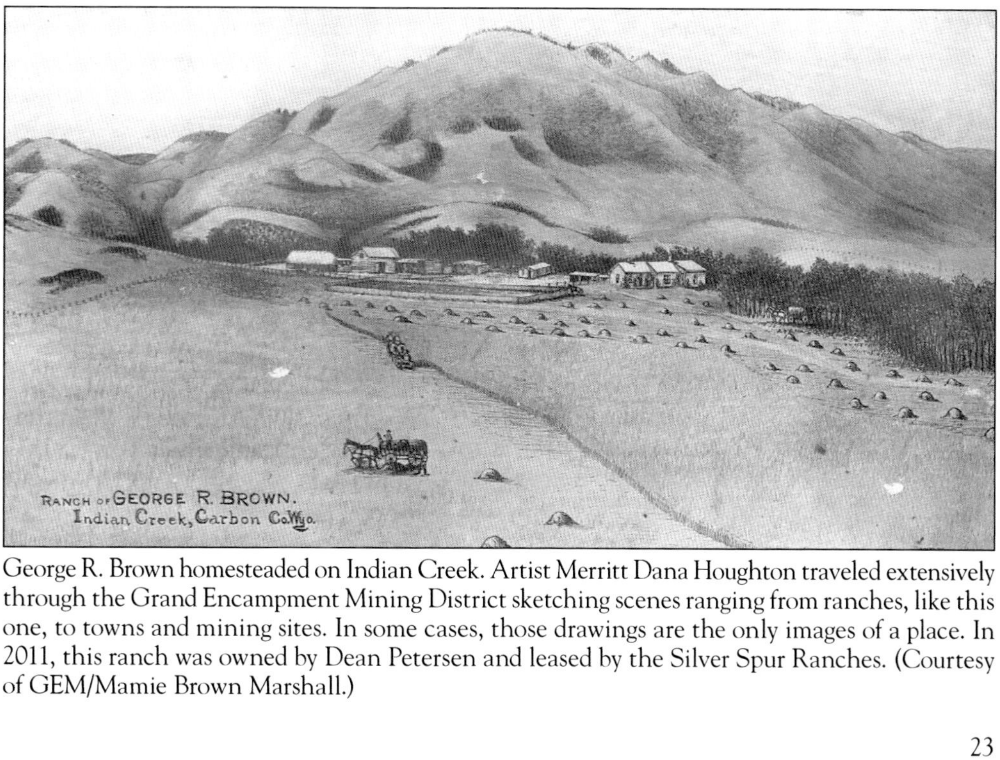

George R. Brown homesteaded on Indian Creek. Artist Merritt Dana Houghton traveled extensively through the Grand Encampment Mining District sketching scenes ranging from ranches, like this one, to towns and mining sites. In some cases, those drawings are the only images of a place. In 2011, this ranch was owned by Dean Petersen and leased by the Silver Spur Ranches. (Courtesy of GEM/Mamie Brown Marshall.)

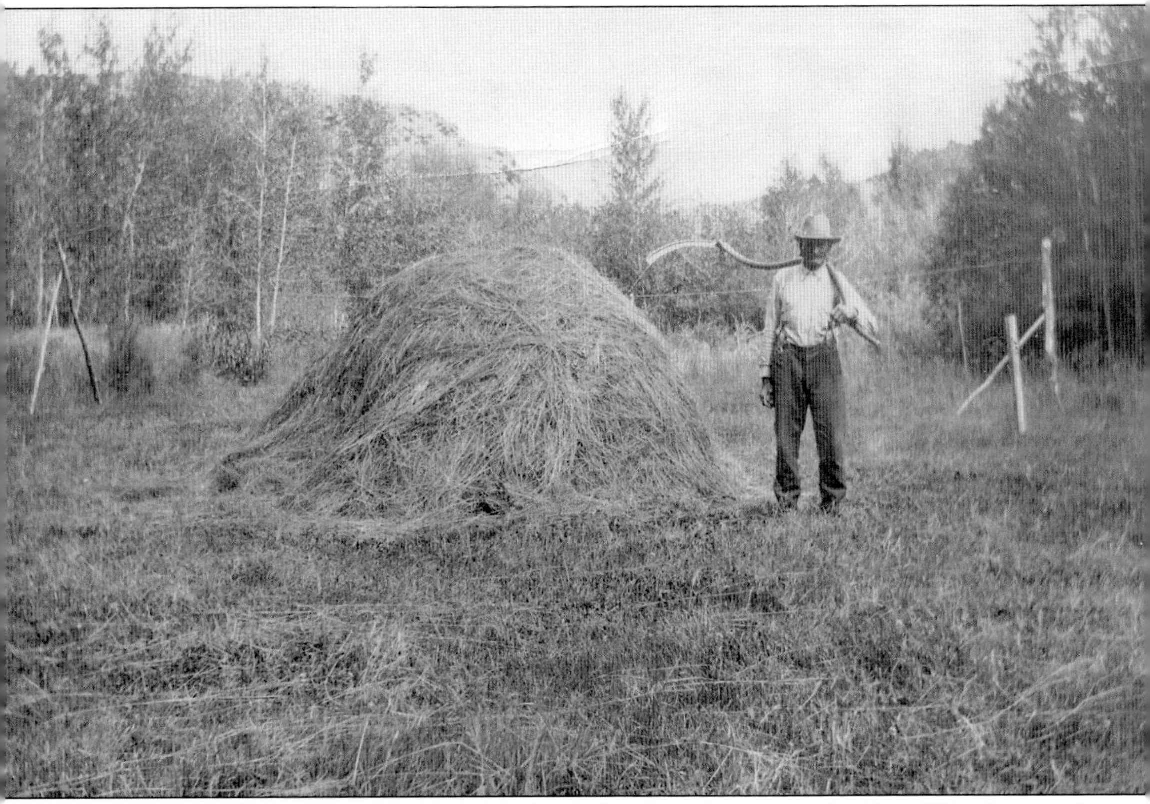

J.W. Fisher holds a scythe, making it likely that he hand cut the nearby pile of hay. This photograph was taken on the Harden Ranch, located on the North Fork of the Encampment River. In 2011, the place was owned by Dick Pickett. (Courtesy of Candy Vyvey Moulton Collection.)

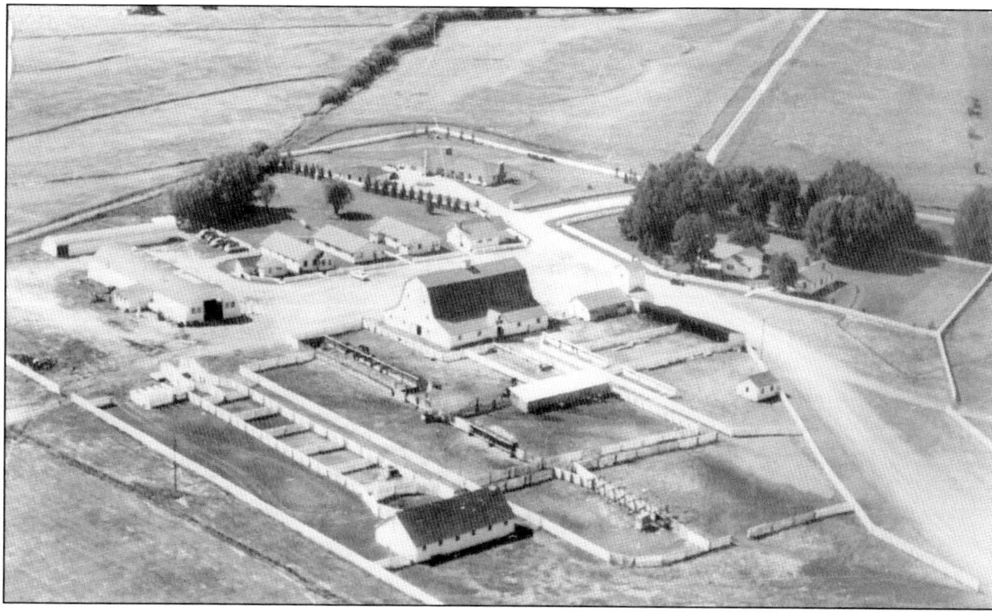

This is an aerial view of Big Creek Ranch, homesteaded by Barney Hunter, who later was joined in partnership by brother Harry and by Ira Casteel. Ira may have come into the operation as the accountant. The ranch was known as Hunter, Casteel, and Hunter. Benjamin C. Hawkes owned the ranch in 1924 and sold to the Gebhard family in 1926. Otto Gebhard had full control until 1941 when he sold out to Wendell W. Anderson. At that time, the ranch was 10,000 deeded acres with grazing rights to another 8,000 acres. In 1967, Anderson sold to Charles C. Gates, whose family retains it today. The current manager is Mark Dunning. George Simons and Otis Moury built the barn in 1909; it burned down in 1924 but was soon rebuilt. Maintenance involves periodic painting, including the episode depicted below, which was a promotion for McMurtry Paint. (Both, courtesy of GEM/Big Creek Ranch Album.)

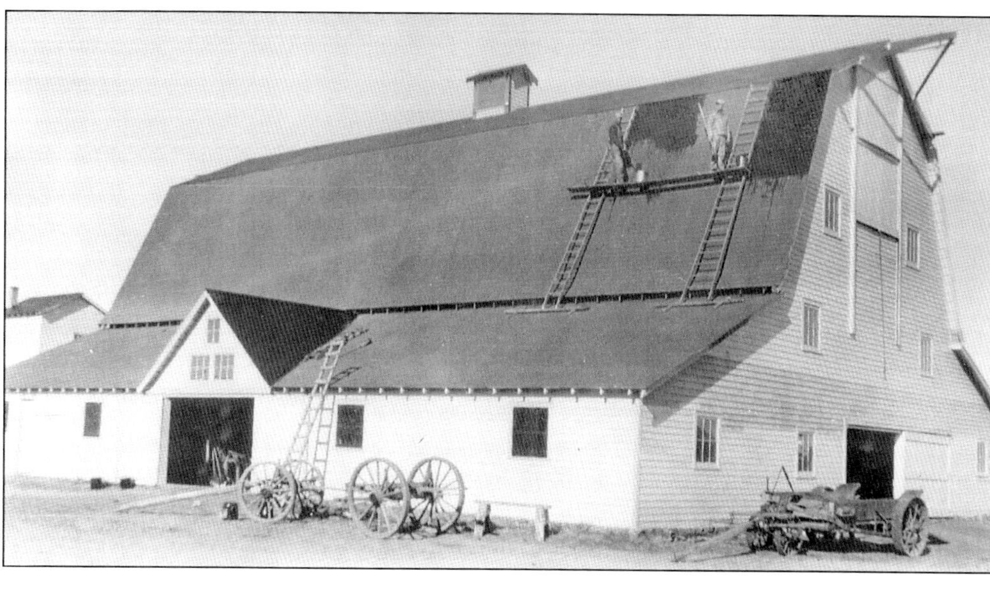

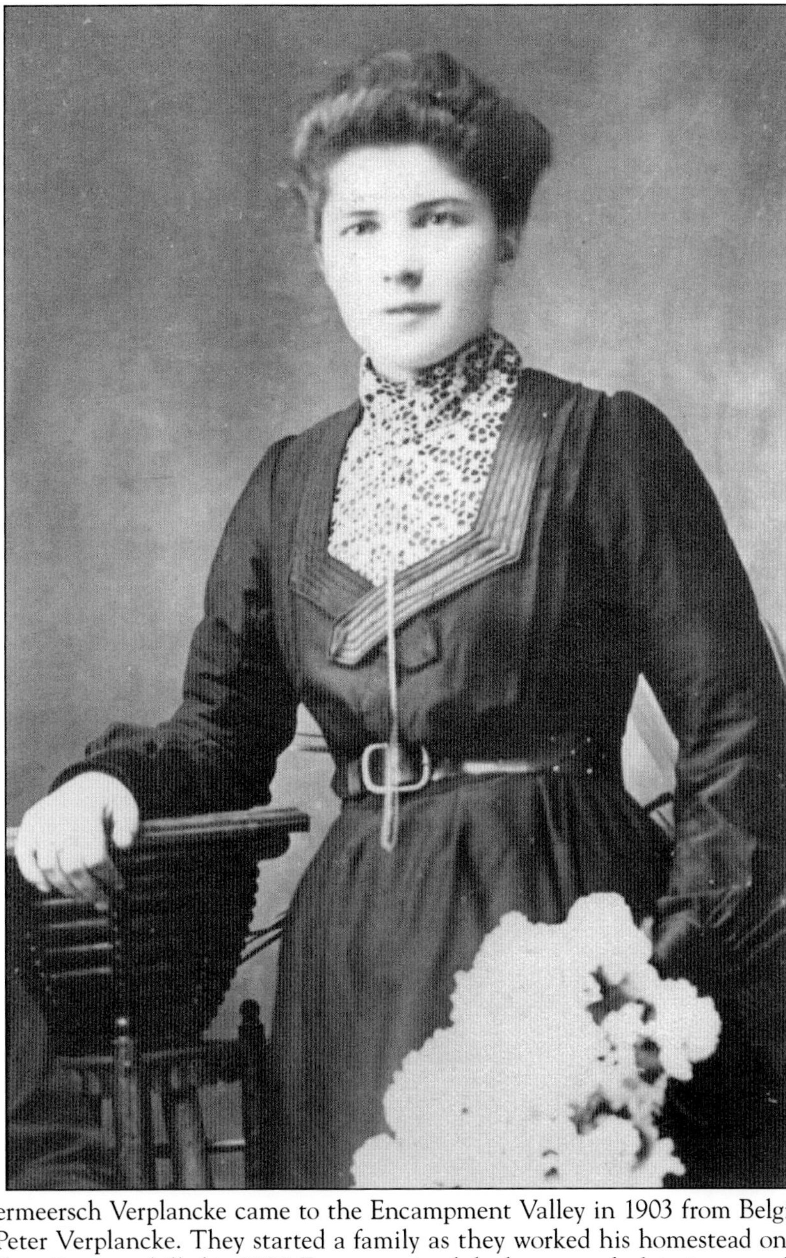

Emma Vermeersch Verplancke came to the Encampment Valley in 1903 from Belgium as the bride of Peter Verplancke. They started a family as they worked his homestead on Antelope Creek. When Peter was killed in 1909, Emma retained the homestead, claiming more land in her own name. This photograph of Emma Verplancke was taken on the day she married her second husband, Charles L. Vyvey. She and Charles continued to expand the ranch. The couple added seven more children to the five Emma and Peter had, making a large family to help with the ranch work. Candy Vyvey Moulton has moved the homestead cabin where her grandmother first lived to her own property up the road from the original location and with family help has restored it. The homestead cabin is the inspiration for the nonprofit organization Candy and her sister Penny Vyvey Walters (along with husbands Steve and Bill) started to preserve history and to serve the Grand Encampment community. Grandma's Cabin provides school supplies and holiday gifts to children. (Courtesy of Candy Vyvey Moulton Collection.)

Peter Verplancke emigrated from Belgium in 1893, taking a homestead on Antelope Creek. He built a log home, cleared sagebrush, planted hay, and engineered irrigation ditches and a reservoir. Having firmly established himself, he returned to Bruges, Belgium, in 1903 and married Emma Vermeersch. He brought her back to Wyoming and the homestead. In 1909, he was fatally injured in a wagon accident. (Courtesy of Candy Vyvey Moulton Collection.)

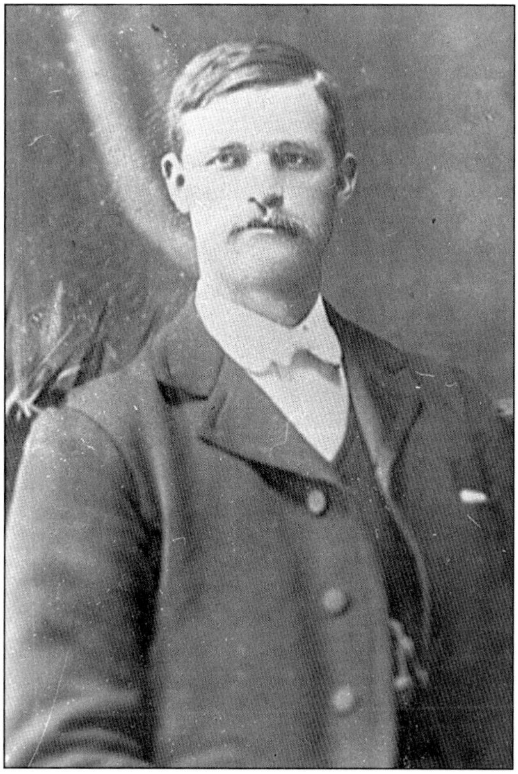

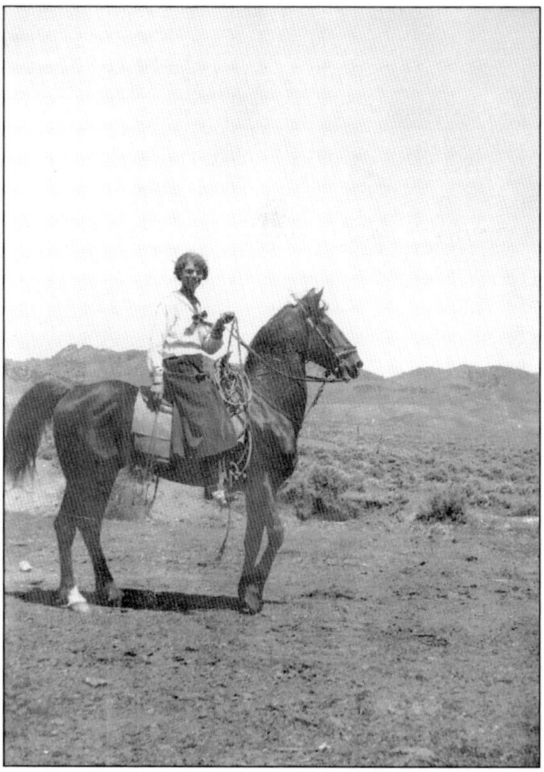

This image depicts Helena Verplancke, eldest daughter of Peter and Emma Verplancke, riding the Big Creek Ranch horse Haffey. She and her sister Lillian were known for their ability to break and train horses. Their half-sister Grace Vyvey Gregory lived at Big Creek Ranch in the 1940s, and their family sold a large number of workhorses to the ranch. (Courtesy of GEM/Big Creek Ranch Album.)

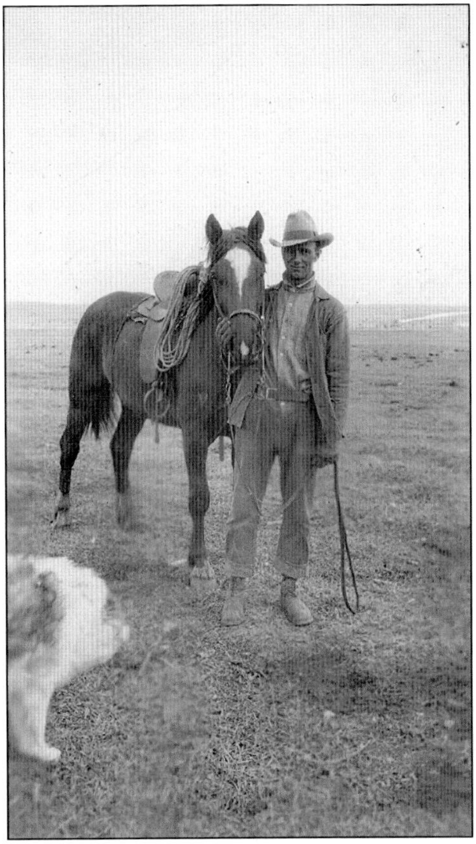

Gordon Turpen appears with his horse and dog. The saddle has oxbow stirrups, a metal device that has fallen out of favor with many modern riders. (Courtesy of GEM.)

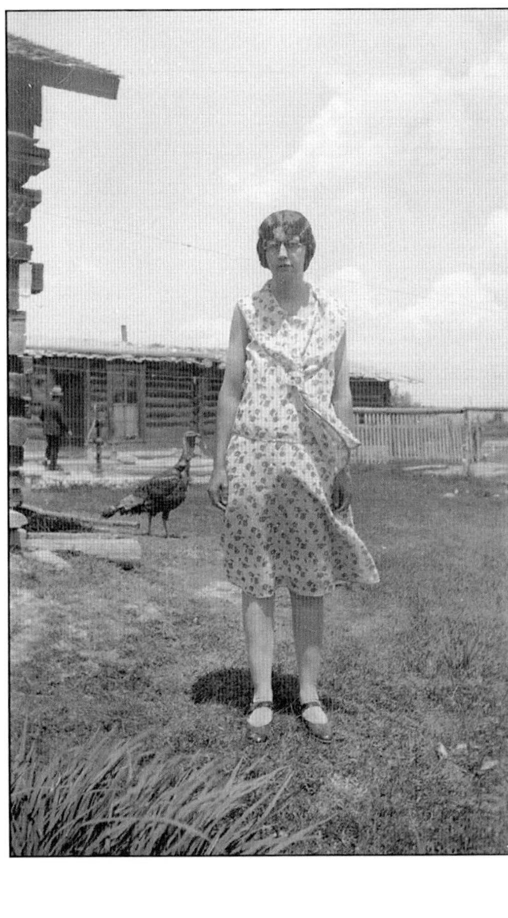

Helen Turpen appears at the ranch house where she raised turkeys and likely other fowl. (Courtesy of GEM.)

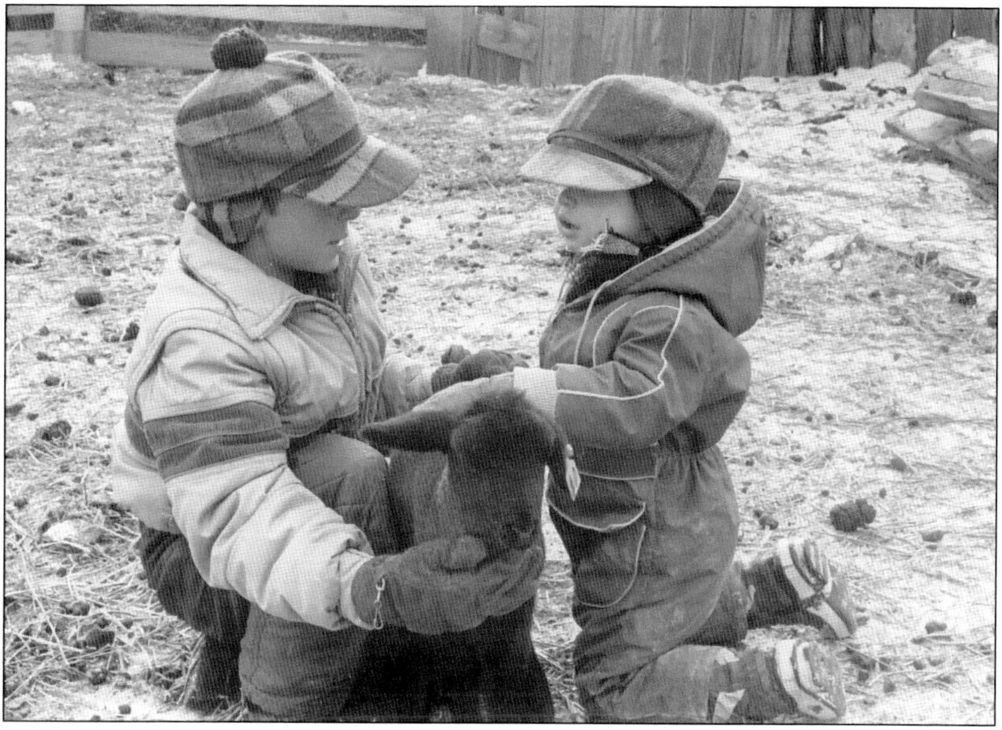

Ben Romios (left) and Shawn Moulton play with a new lamb on the Romios Ranch in 1985. Although cattle have always been the predominant livestock raised in the Encampment Valley, some ranchers also had small flocks of sheep. But as the market for lamb and wool declined (and losses to predators, such as coyotes, increased), most ranchers sold off their sheep and added to their cattle numbers. (Courtesy of Candy Vyvey Moulton Collection.)

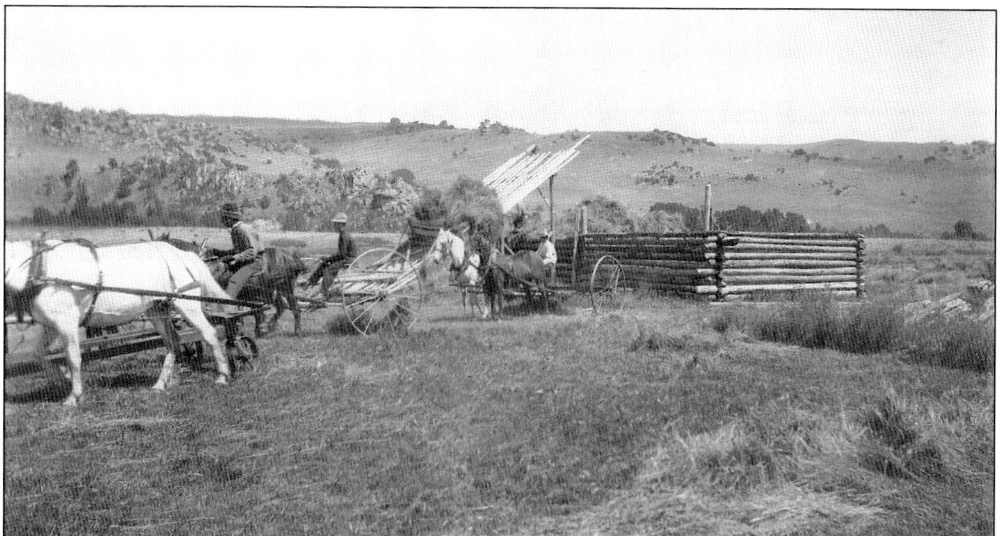

In the country where snow generally falls before Thanksgiving and can stay on the ground until early May, cutting and stacking hay for winter feeding of livestock is critical. Here, a hay crew uses horse-drawn equipment for the task. Unfortunately, photographer J.W. Fisher did not frame his image to include the lead team's heads. (Courtesy of Candy Vyvey Moulton Collection.)

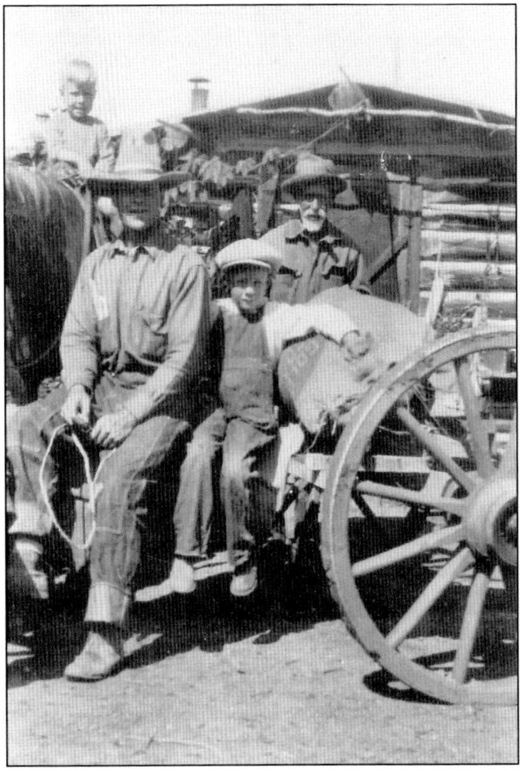

This image depicts three generations of the Higby family, including, from left to right, Larry, his father Lester, brother Warren, and grandfather Lawrence. This photograph was likely taken at the Reed Higby ranch, which in 2011 is the Sky Meadows Ranch. At one time the ranch took in guests, but it was (and is) also a working cattle ranch. (Courtesy of GEM/Larry Higby.)

Ross Armstrong (left) was foreman of Big Creek Ranch from 1929 to 1942 during the period when Otto Gebhard (right) owned the ranch. (Courtesy of GEM/Big Creek Ranch Album.)

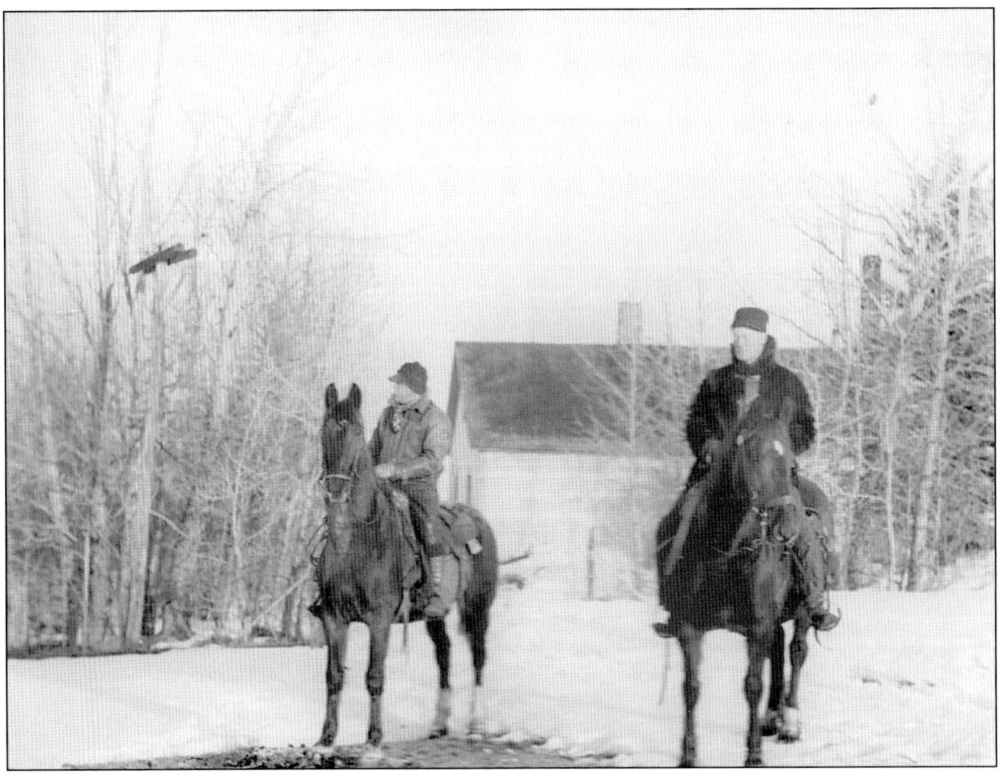

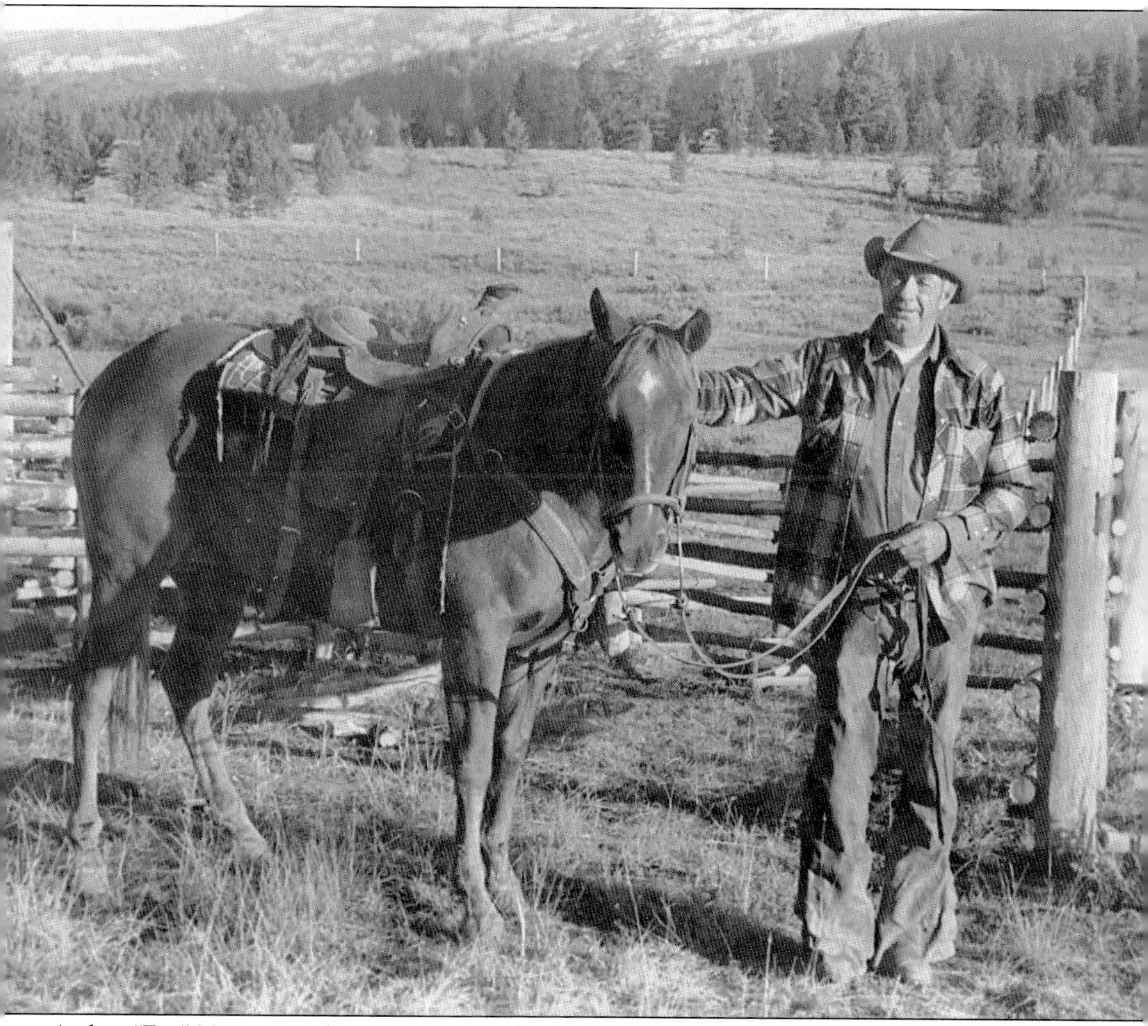

Arthur "Fox" Vyvey was the youngest son of Charles and Emma Vyvey. Fox, as he was always known, was reared on his parents' homestead, and later operated it as VX Ranch with his wife, Betty M., brother Albert, and Albert's wife, Phyllis. As a six-year-old, Fox wanted to impress the Big Creek cowboys because he wanted to grow up to be just like them. When he saw the cowboys ride over the hill and toward the Vyvey ranch house, he ran out to a well casing in the yard and stuck his foot down it. He captured the attention of the cowboys alright, as his foot became stuck. They laughed at his predicament, which was finally eased when his new shoe was cut from his foot. The VX Ranch had 3,500 deeded acres and ran cattle on forest-grazing allotments in Wyoming on Billy Creek and Hog Park and in Colorado's Big Red Park. This photograph of Fox was taken in Hog Park. He was presented the Grand Encampment Cowboy Gathering Pioneer Award in 2005. (Courtesy of Candy Vyvey Moulton Collection.)

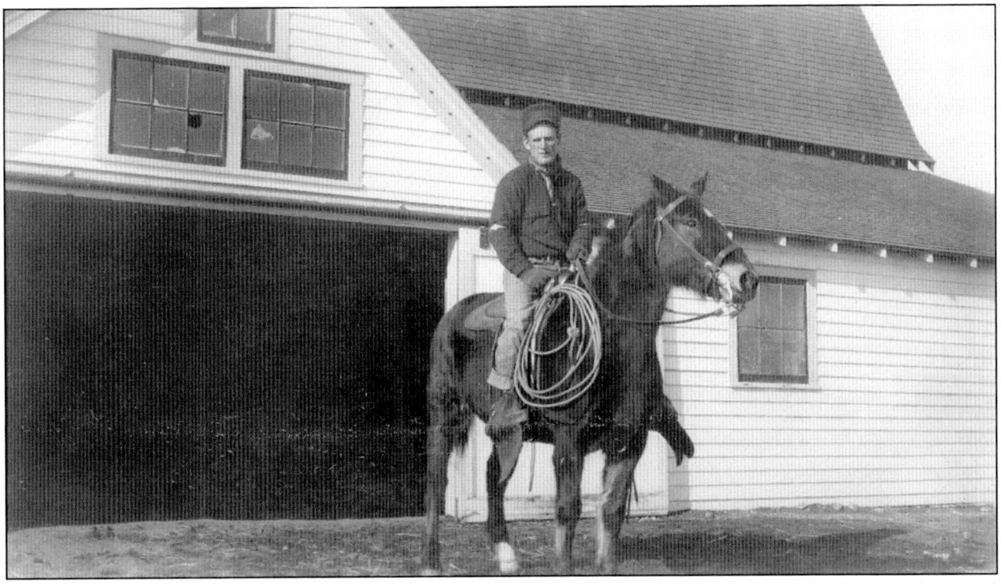

Melvin "Greg" Gregory worked at Big Creek Ranch in the 1940s. Best known for his mechanical ability, he fashioned equipment and self-opening gates. Here, he is riding one of the ranch horses. (Courtesy of GEM/Big Creek Ranch Album.)

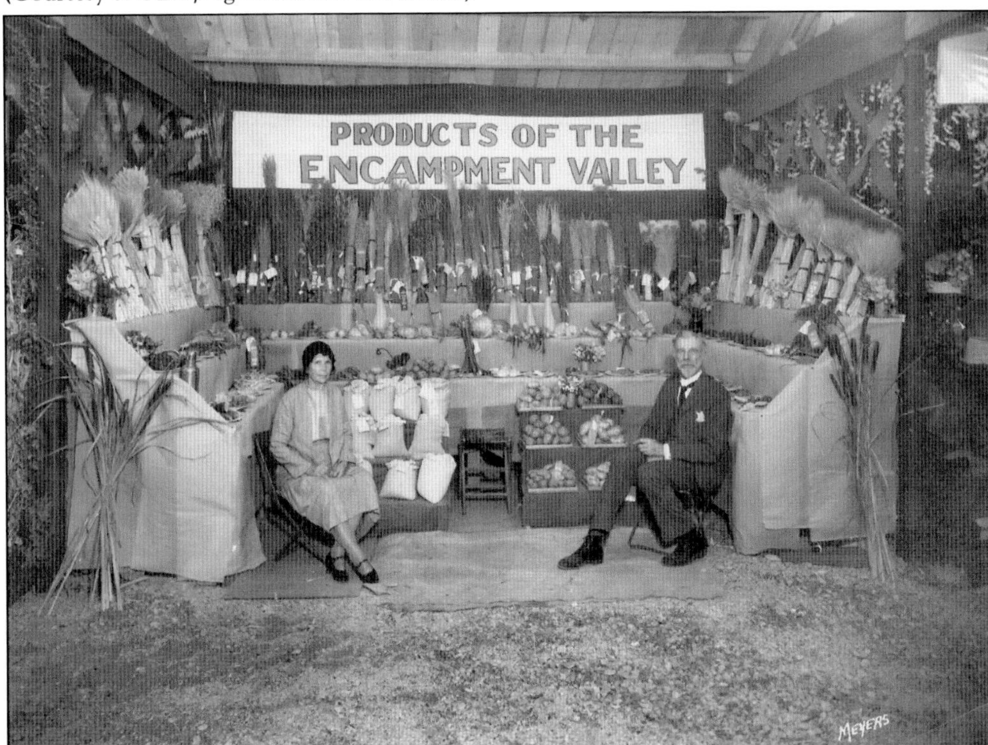

Nellie Reynolds and Joshua R. Rollman show off products of the Encampment Valley at the Carbon County Fair in 1930. In addition to a variety of hay and grain products, the display includes potatoes, cabbage, turnips, rhubarb, cucumbers, squash, beets, onions, and flowers. (Courtesy of GEM/Fannie Wolfard.)

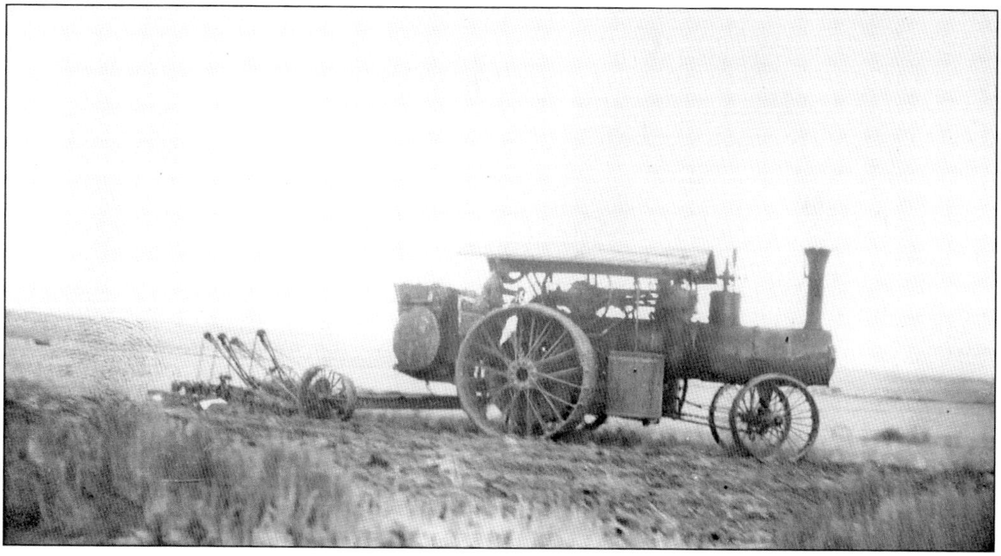

Mechanization enhanced farming operations for valley ranchers. Hardware store owner W.M. Englehart sold the steam tractor shown above to Archie Anderson in about 1915. Archie and his brother Ed Anderson also had three other early tractors in the valley, which they showed off by churning the ground in front of the E&H Building in Encampment. The Andersons were farmers rather than ranchers, and they used their tractors for working fields. When they began planting dryland crops, many of the ranchers who irrigated their fields told the Andersons that dryland crops would not be productive, but with an efficient system of crop rotation in which each field was allowed to lay fallow one year and produce the next, the Anderson Farms successfully raised winter wheat for more than 70 years. (Courtesy of Lora Nichols Collection.)

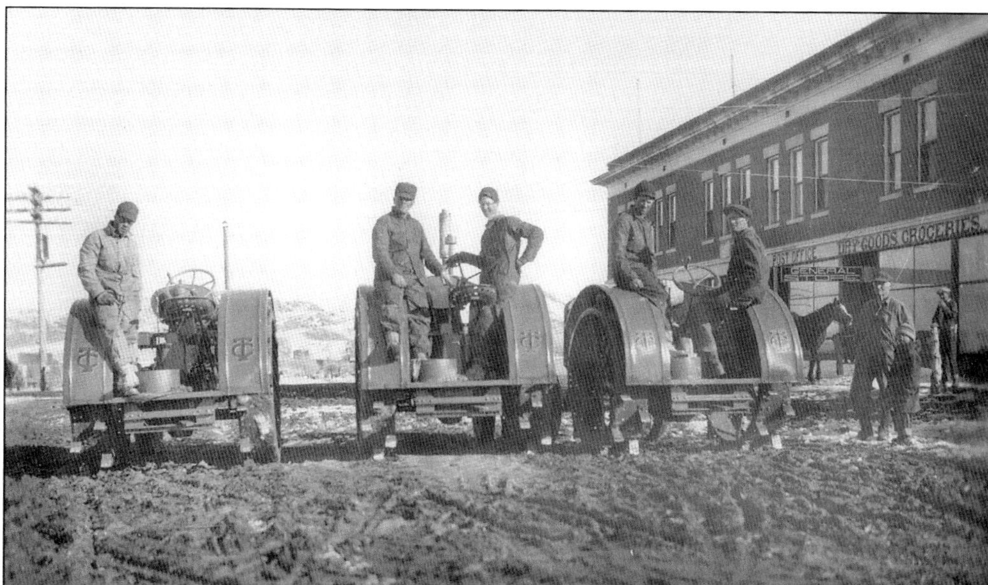

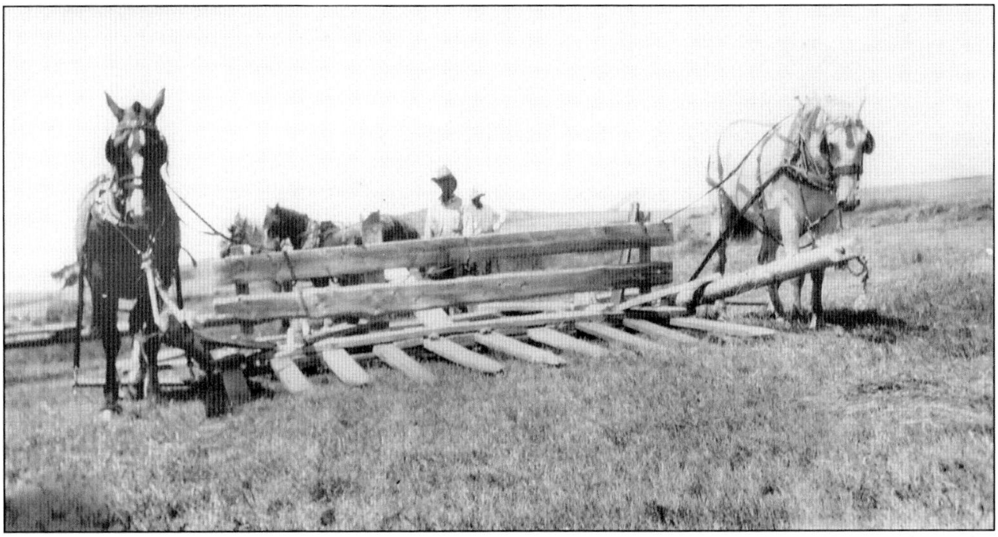

A good portion of summer is filled with haying operations throughout the valley. Back in the days of muscle power, ranches utilized teams of animals to operate a variety of equipment, such as this sweep being managed by Ellis Herring (foreground) and Doc Culleton working on the Hardin Ranch. (Courtesy of Betty Herring Vyvey Collection.)

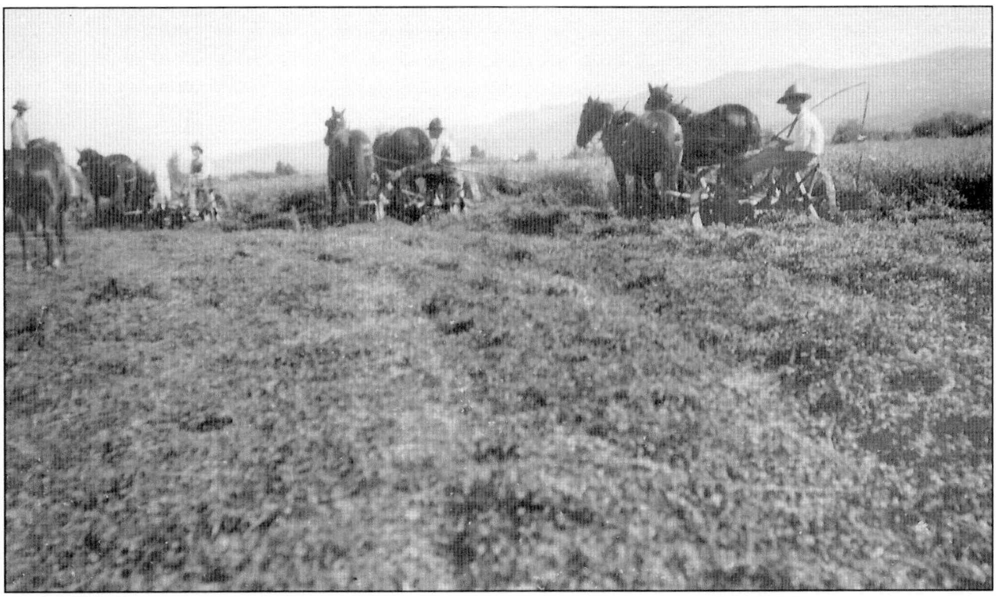

Guy Pool, a brother of Alwilda Pool Platt, homesteaded on Little Beaver Creek. This hay mowing operation on the Pool place was being done on July 20, 1921. At the time, the land was part of the J.W. Bingham Ranch. The Pool Ranch is now owned by descendants of Alwilda Pool Platt. (Courtesy of GEM/Grant Forney.)

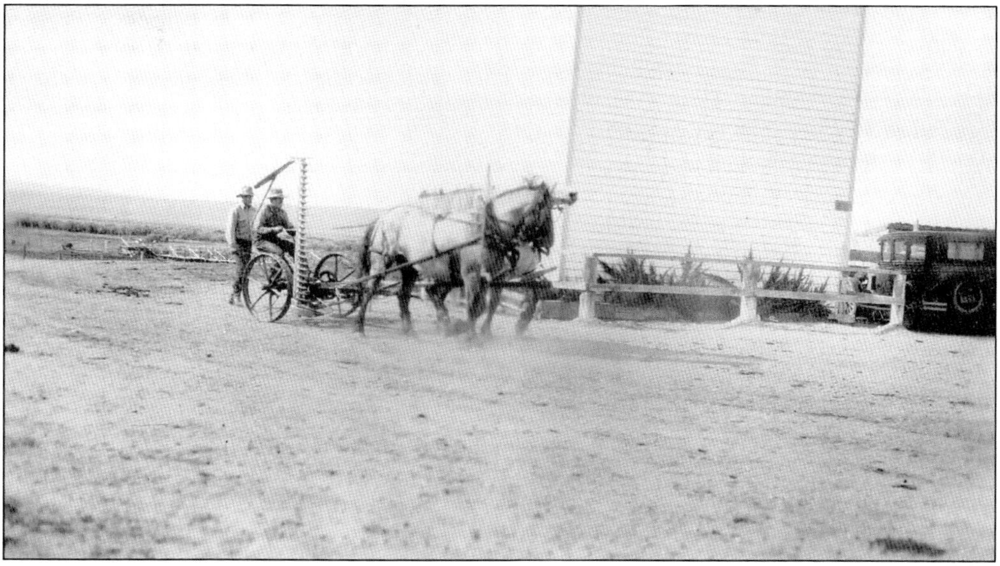

In this image, two workers move a horse-drawn mowing machine at Big Creek Ranch. That ranch, with its many acres of hay ground, had dozens of mowing machines and therefore, dozens of teams of horses to pull them. Many of the Big Creek Ranch workhorses were Percherons, Clydesdales, and Belgians, the latter raised by Charles Vyvey of the VX Ranch. (Courtesy of GEM/Big Creek Ranch Album.)

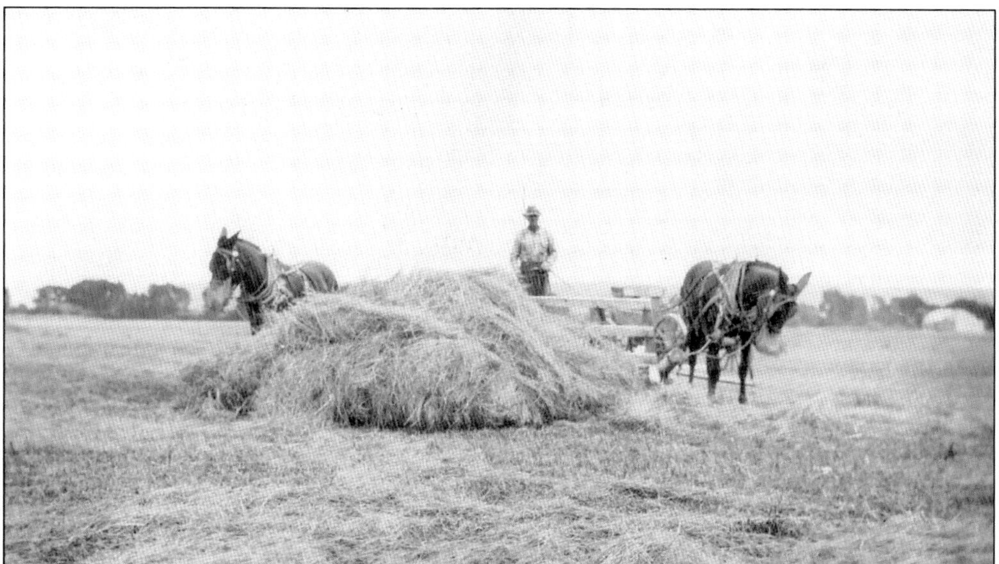

This image depicts haying at the Bill Sidley Ranch using a horse-drawn sweep. This ranch is better known as the Silver Spur. These mules have on nosebags. The driver is unidentified, but it could be Sam Verplancke. (Courtesy of GEM.)

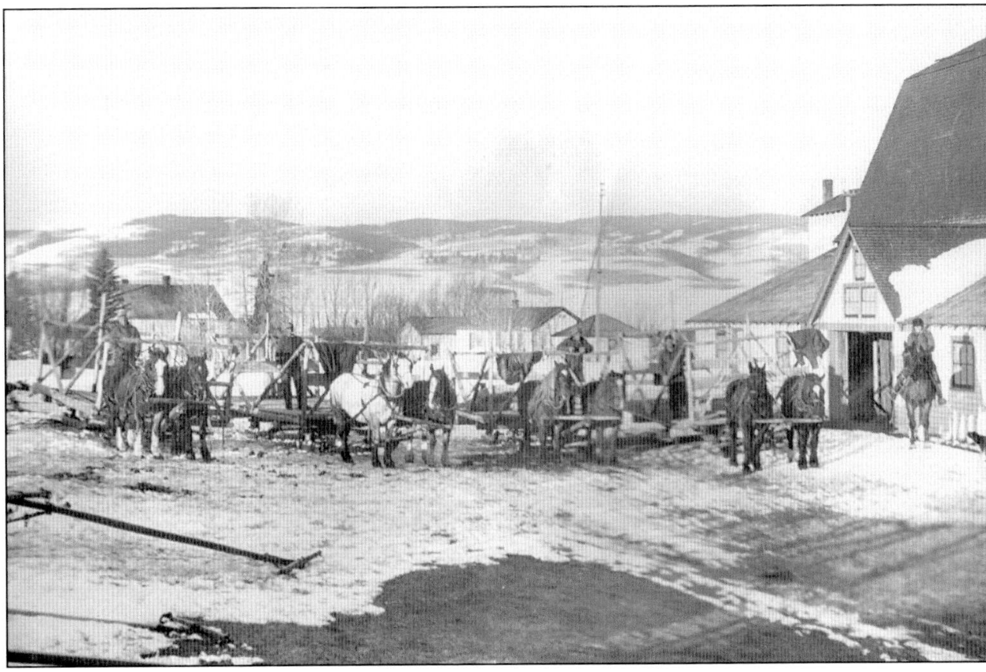

A winter feeding crew (above) prepares the hay sleds at Big Creek Ranch. During their earlier ownership, Hunter, Casteel, and Hunter owned many ranches in the Encampment Valley, including Big Creek Ranch, Bear Creek Ranch, Big Creek Park Ranches, Huston Ranch on Cow Creek, Sterrett Ranch on Brush Creek, Kuykendahl Ranch on the North Platte River, and the Canyon Ranch (Parr Ranch) on the Encampment River. Below, Vergal Aydelott runs the hay sweep at Big Creek Ranch around 1940. (Both, courtesy of GEM/Big Creek Ranch Album.)

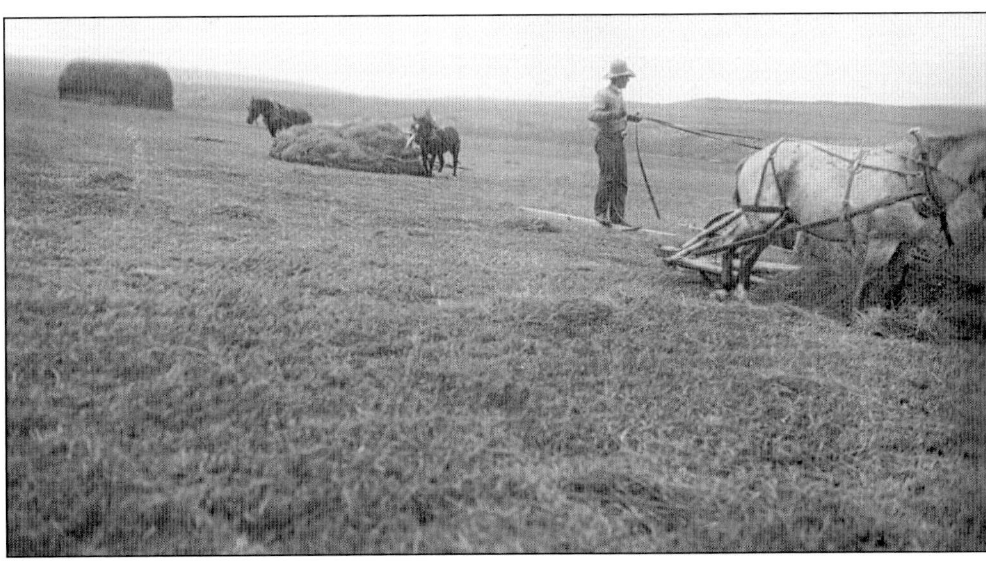

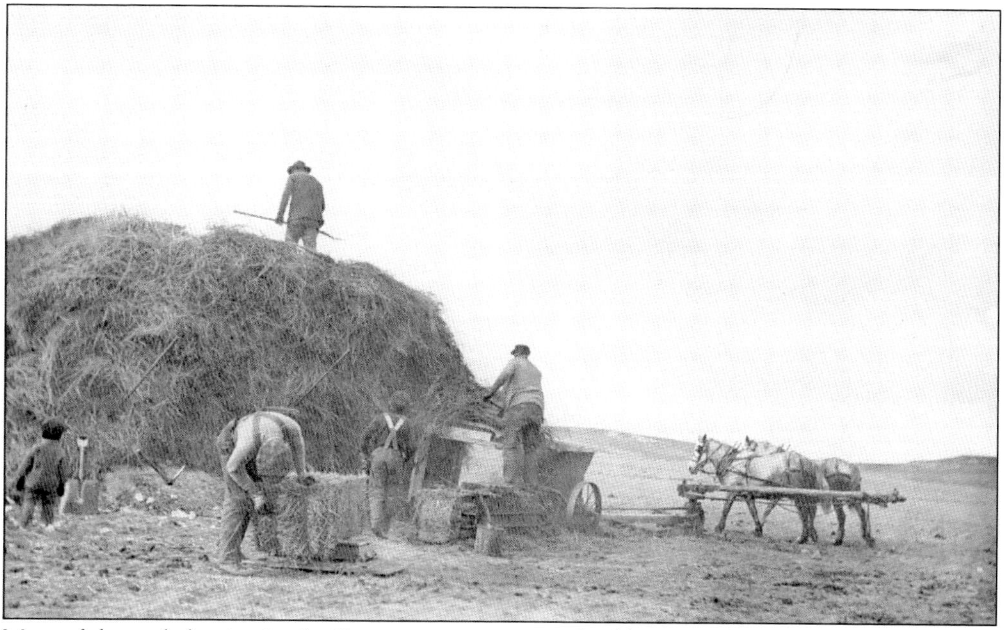

Most of the early haying in the Encampment area involved loose stacking of the hay, but balers eventually came into use, as shown here. Today's ranchers harvest hay using a variety of equipment from big square bales weighing 1,500 pounds, to round bales of 1,000 pounds, and small square bales averaging about 80 pounds. Very few area ranchers still loose stack hay, and none use horse-drawn implements. (Courtesy of GEM.)

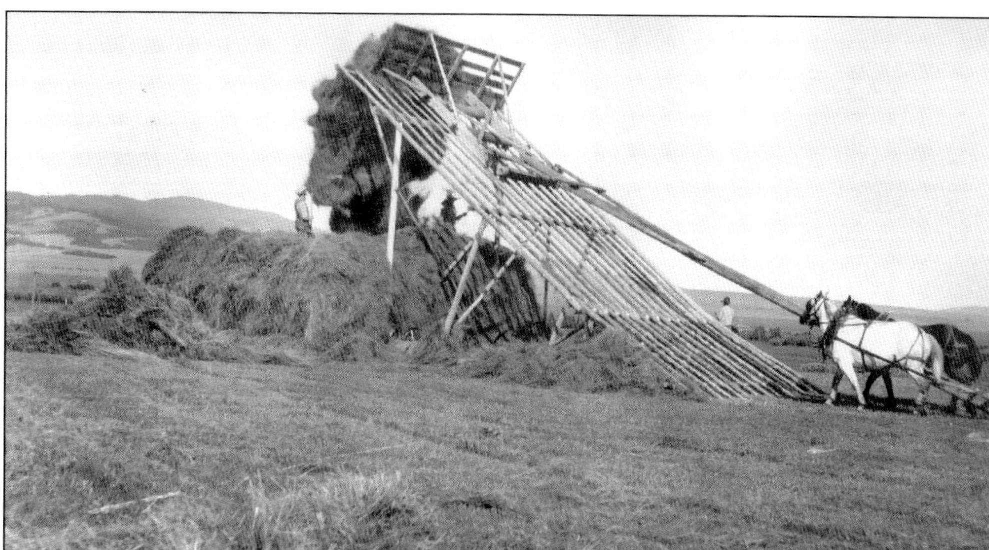

A team of horses provides the power to drive the pusher up a beaver-slide stacker and build a haystack on Big Creek Ranch. (Courtesy of GEM/Big Creek Ranch Album.)

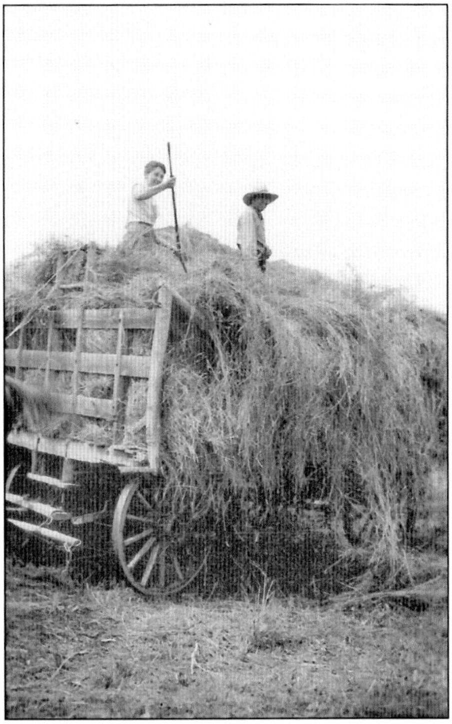

Harley Moore has a full load of hay on this wagon. He has a woman helper, perhaps his wife, Inez. It was very common on the family ranches for wives and children to work beside husbands and fathers. On most Encampment ranches, daughters were treated no differently than sons; all were expected to do their share of the work, whether that involved managing livestock or harvesting crops. (Courtesy of GEM.)

In this image, workers move hay from a loaded wagon to the mow of the barn at Big Creek Ranch around 1940. At the time of this photograph, Otto Gebhard owned the ranch. (Courtesy of GEM/Big Creek Ranch Album.)

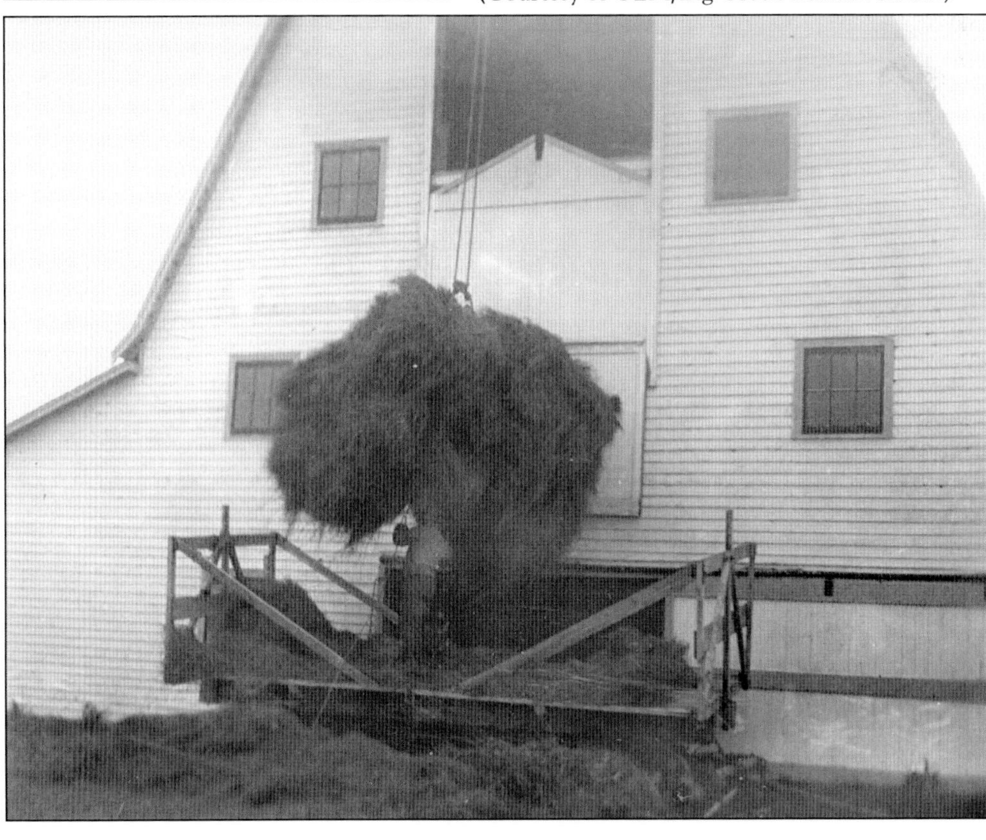

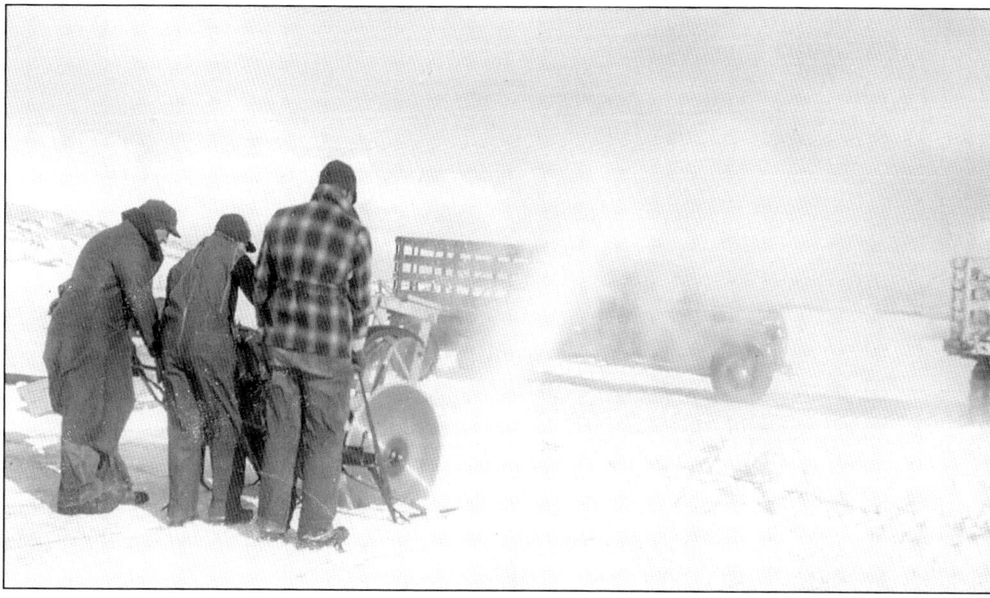

Ross Armstrong, Melvin Gregory, and Ernie Hubenka cut ice on Vyvey Reservoir for Big Creek Ranch. Ross and Melvin built the ice-sawing machine in about 1940. It was common practice in the days before refrigeration to cut ice from lakes, reservoirs, or streams, and stack it in icehouses where it was insulated in sawdust and therefore preserved for use in warmer months. (Courtesy of Grand Encampment Museum/Big Creek Ranch Album.)

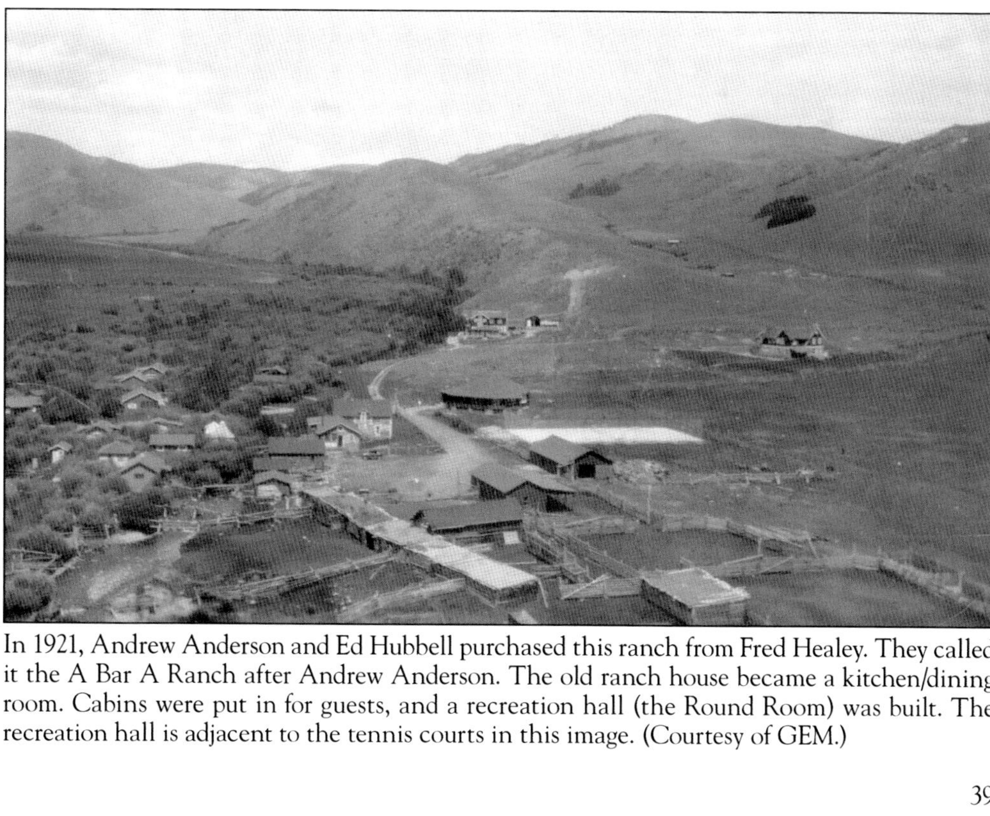

In 1921, Andrew Anderson and Ed Hubbell purchased this ranch from Fred Healey. They called it the A Bar A Ranch after Andrew Anderson. The old ranch house became a kitchen/dining room. Cabins were put in for guests, and a recreation hall (the Round Room) was built. The recreation hall is adjacent to the tennis courts in this image. (Courtesy of GEM.)

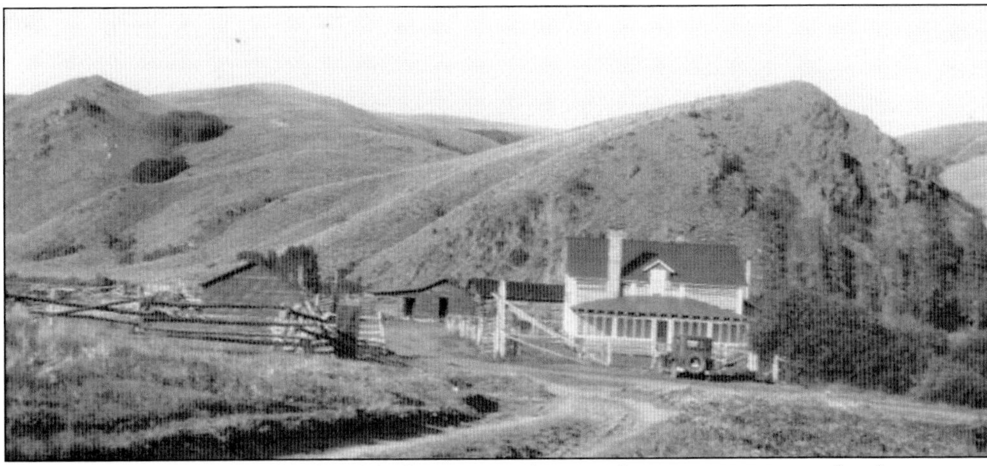

From the start, Anderson and Hubbell envisioned a grand visitor experience for their guests. The A Bar A originally advertised itself through mass mailings to the nation's elite. They took their mailing list straight out of the popular *Who's Who*. Being next to national forest lands, they incorporated these large tracts of unspoiled acres in their excursions. (Courtesy of GEM.)

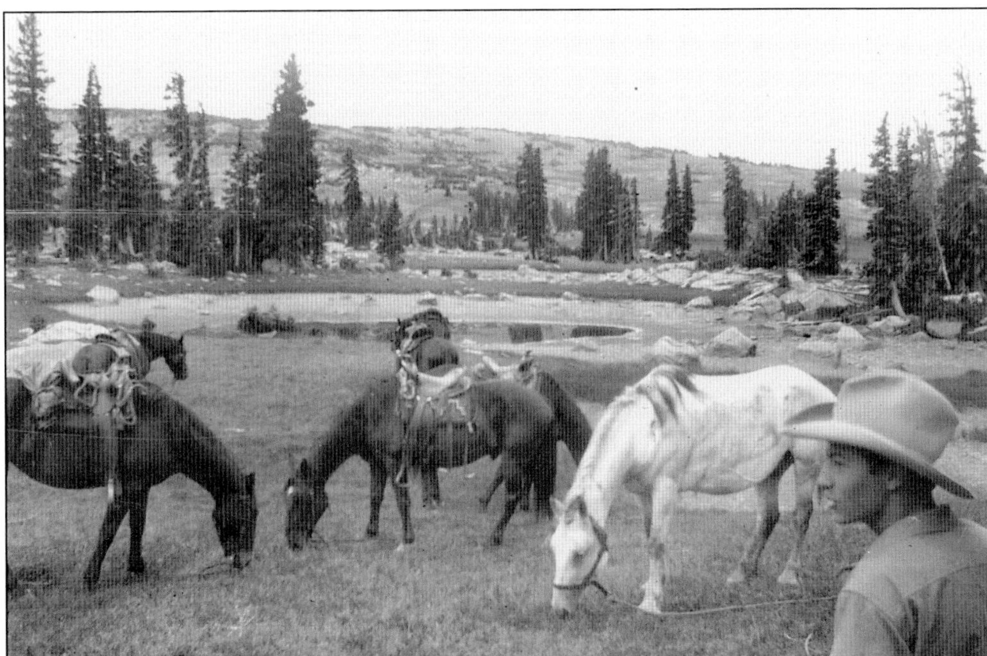

A young wrangler keeps tabs on a string of dude horses at a high mountain lake. A Bar A Ranch provided a variety of experiences to its guests. Doc Culleton often led horseback expeditions into the backcountry. Horses, such as these, were selected for their suitability to carry inexperienced riders. Horseback riding remains a popular attraction at the A Bar A Ranch. (Courtesy of GEM.)

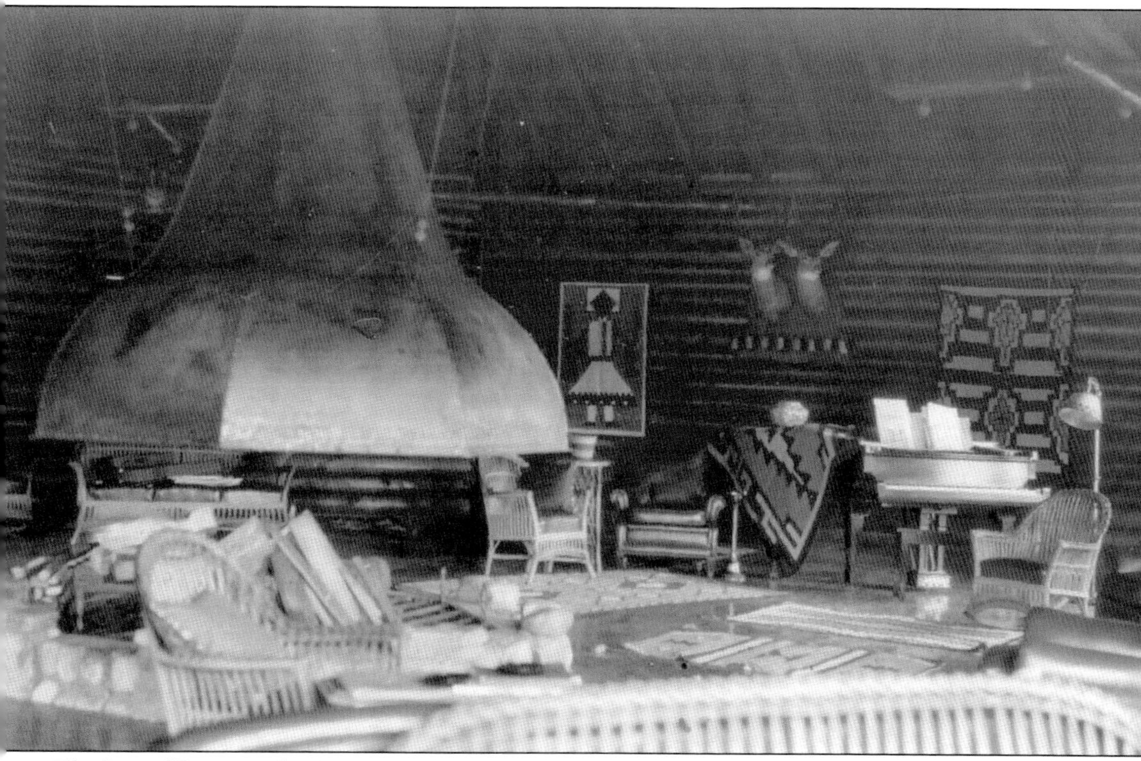

The Round Room at the A Bar A Ranch has always served visitors as a place to relax, play games, and listen to music. Formal balls were held here with music provided by Bill Kuntzman's Orchestra. The room is round like a Navajo *hooghan* and is decorated with Navajo rugs and other fine art. The couches, chairs, lamps, and tables were constructed by Thomas Molesworth, an important furniture maker from Cody, Wyoming, who created a new style of furnishing that today is highly prized (and highly valued). Today's ranch has some original Molesworth pieces, as well as replica-style furniture crafted by Steve Moulton. The circular stove hood is operated using a system of pulleys and cables, easily allowing smoke to be drawn upward when there is a fire in the circular building. (Courtesy of GEM.)

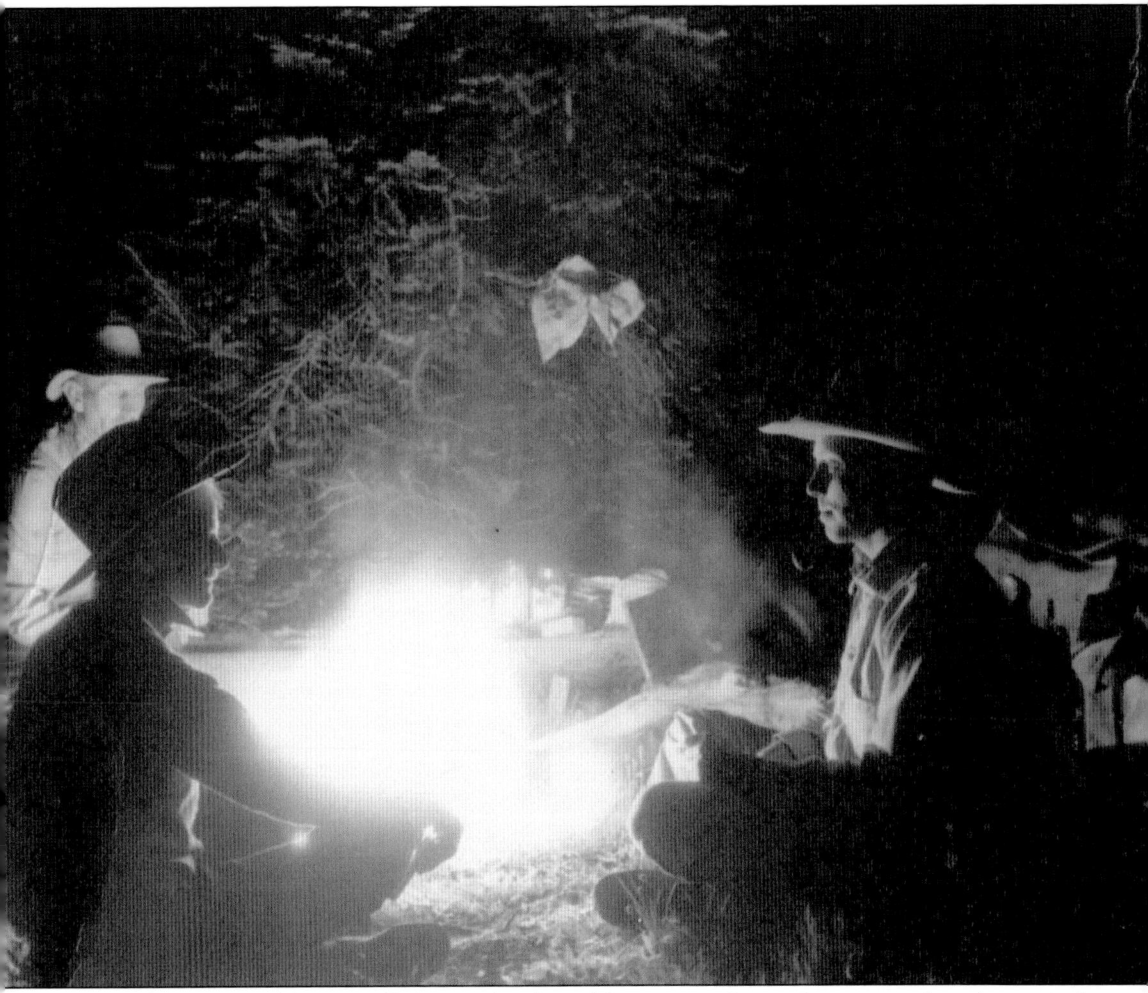

It is almost possible to smell the sagebrush and burning cedar as this group of cowboys winds down their day at the A Bar A Ranch. The fire pops and snaps as a coyote howls somewhere in the distance. Could any night be so perfect? (Courtesy of GEM.)

Three

Industrial Revolutions

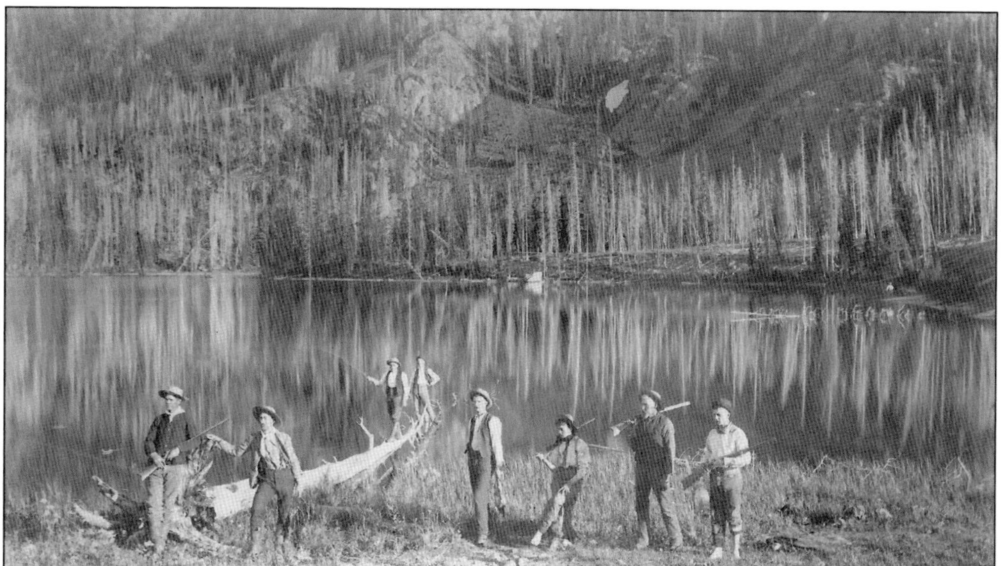

Battle Lake Creek fed the lake of the same name on the western slope of the Continental Divide and attracted both fishermen and men with guns who may have been hunting in the area. In the right mid-ground of the image, an angler has hooked something, hopefully not a branch. The name *Battle* comes from an 1841 fight involving Indians and trappers. This photograph is by E.F. Bunn, of Fort Collins, Colorado. (Courtesy of GEM/Wilbur Hugus.)

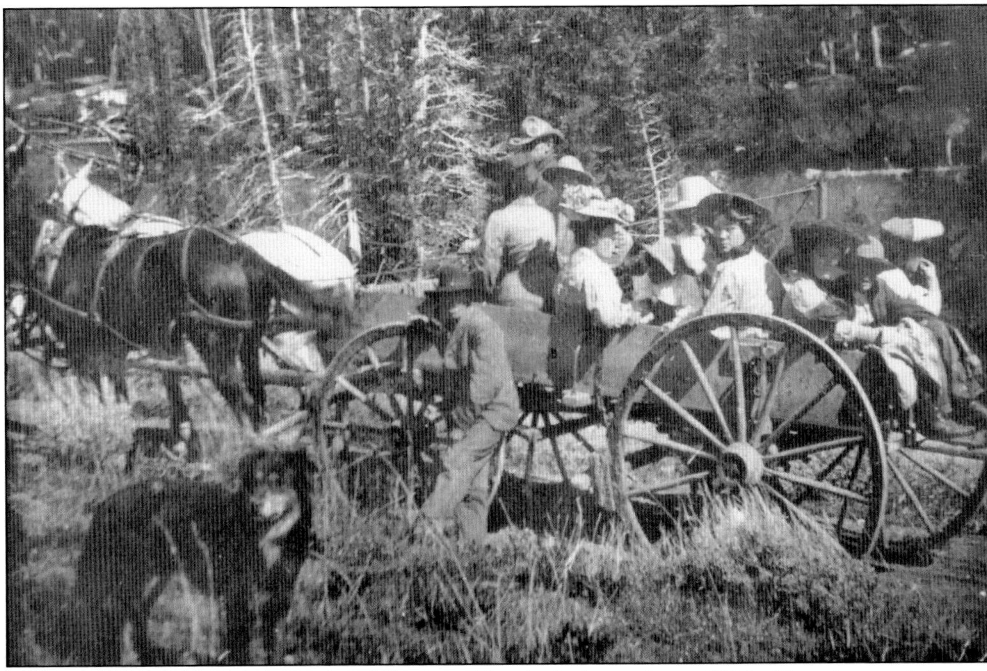

This image shows a group going fishing at Battle Lake in June 1908. Hunting and fishing became industries in the area during the 19th century. Outdoor recreation continues to attract individuals who like to hunt, fish, camp, boat, ride, ski, sled, or hike. The Continental Divide National Scenic Trail has a trailhead just east of the lake at the top of the divide. (Courtesy of GEM/Charles Fletcher.)

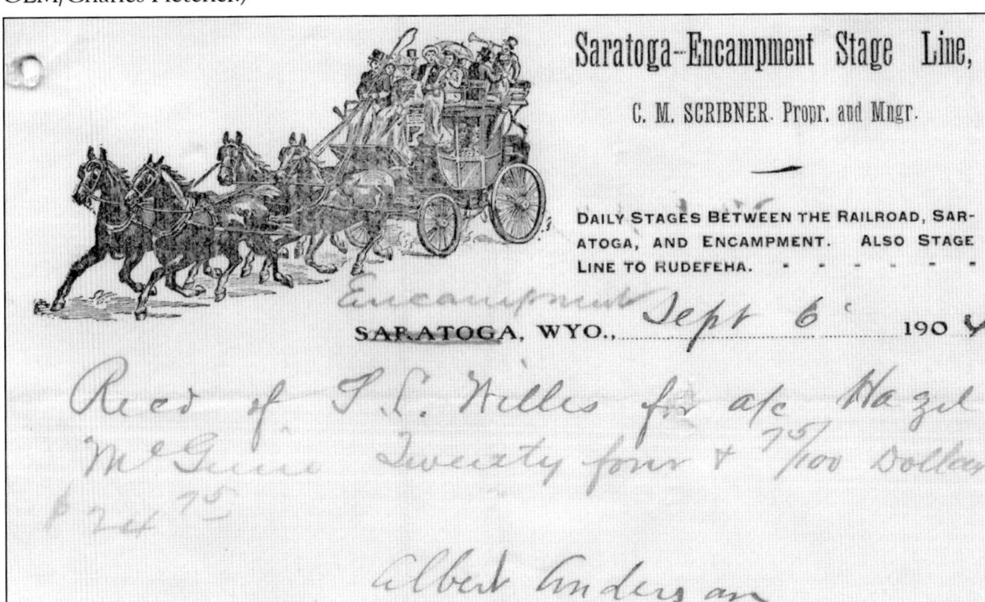

Saratoga-Encampment Stage Line,

C. M. SCRIBNER. Propr. and Mngr.

DAILY STAGES BETWEEN THE RAILROAD, SARATOGA, AND ENCAMPMENT. ALSO STAGE LINE TO RUDEFEHA.

Encampment SARATOGA, WYO., Sept 6 1904

Rec'd of G.L. Willis for a/c Hazel McGuire Twenty four & 75/100 Dollars

$24.75

Albert Anderson

The Lake Creek Stage Company operated between Walcott Junction and Grand Encampment with stops at the Lake Creek Stage Station and in Saratoga. This receipt is for service on September 6, 1904, and reads, "Rec'd of G.L. Willis for Hazel McGuire twenty-four & 75/100 dollars $24.75 Albert Anderson." (Courtesy of GEM.)

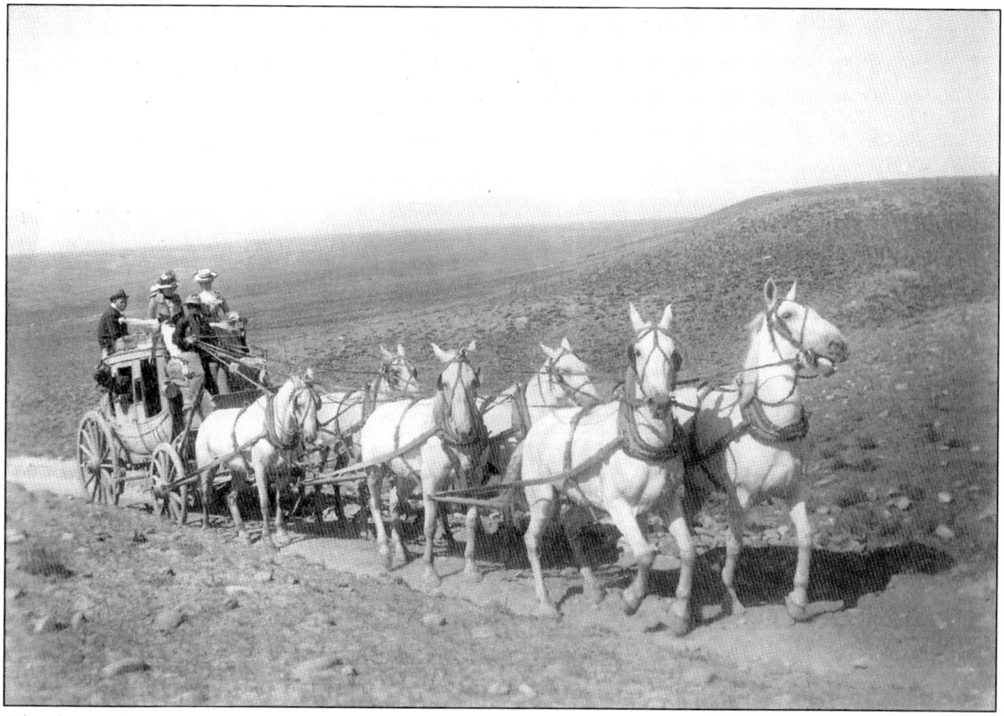

Charles Wilcox became one of the most skilled and well-known stagecoach drivers in the Grand Encampment Mining District and Saratoga area. Bound for Elwood in 1903, Wilcox drives the "White Six," a team of matching horses. Now a ghost town, Elwood was located about six miles west of Grand Encampment. This photograph was given to Tom Elwood by Charles Wilcox and donated to the museum by Ben Culleton. (Courtesy of GEM.)

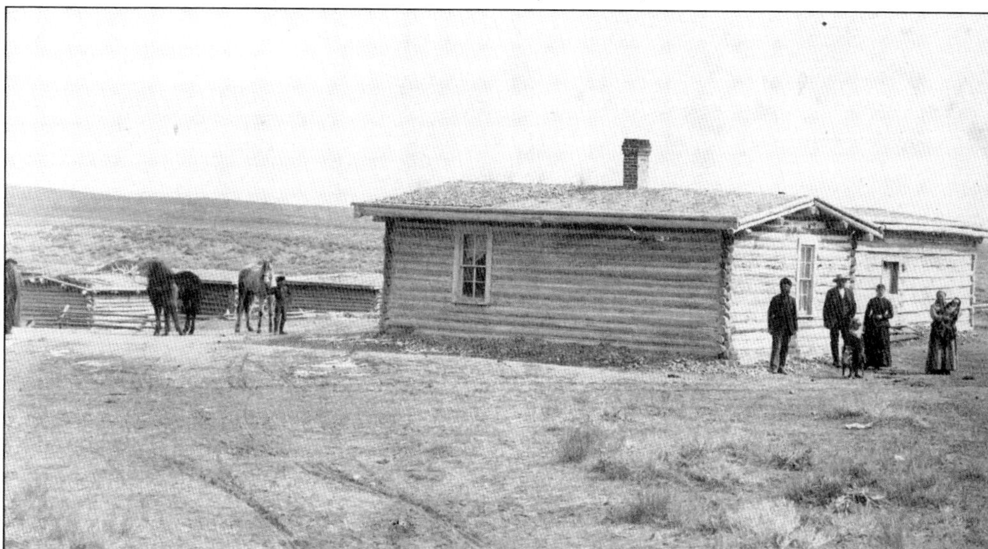

Shown around 1890, the Lake Creek Stage Station stood north of Saratoga and served traffic traveling the 40-mile route on the Union Pacific Railroad between Walcott Junction and Grand Encampment. Tired teams were replaced with fresh animals at such stations. This station building is now at the Grand Encampment Museum complex. (Courtesy of GEM.)

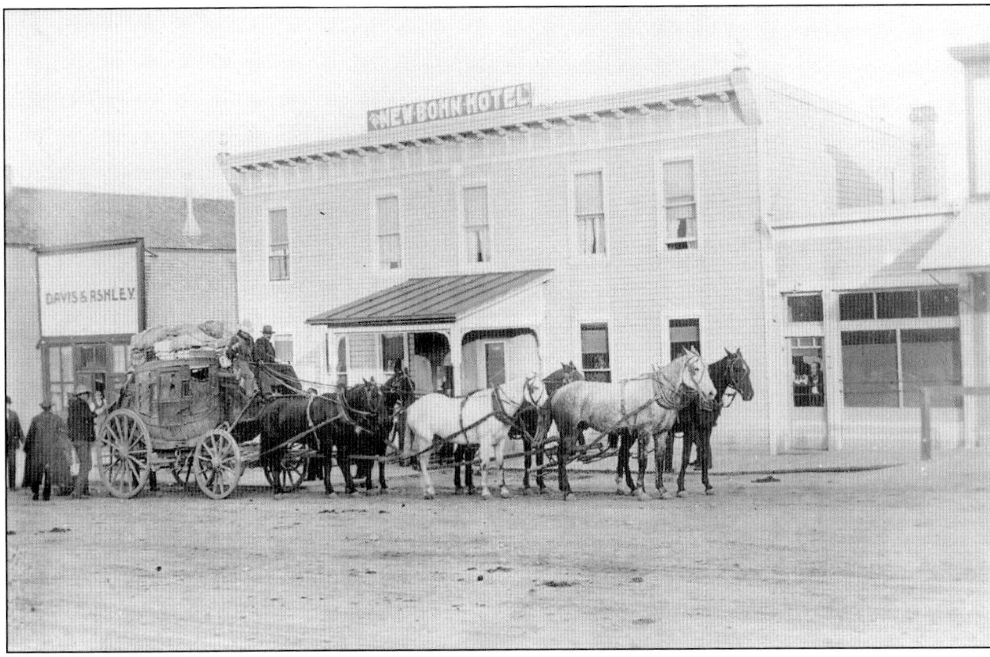

Daily stagecoach service ran between Walcott Junction and Grand Encampment during the peak years of the copper-mining boom. The photograph above shows the stage in front of the New Bohn Hotel. It is not known what day the stagecoach and spring wagon (below) met at the livery barn in Encampment, but photographer J.W. Fisher identified the time as 5:00 p.m. More than one stagecoach served Grand Encampment, as is evident by comparing the coaches in these two photographs. (Both, courtesy of Candy Vyvey Moulton Collection.)

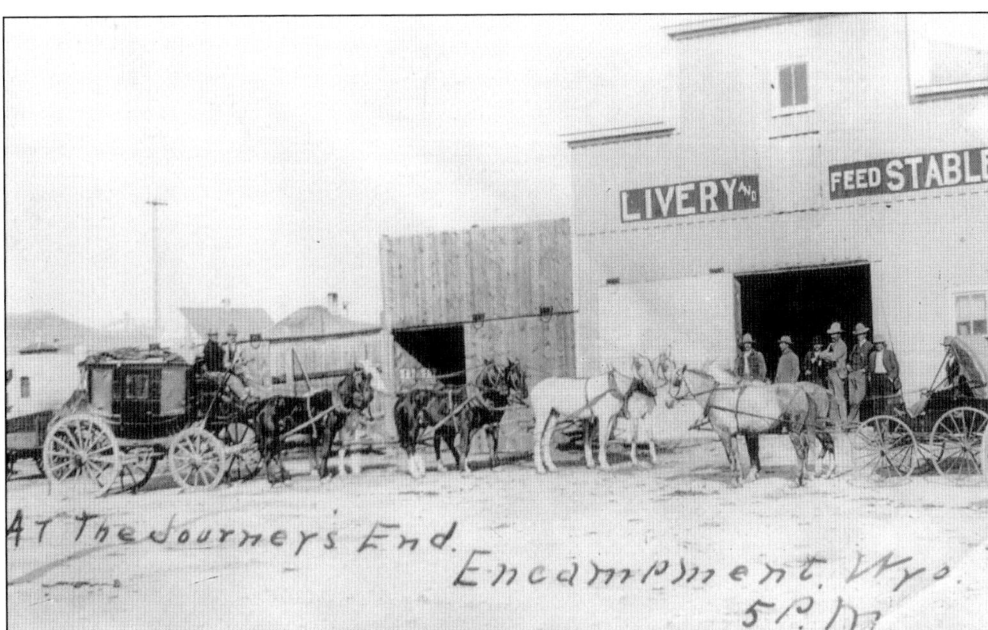

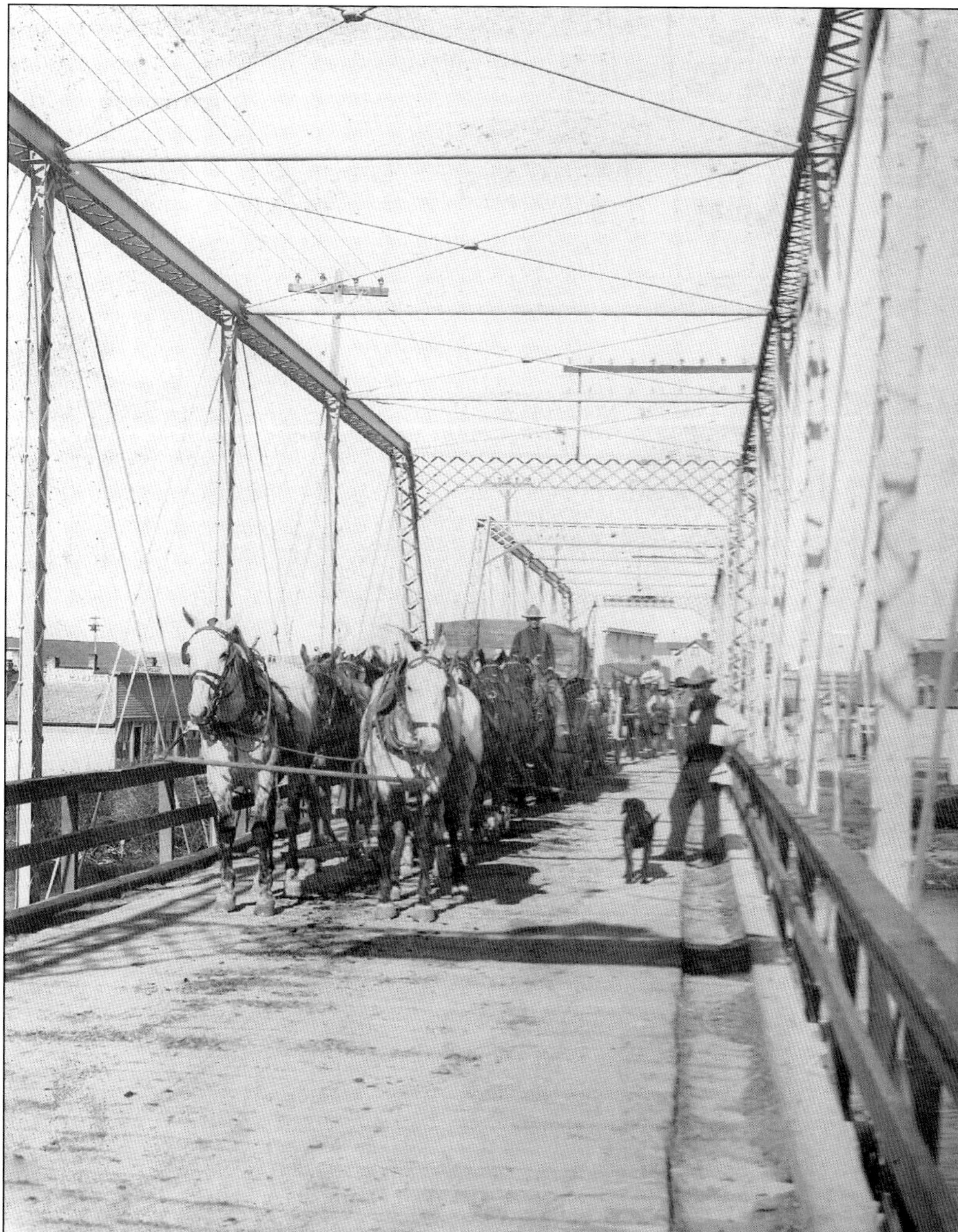

"Gee-String" Jack Fulkerson, seated on wheel team horse, drives his eight-horse hitch across the North Platte River Bridge in Saratoga in 1906. This fine freighter earned his nickname because he handled his horse or mule teams using a single jerk line that controlled the lead animals. Rigs like this carried almost all goods in and out of the valley until 1907. (Courtesy of GEM/ Geraldine Walker.)

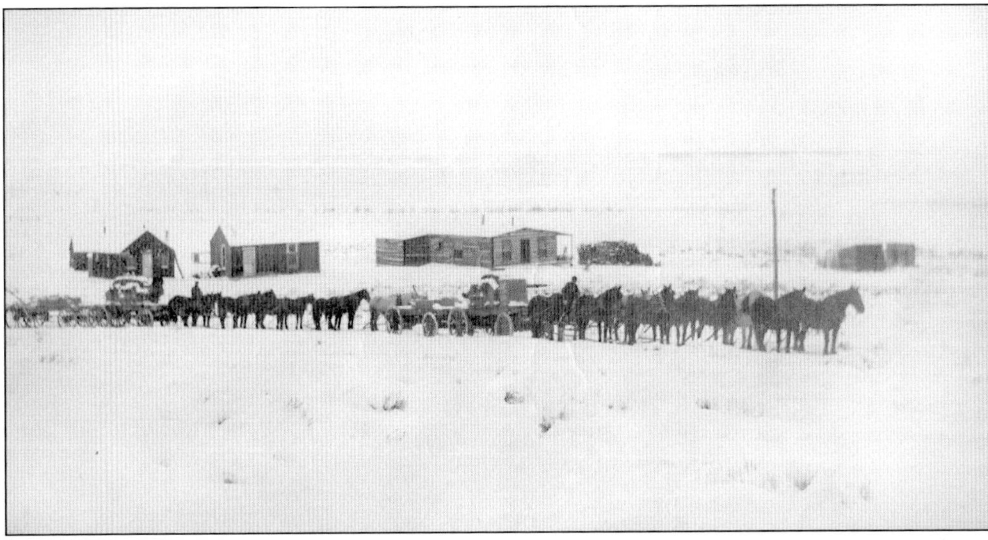

These 10-horse teams each pull two wagons full of supplies. Overall, hauling capacity of horse teams is similar to mule teams, except that larger breeds, such as the Percherons and Clydesdales, were favored at the Big Creek Ranch. Lead horses were specially trained to understand directional commands of *gee*, meaning "left," and *haw*, meaning "right." Reins supplemented the driver's control. It is uncertain where J.W. Fisher took this photograph. (Courtesy of Candy Vyvey Moulton Collection.)

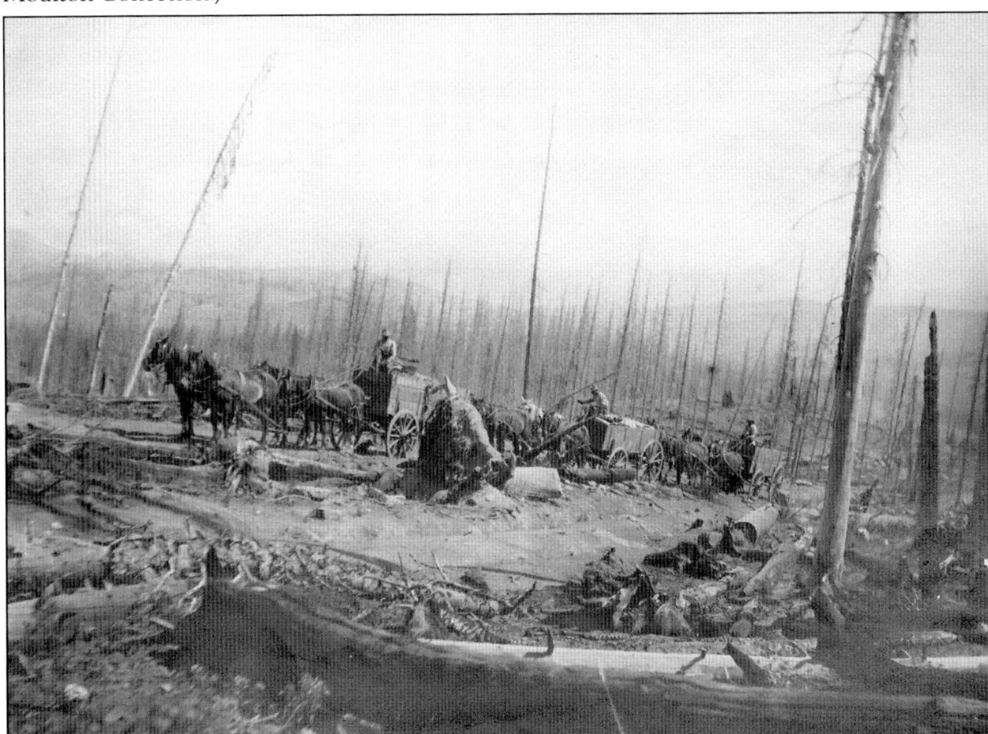

Tom Strand is one of the drivers, as three freight wagons of supplies are hauled to Hog Park Tie Camp where workers cutting railroad ties lived. This photograph was likely taken around 1903. There is evidence of forest fires that had burned the region. (Courtesy of GEM/Myrtle Peterson.)

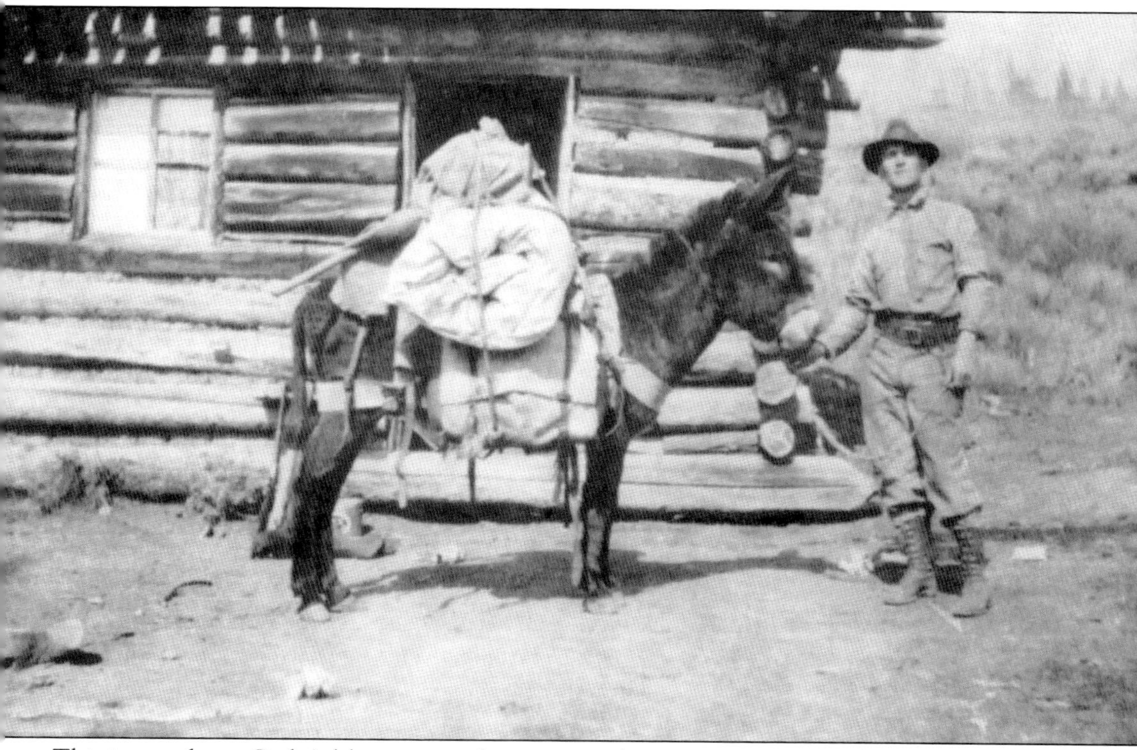

This image shows Carl Ashley apparently preparing for a prospecting expedition. The sturdy burro is piled high with a tent, camping gear, tools, and ore bags. Near the burro's back legs are a can of blasting powder and a rifle. Hardy prospectors searched the area diligently and discovered the mineral wealth that brought the mining industry to the Encampment Valley. (Courtesy of Candy Vyvey Moulton Collection.)

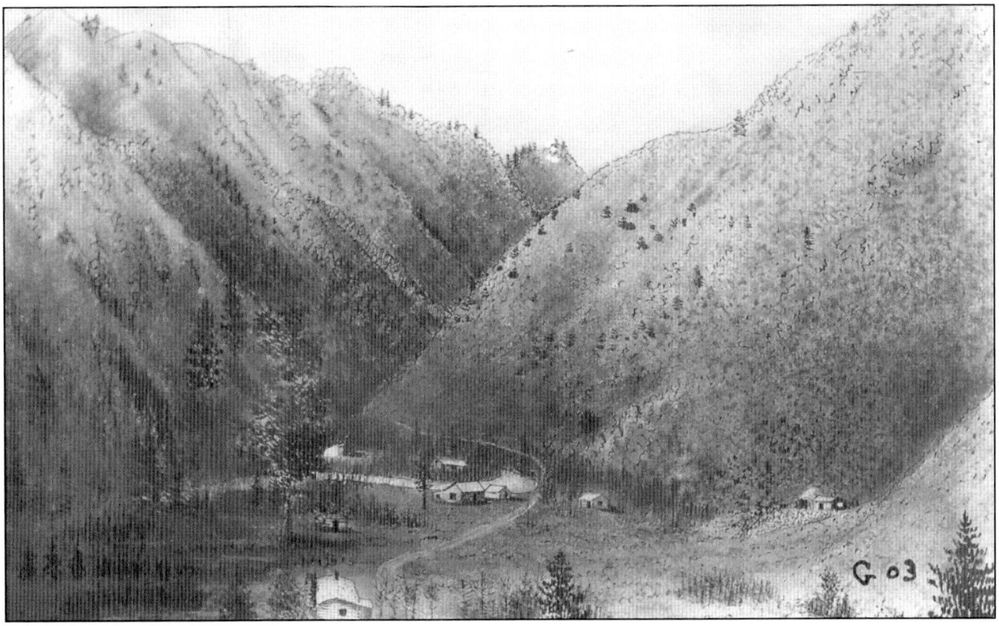

M.D. Houghton spent a considerable amount of time in the Grand Encampment Mining District sketching the various mining camps and communities for publications, such as his *Portfolio of Views*. This is one of his drawings of a mining district camp. (Courtesy of GEM.)

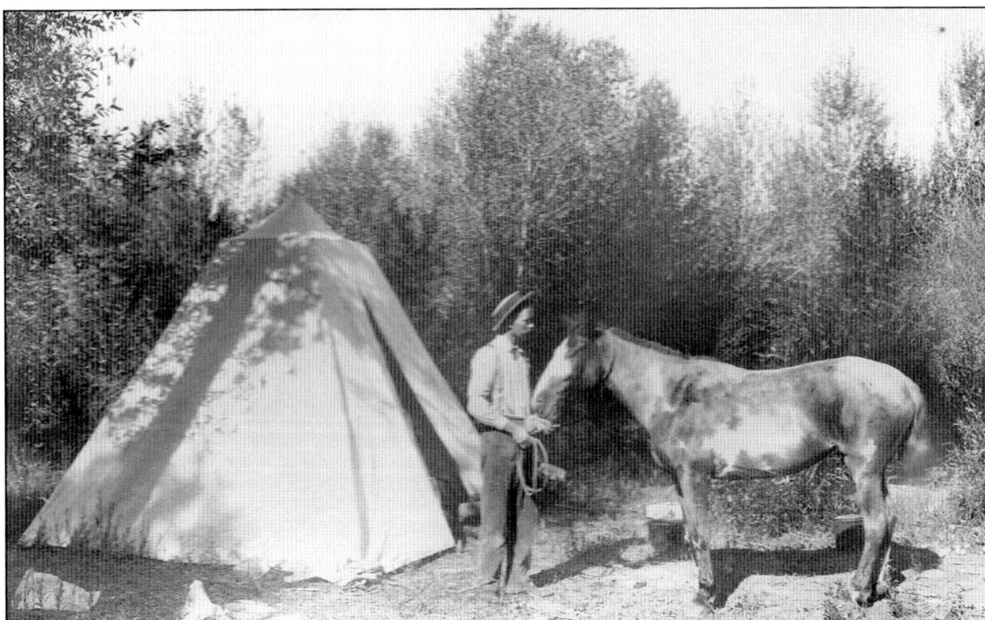

Many miners were forced to camp near their work. Until communities could be built, small campsites dotted the Encampment Valley. In this early-19th-century image, an unknown man poses in front of his tent with his horse. (Courtesy of GEM/Hila Parkison.)

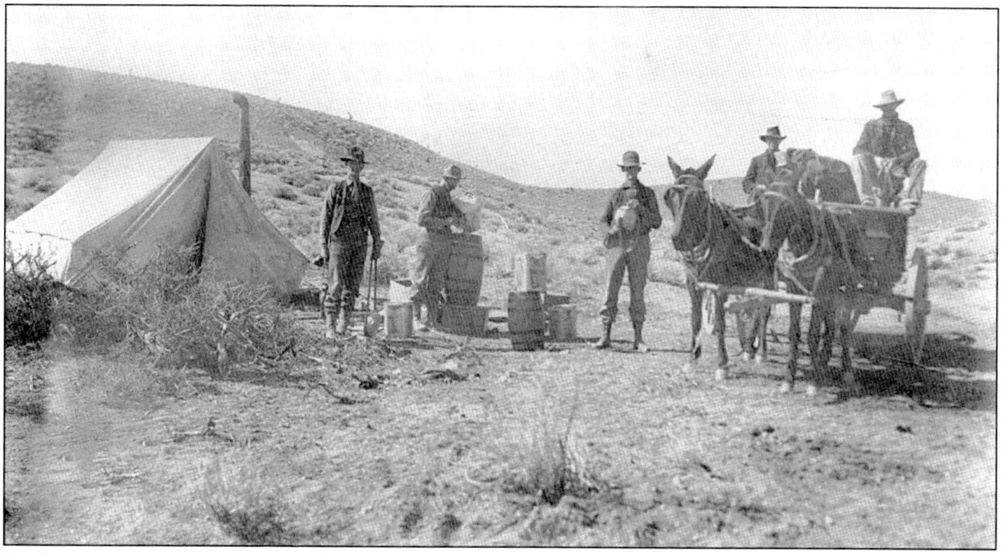

In this image, miners apparently are restocking their water supplies. The man second from the left appears to be pouring water from a large, tinned container while the men on either side of him bring out their canteens. Dry camps like this were often necessary to keep the miners near the diggings. (Courtesy of GEM/Hila Parkison.)

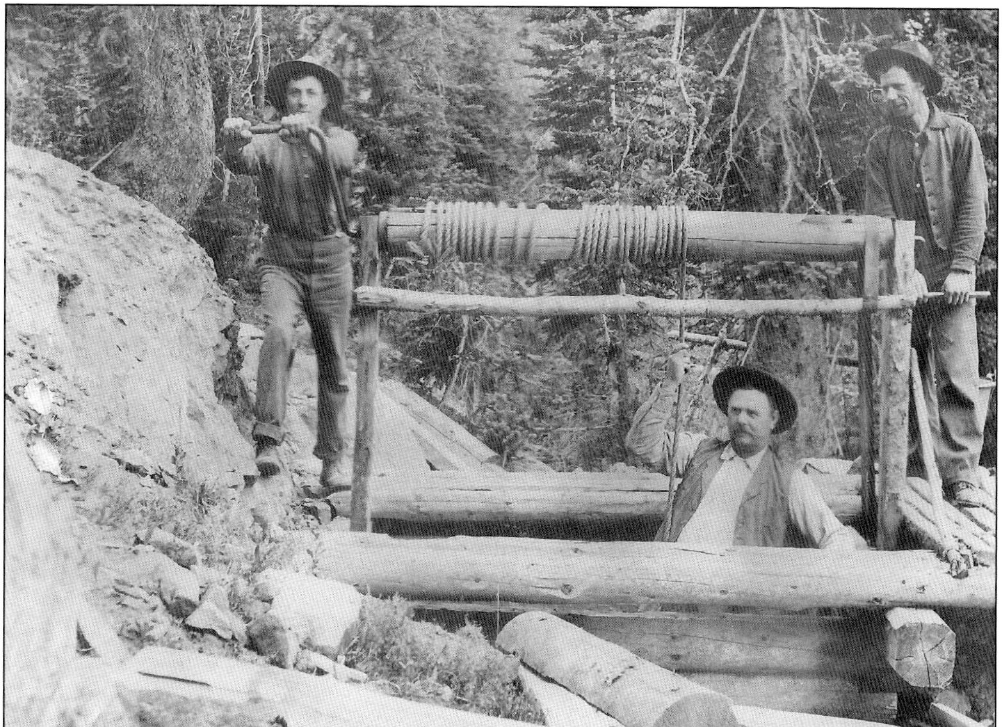

Dick Parr (right) and an unidentified man lower Omar Dunbar into a mine shaft. The discoloration at the top of the photograph is a stain from a fire at the Ellis Herring home that claimed the lives of two of the Herring children (Lloyd and Kenneth). Only a few possessions were saved, including such items as this photograph. (Courtesy of GEM/Gladys and Ellis Herring family.)

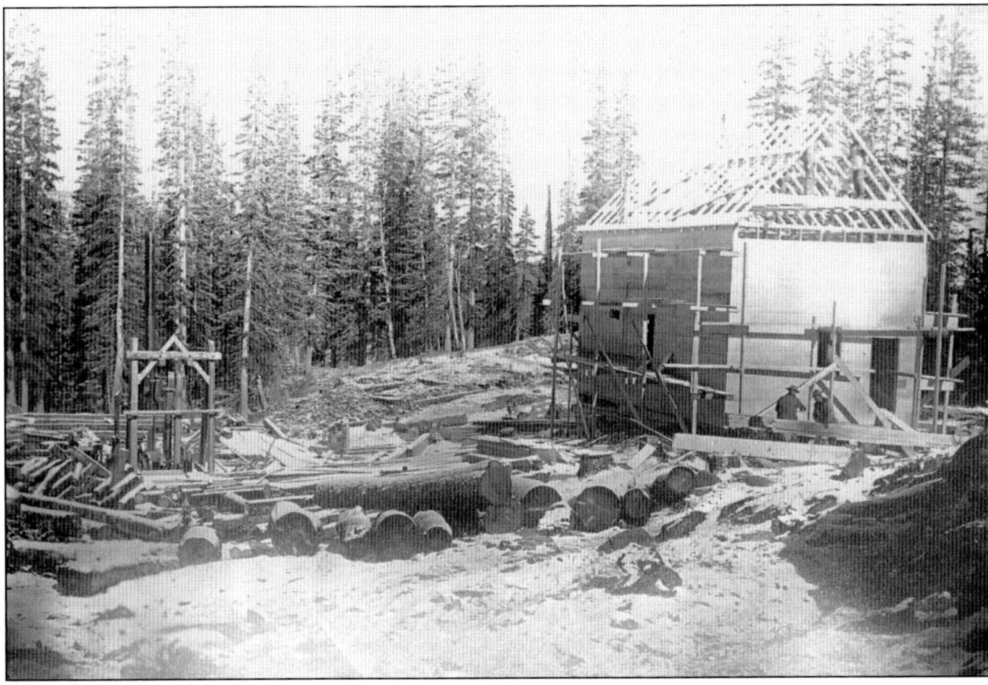

This image depicts construction on new buildings at a mining property on Monday, September 5, 1910. The location is thought to be the Batchelder Mine. Planks, boards, and beams apparently are processed at the steam-powered mill at left. Trees were cut locally and brought to the mill for processing. (Courtesy of GEM.)

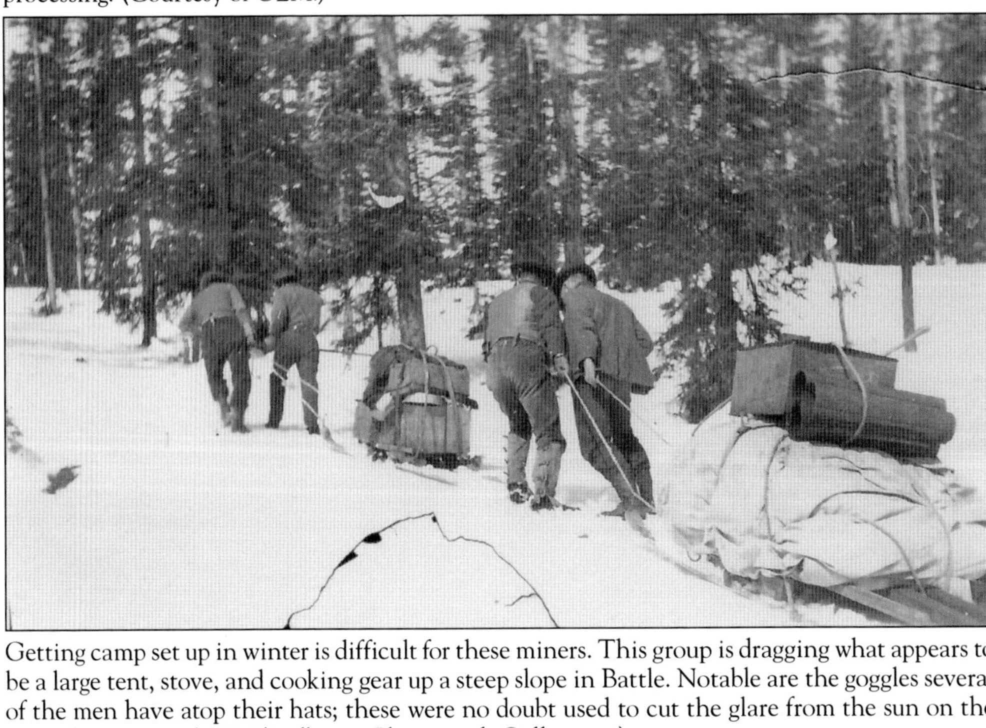

Getting camp set up in winter is difficult for these miners. This group is dragging what appears to be a large tent, stove, and cooking gear up a steep slope in Battle. Notable are the goggles several of the men have atop their hats; these were no doubt used to cut the glare from the sun on the snow. (Courtesy of GEM/Ledbetter Photograph Collection.)

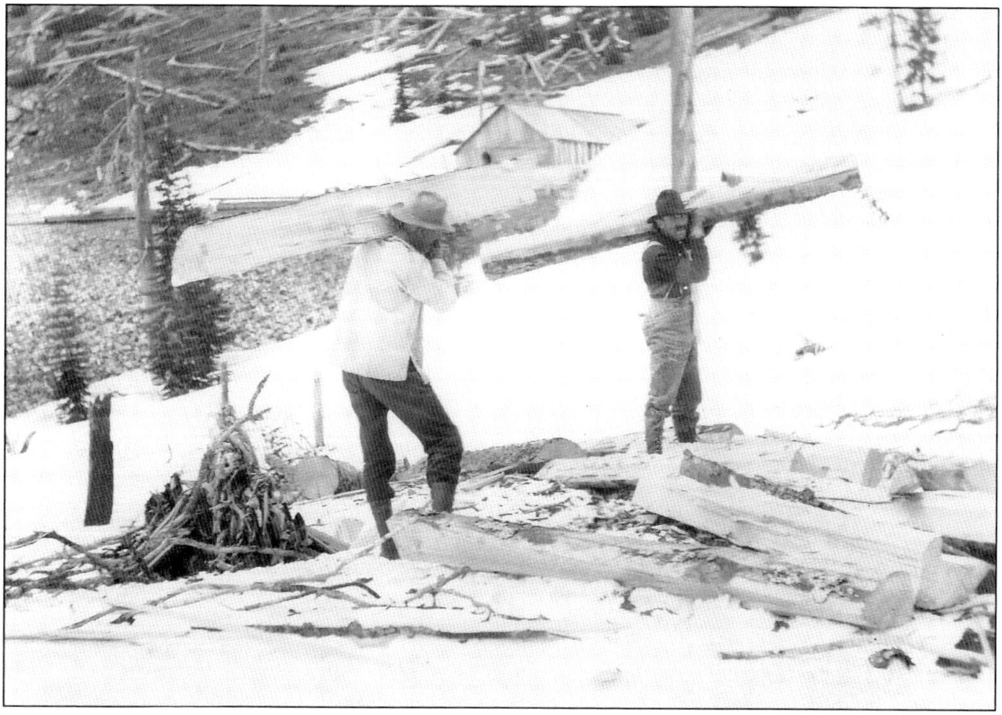

Jack Ledbetter (back to camera) and Russ Ledbetter (right) pile timbers at the Portland Mine tunnel. The timbers are used to brace the tunnel and reduce the risk of collapse. The Ledbetter brothers lived in Battle during the mining operations but later moved to Saratoga where they became prominent residents. (Courtesy of GEM/Ledbetter Photograph Collection.)

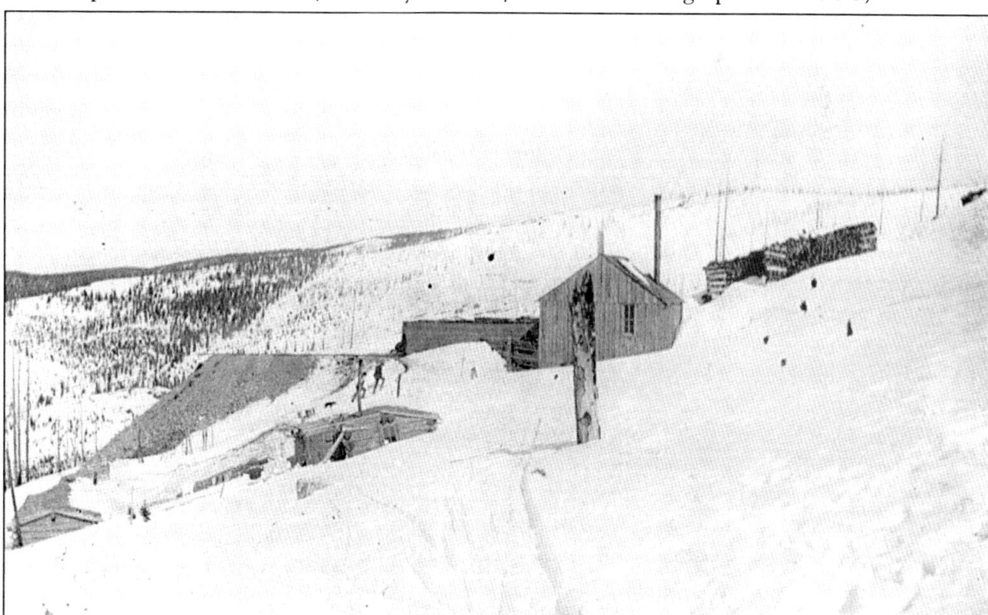

Workers traverse a snow-covered roof at the Batchelder Mine. The hills immediately surrounding the mine have been denuded of trees, which were used to build the structures and provide fuel for the miners. (Courtesy of GEM.)

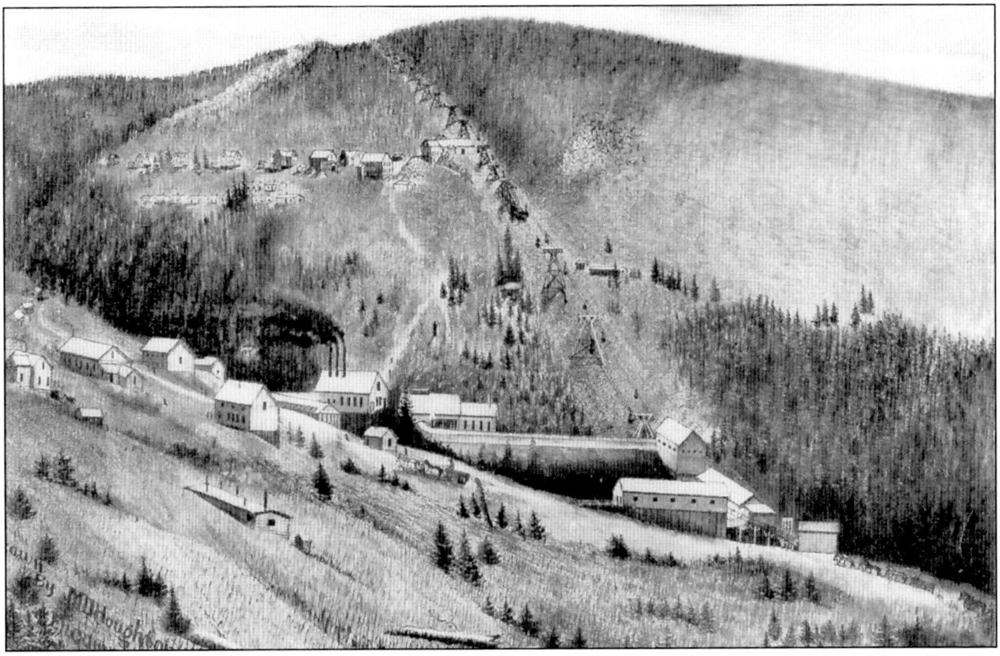

Merritt Dana Houghton sketched the Ferris-Haggarty Mine for inclusion in his *Portfolio of Views*. The caption reads, "The Ferris-Haggarty mine is the base, not only of the North American Copper Company's heavy investments but is also the direct cause of an increase in all branches of industry in this part of Wyoming, to the extent of several hundred per cent." (Courtesy of Candy Vyvey Moulton Collection.)

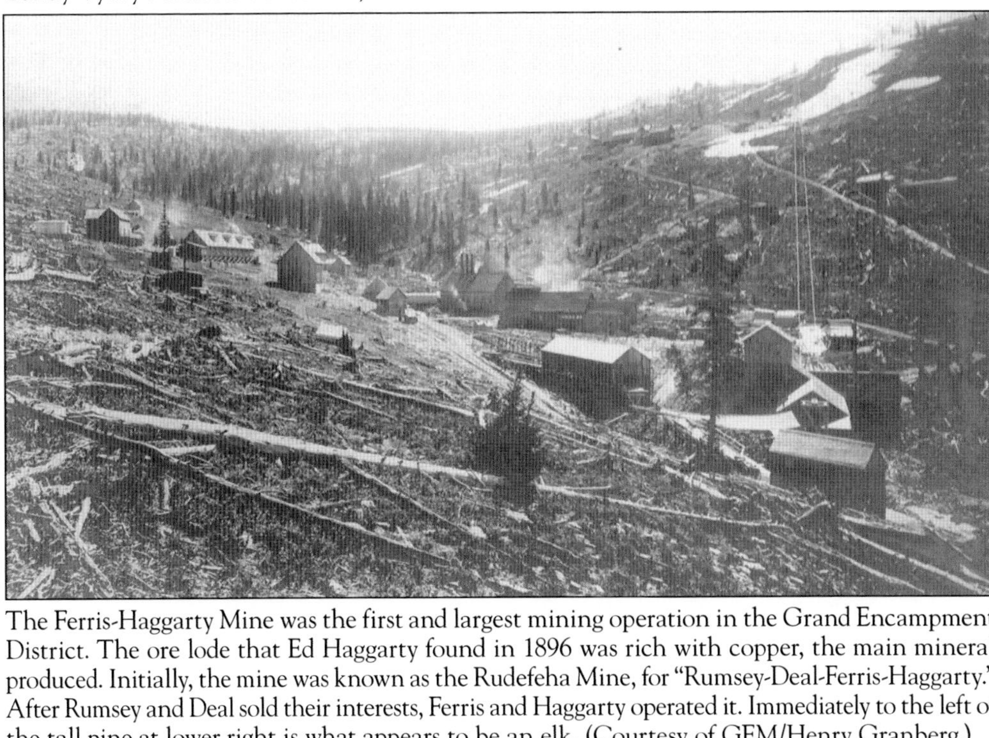

The Ferris-Haggarty Mine was the first and largest mining operation in the Grand Encampment District. The ore lode that Ed Haggarty found in 1896 was rich with copper, the main mineral produced. Initially, the mine was known as the Rudefeha Mine, for "Rumsey-Deal-Ferris-Haggarty." After Rumsey and Deal sold their interests, Ferris and Haggarty operated it. Immediately to the left of the tall pine at lower right is what appears to be an elk. (Courtesy of GEM/Henry Granberg.)

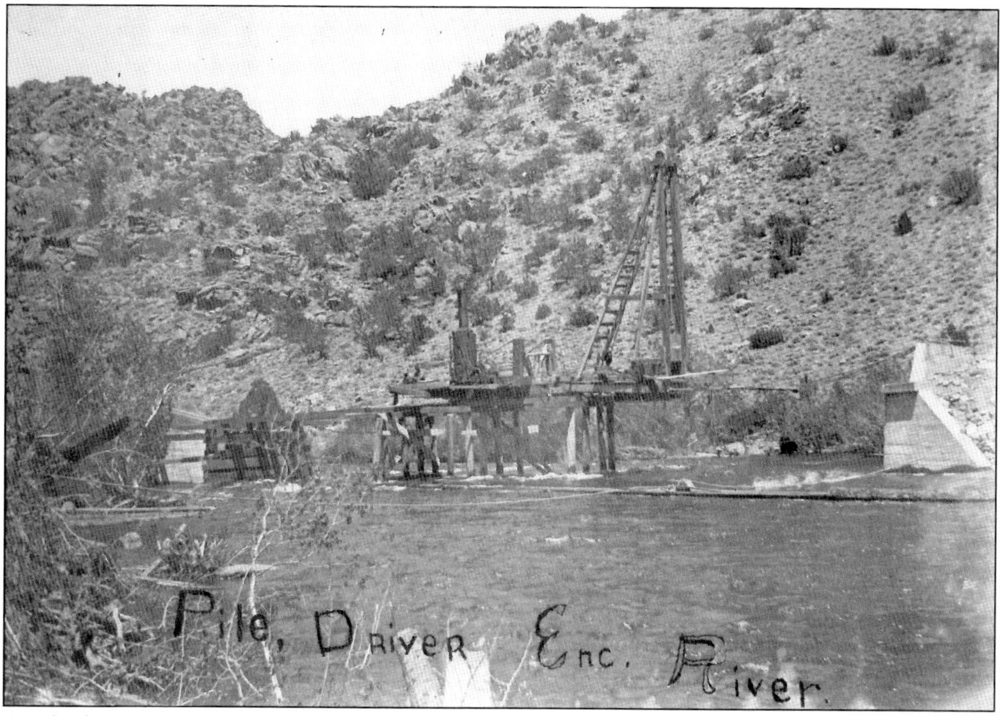

A pile driver hammers supports into the bed of the Grand Encampment River. Such supports were necessary for bridges and pipeline abutments. The steam-powered equipment in this image is thought to be working on abutments. (Courtesy of GEM.)

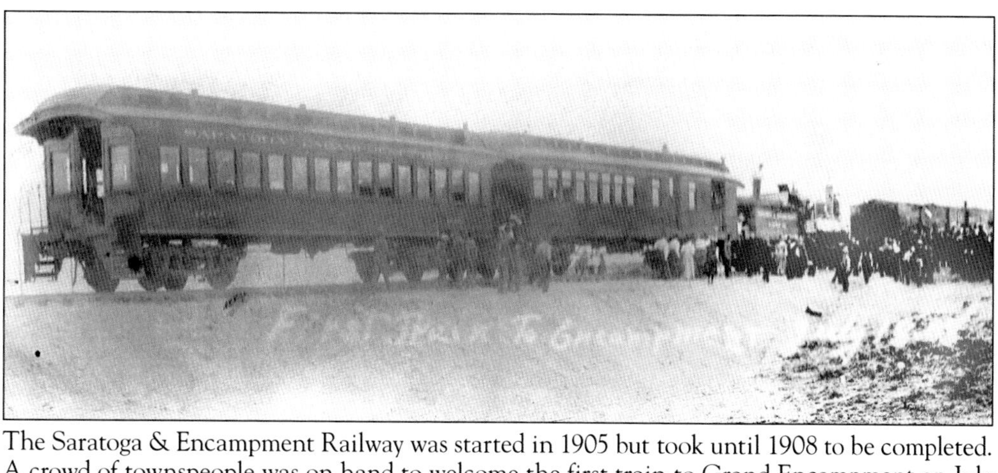
The Saratoga & Encampment Railway was started in 1905 but took until 1908 to be completed. A crowd of townspeople was on hand to welcome the first train to Grand Encampment on July 15, 1908. The line connected with the Union Pacific Railroad in Walcott and had a troubled history, eventually being given to the Union Pacific Railroad in 1928. (Courtesy of GEM.)

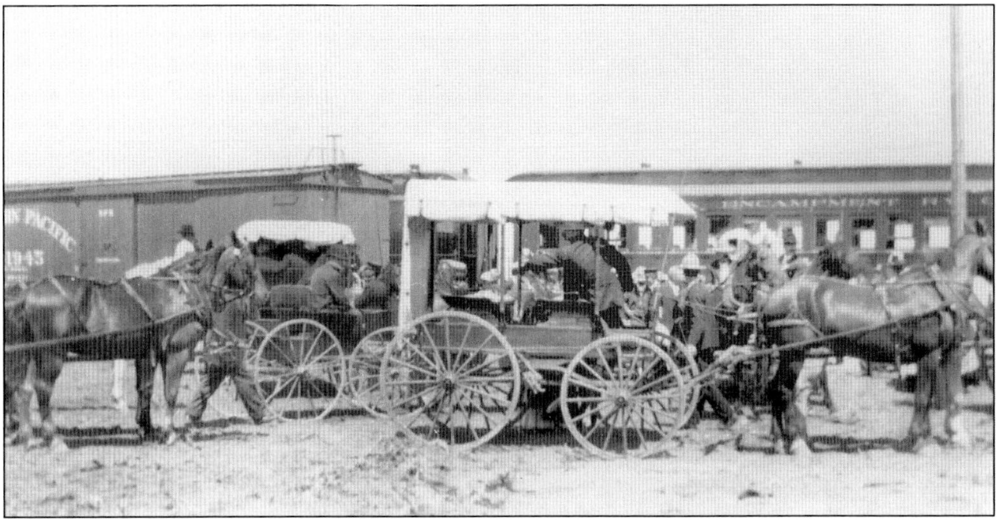

As is obvious in the energetic crowds supporting Railroad Day 1908, the Saratoga & Encampment Railway was of tremendous importance to the local economy. The line was started by private investors to serve the copper mining industry but found new business when the smelter closed. Purchased by Morse Machinery and Supply, the railroad survived numerous attempts to abandon it by the owners, operating for years in court-ordered receivership. (Courtesy of GEM/Bahs Cruse.)

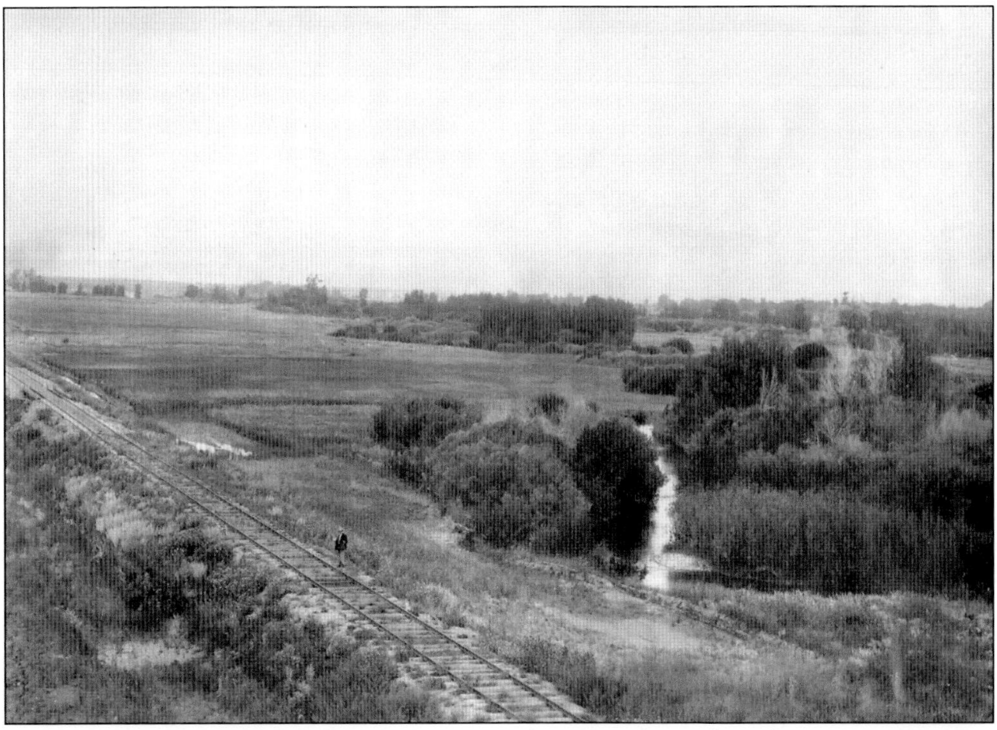

Getting a railroad was not easy. Five companies vied to put in the tracks with promotions starting in 1901. The investors of the Saratoga & Encampment Railway had the right stuff and managed to finish the task though others had years of a head start. This image shows the tracks of the Saratoga & Encampment Railway at Cow Creek, eight miles north of Encampment. (Courtesy of GEM.)

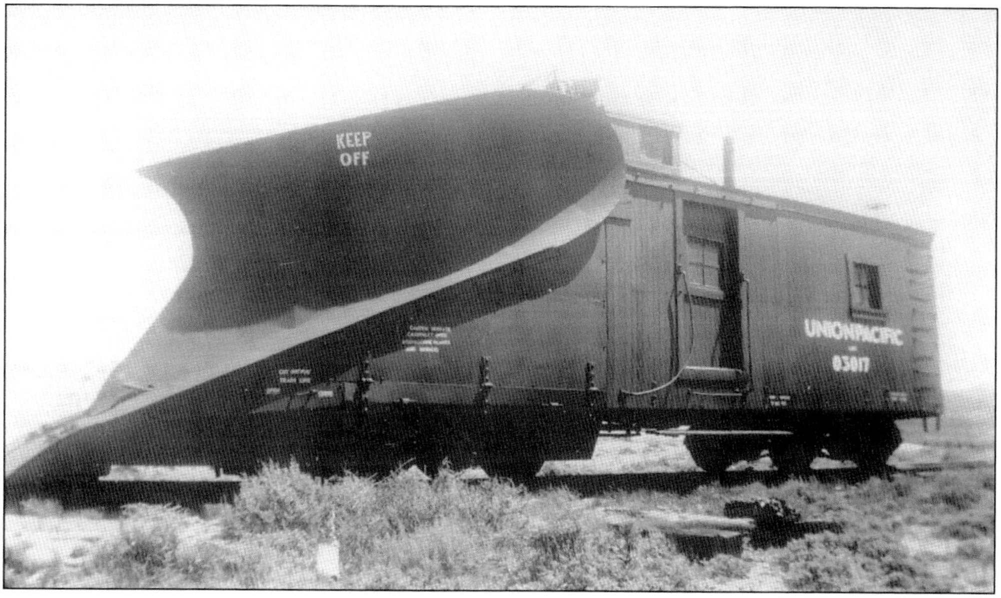

The Saratoga & Encampment Railway arrived at the smelter on July 15, 1908, bringing rail service to Grand Encampment and drawing a large crowd of people for the celebration. Plummeting copper prices closed the smelter shortly after the railroad arrived, taking away the primary impetus for the line's existence. This is one of the snowplows used on the line after the Union Pacific took control. (Courtesy of Candy Vyvey Moulton Collection.)

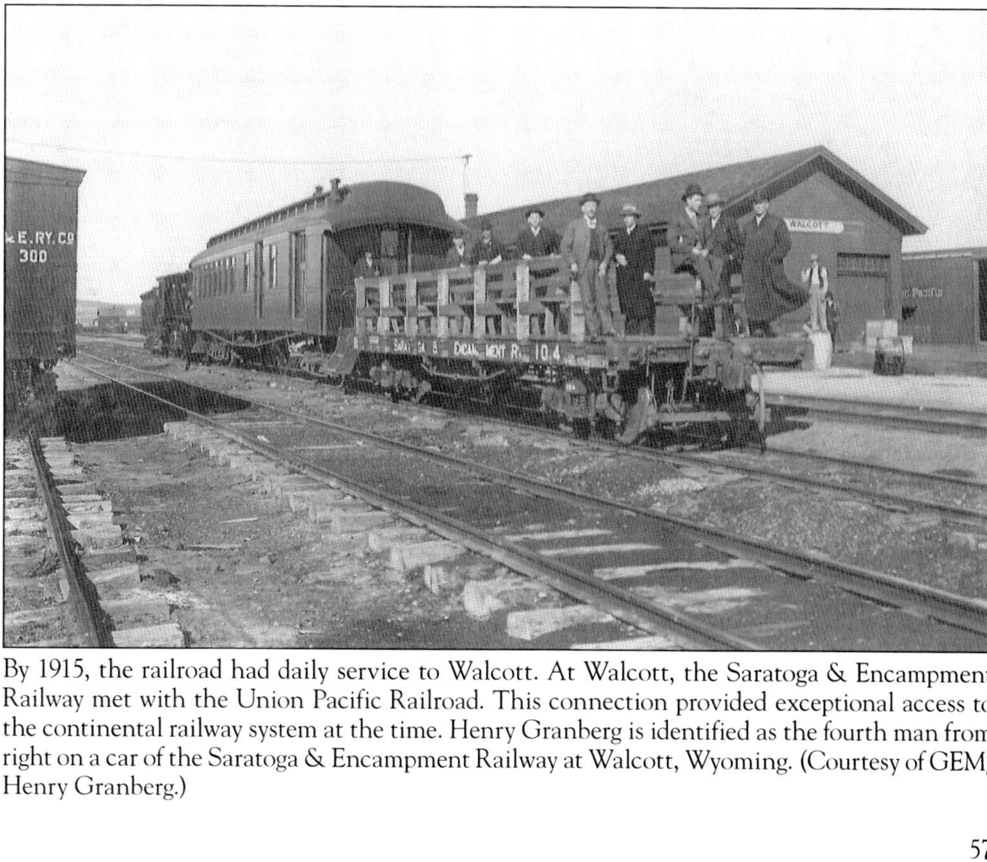

By 1915, the railroad had daily service to Walcott. At Walcott, the Saratoga & Encampment Railway met with the Union Pacific Railroad. This connection provided exceptional access to the continental railway system at the time. Henry Granberg is identified as the fourth man from right on a car of the Saratoga & Encampment Railway at Walcott, Wyoming. (Courtesy of GEM/ Henry Granberg.)

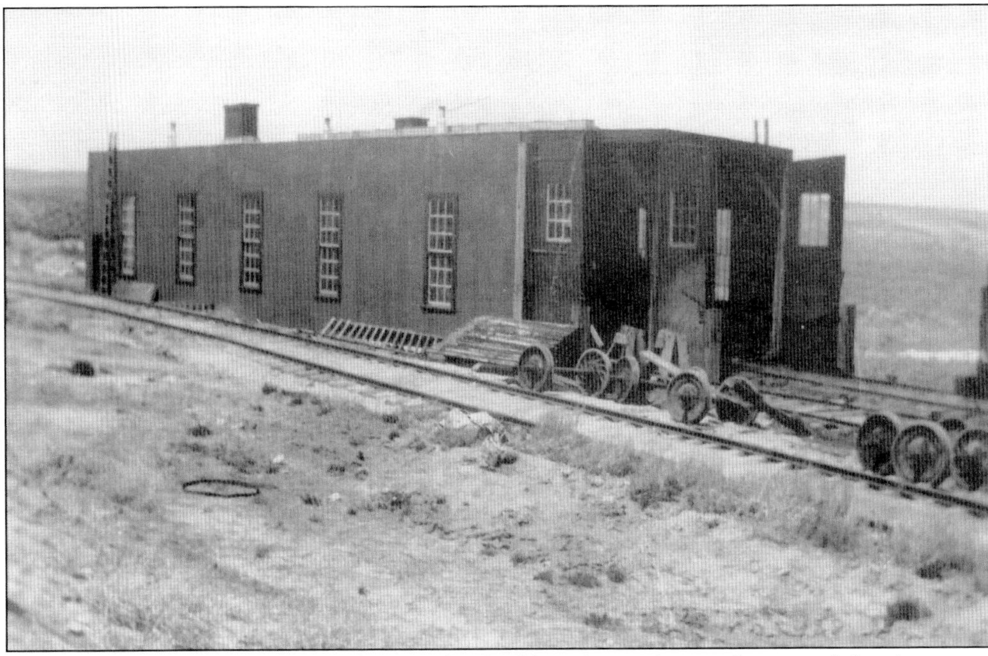

Though technically not a roundhouse, this building located near the site of the American Copper Company Smelter effectively served as one for the two engines used by the Saratoga & Encampment Railway. The building was used to house and repair the trains as well as to pull rolling stock off the tracks. (Courtesy of GEM/Alan Barka.)

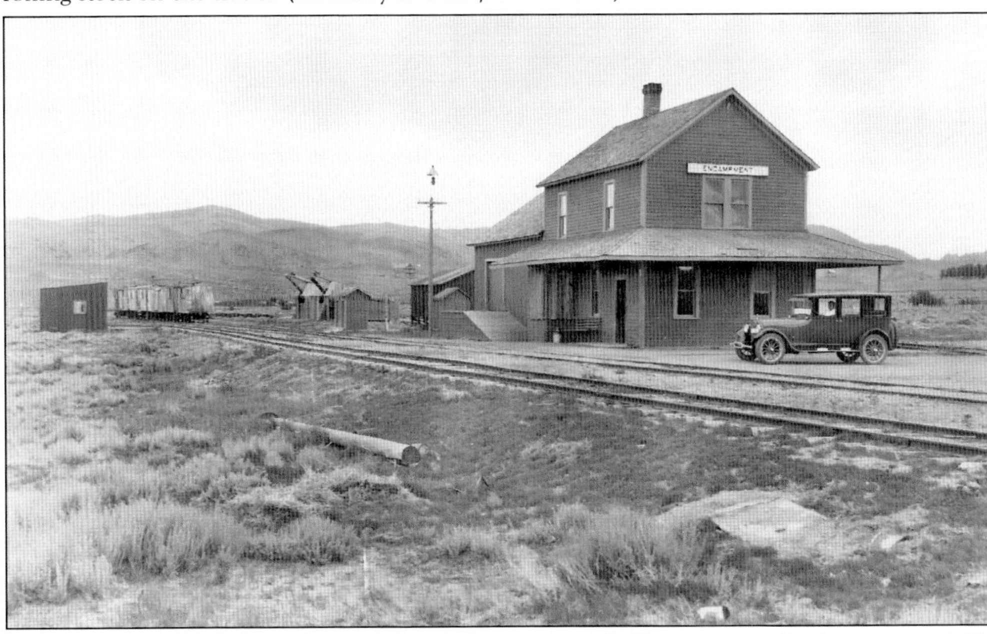

Affectionately called the "Slow and Easy," the Saratoga & Encampment Railway was quickly seized upon by the livestock industry as an economical way to get products to markets. The scales and stockyards near the Encampment depot pictured here quickly became a local fixture and a subject of heated debate when the scales were scrapped by the owners in 1967. (Courtesy of GEM/Dr. Scott Thomas.)

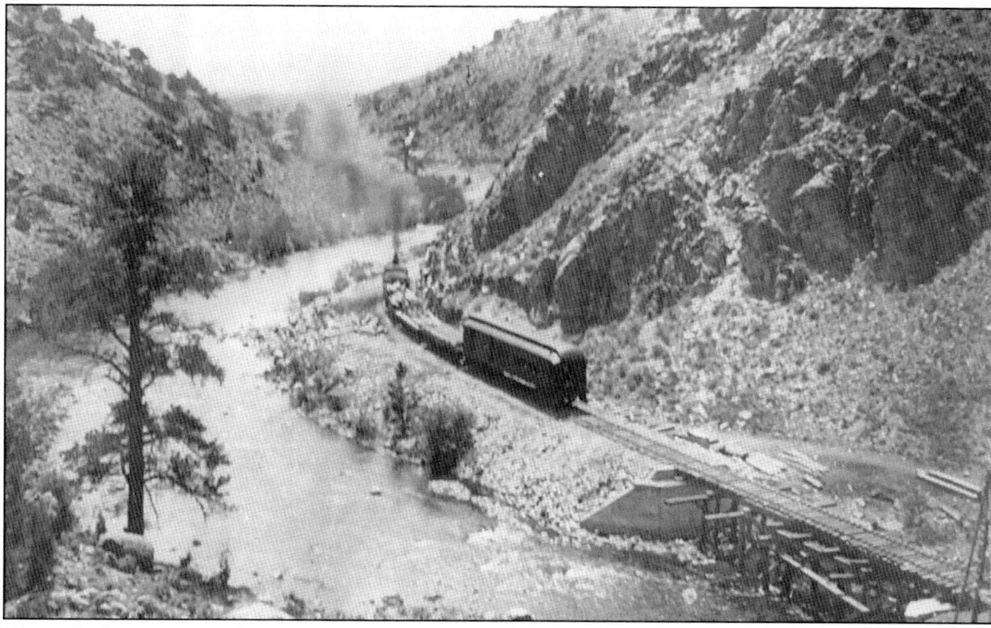

Though the scene of the Encampment River and Baggott Rocks suggests tranquility, the Slow and Easy did not have a prosperous life. Its owners tried repeatedly to close the line only to be forced to remain open. Carbon County residents bought the line and gifted it to the Union Pacific Railroad, provided the line remain open in perpetuity. That did not happen. In spite of protest, it ceased operation in 1974. (Courtesy of GEM/Cecil Ryan.)

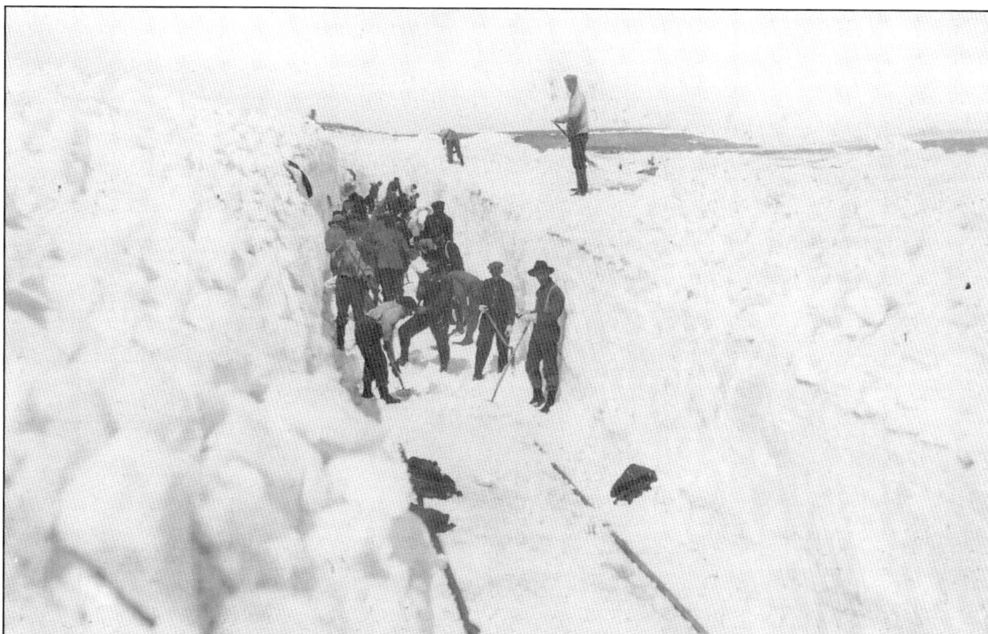

While the technology existed in 1917 to plow snow from tracks, the deep snows of that winter apparently foiled the machines. Here, a hand crew clears the track the old-fashioned way, using shovels with some muscles behind them. This appears to be a drift area, as the snows on the neighboring hills have been mostly removed by the wind. (Courtesy of GEM.)

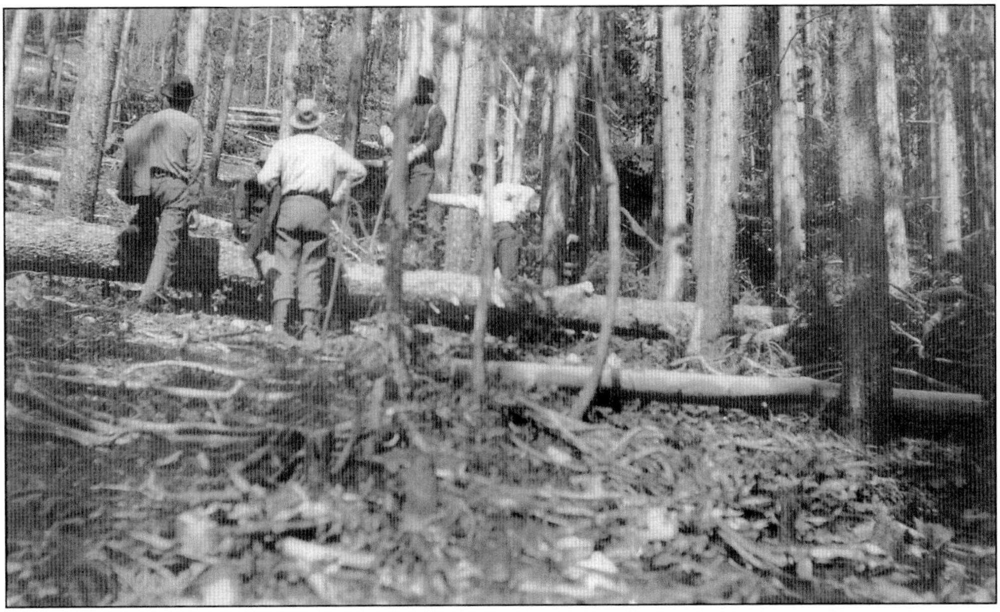

The production of railroad ties, called tie hacking, became a major employer in the Encampment area. The men who did the laborious work of cutting trees, shaping ties, and then floating them to rail junctions were called tie hacks. These are tie hacks cutting trees near Billy Creek Tie Camp. This operation was promoted by Ed Hoyt Parkison, so the camp is sometimes called Parkison's. (Courtesy of GEM.)

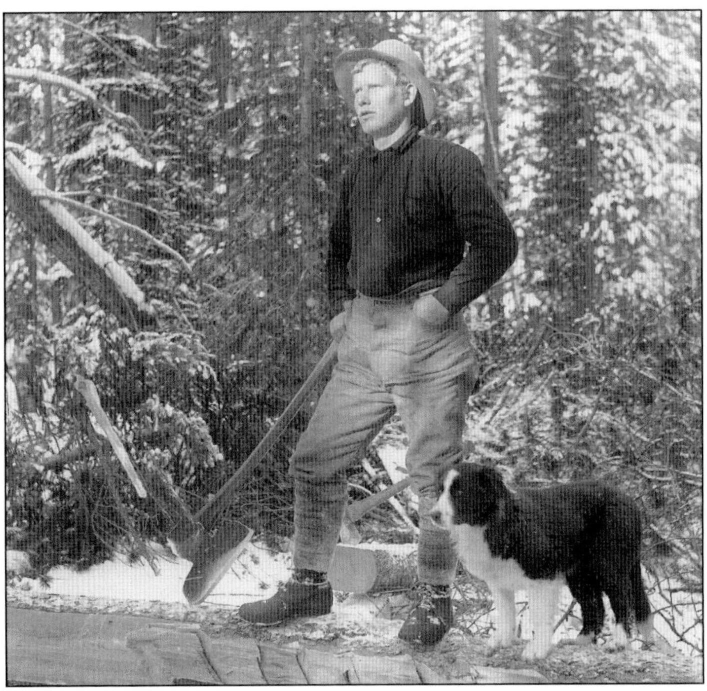

Ole Fuglaar with his dog and broadax present the archetypical image of a rugged tie hack. The log on which Ole stands shows the deep cuts of the initial shaping of a log into a tie. Much of the tie hack's work is done in the winter months with transportation to market on the swollen streams and rivers of spring. (Courtesy of GEM.)

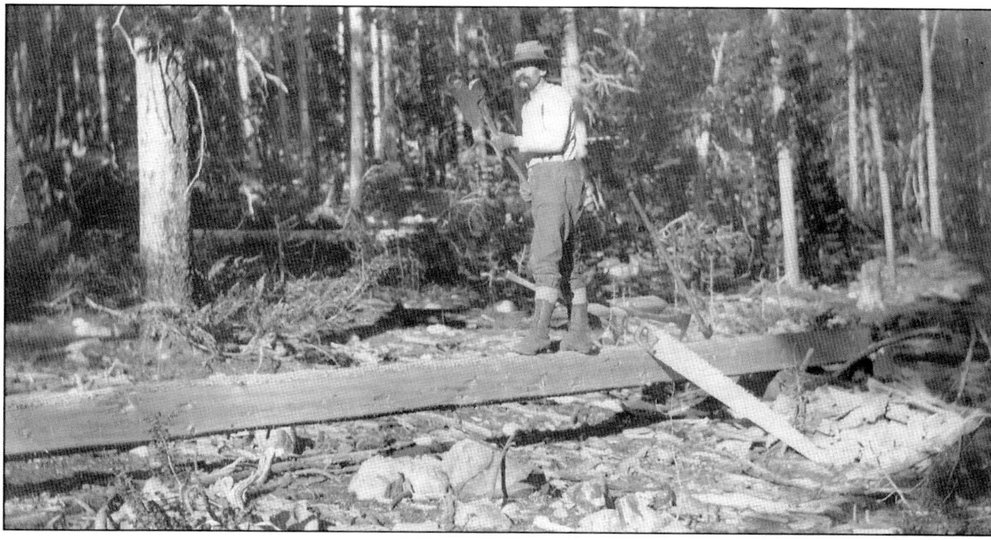

Above, John P. Oxford wields a broadax as he cuts a tie. His daughter was Sylvia Oxford Ethell. Sylvia spent the 1904–1905 winter in the Carbon Timber Company Camp at Hog Park. She later wrote in *Winter Moods of 1904–05* that Carbon Timber Company, with Dan Wilt as the superintendent, "employed about one thousand men, divided into numerous 'camps,' allotted certain portions of timber to be cut into ties and delivered to a landing field on the bank of the Encampment River to await the spring drive that would carry them to Fort Steele. It was the job of the Inspector P.O. Shortt to count and grade all these ties, each cutter having a brand on each tie that must be accounted for." Below, a typical tie camp at winter's end is stacked high with ties for the spring drive. (Courtesy of GEM/Ferris Album.)

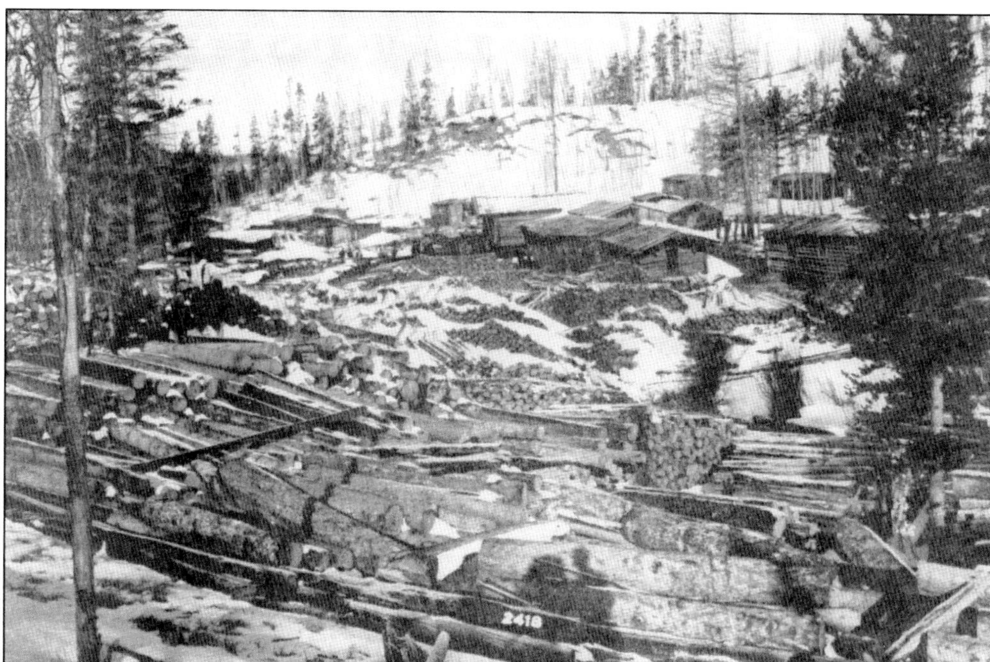

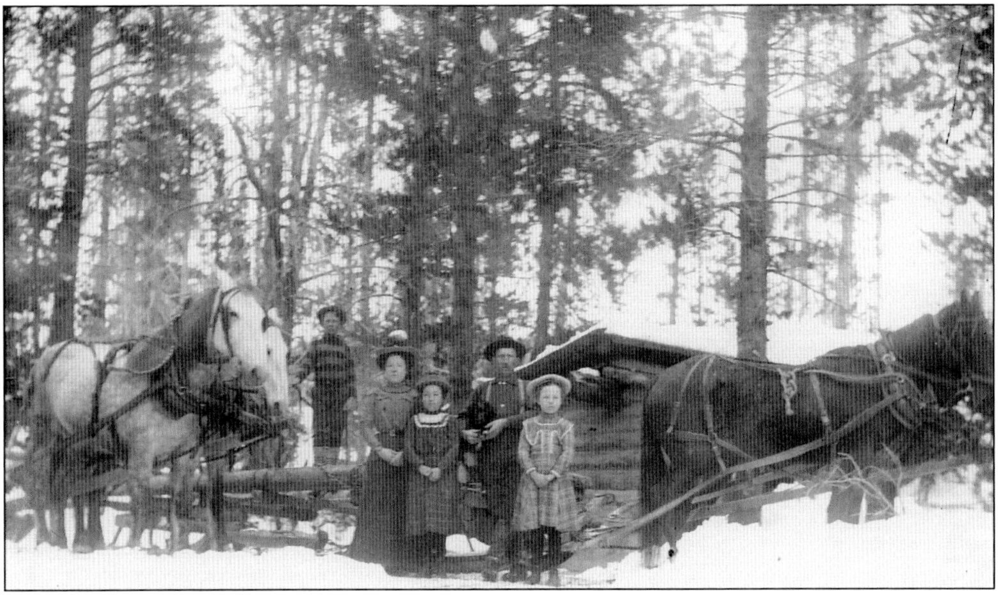

Tie hacks often brought their families into the camps to share the long winters. Here is the W.A. Ralston family at Hog Park Tie Camp in 1902. From left to right are Lester Ralston (boy on ties), Della Ralston (Shawver), Lulu Ralston (Roush), William Ralston, and Mae Ralston (later married Claude May). (Courtesy of GEM/Ferris Album.)

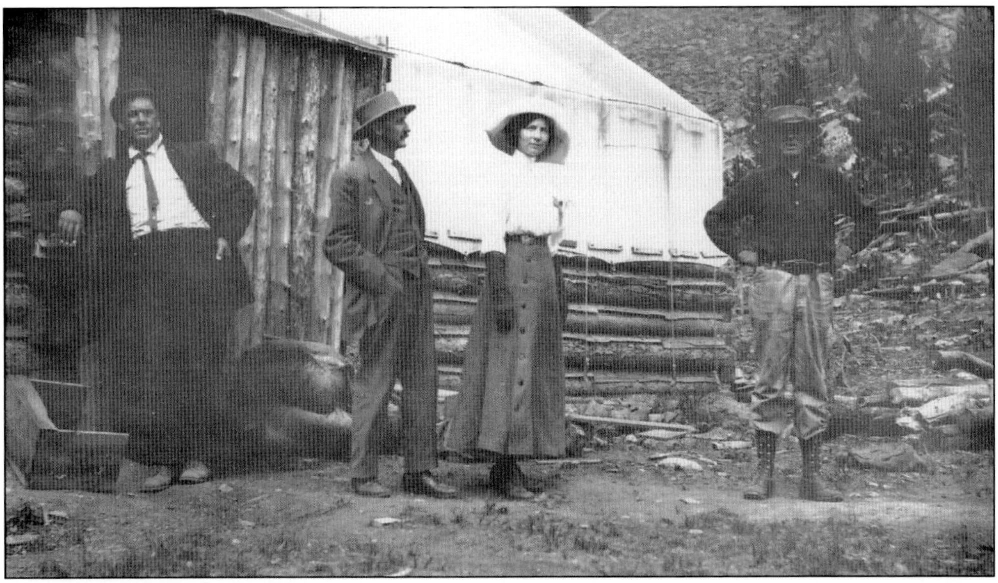

In this image taken at the Billy Creek Tie Camp, the well-dressed couple in the middle is identified as Mr. and Mrs. Stewart. One of the other two men is identified as Charley Martin; the remaining man has yet to be identified. (Courtesy of GEM.)

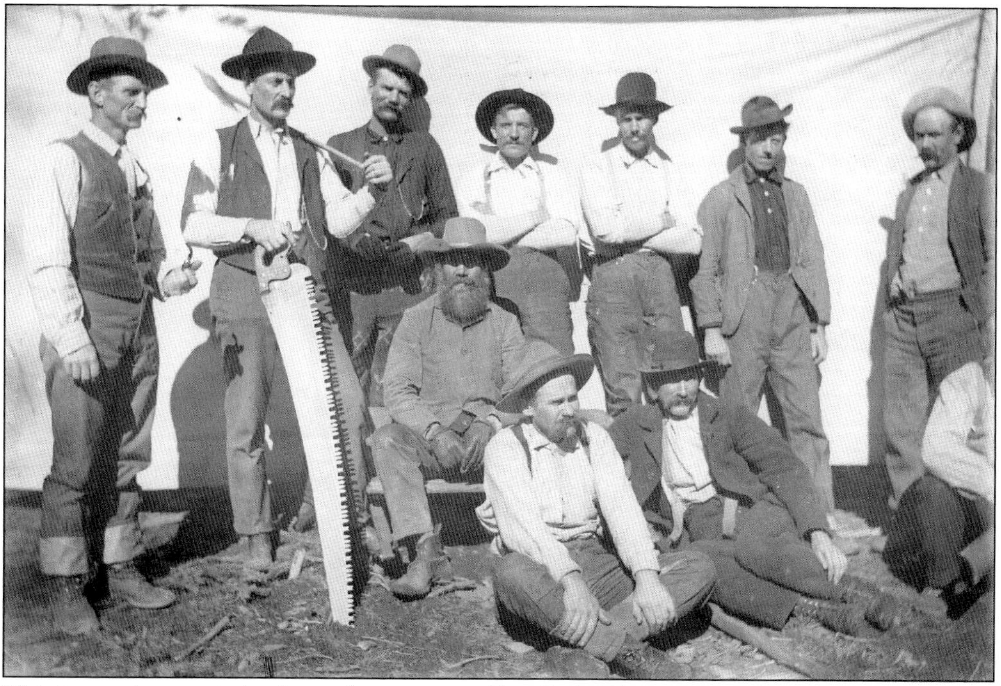

This image depicts tie hacks in their camp at Hog Park. The man standing third from right is James Wellington Clements, who later became a mayor of Encampment. Others who can be identified are a man known as Green River (standing far left) and Billie Carlson (third from left). Some identify the man with dark jacket sitting on the ground as Olaf Olson. (Courtesy of Grand Encampment Museum Photograph Collection.)

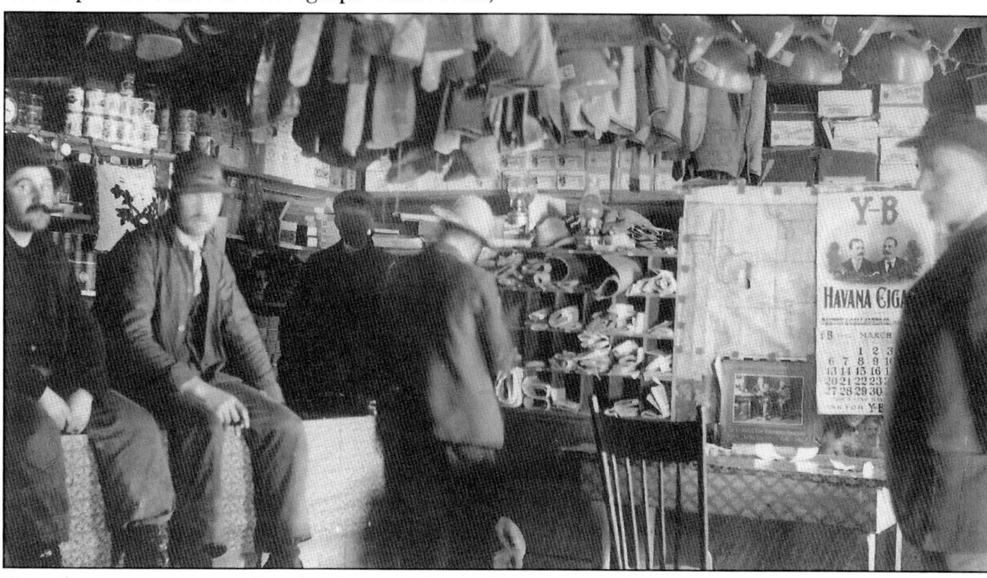

Providing necessary supplies for the workforce, the interior of the commissary at the Hog Park Tie Camp operated by Carbon Timber Company shows the basic items needed in camp. This March 1904 image depicts boots, hats, helmets, alarm clocks, pocket watches, dried oats, canned tomatoes, corn starch, coffee, coffee pots, oil lamps, shoes, blankets, pillows, and many other useful items. No doubt the company charged inflated prices for all merchandise. (Courtesy of GEM.)

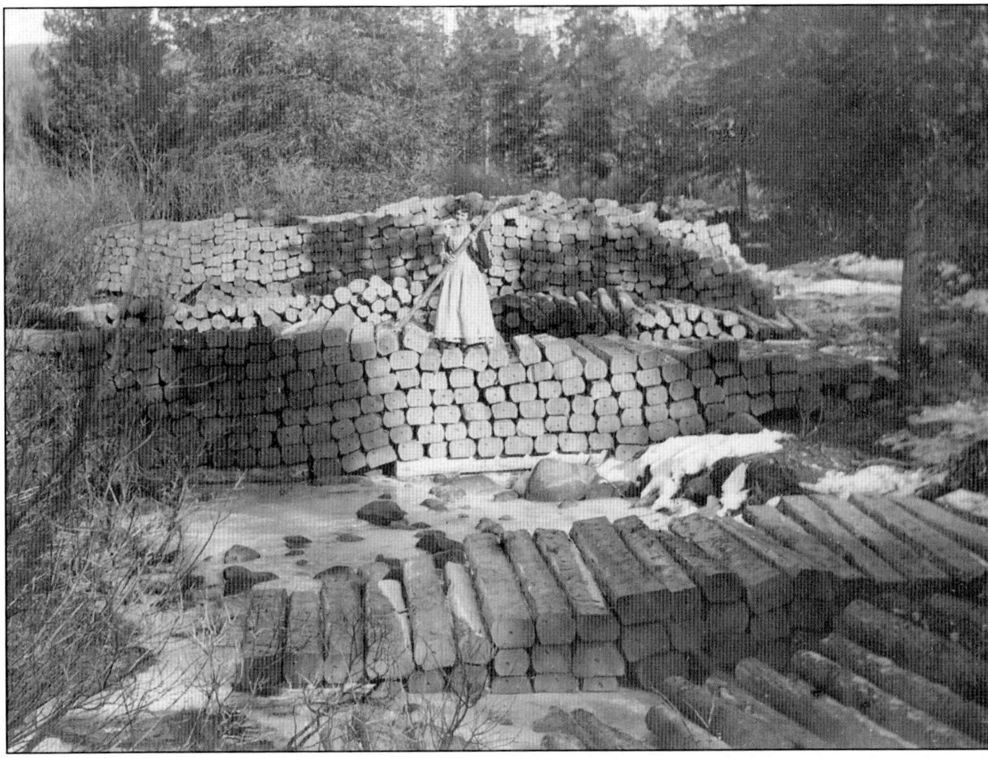

The work of a winter piles up as spring approaches. Although this woman holds a pike pole and stands on a deck of ties, it is unlikely she was working, as she does not appear to be appropriately attired for the job. These ties are ready for the great spring tie drive. (Courtesy of GEM/Ferris Album.)

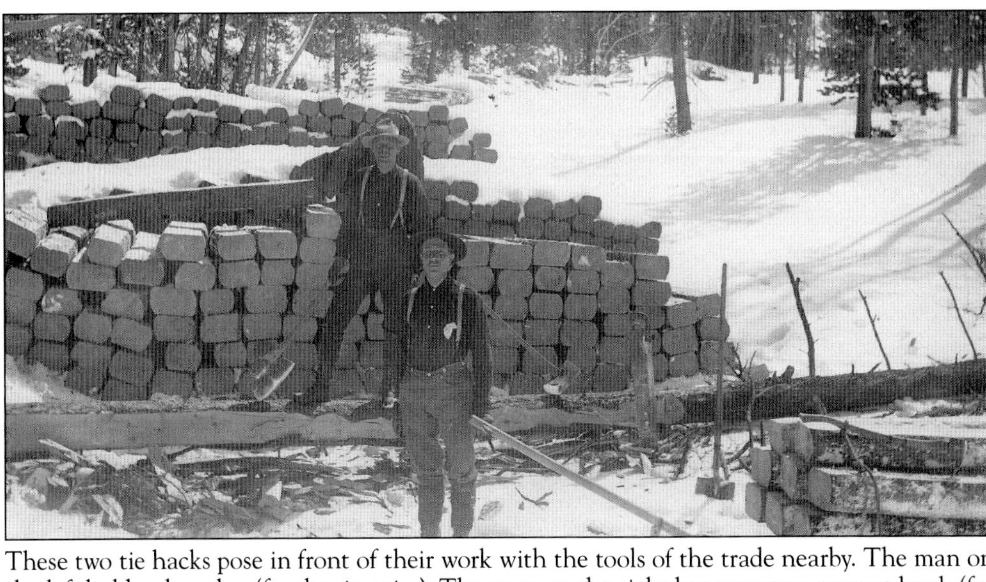

These two tie hacks pose in front of their work with the tools of the trade nearby. The man on the left holds a broadax (for shaping ties). The man on the right has a peavey, or cant hook (for positioning logs), immediately before him and a double-bladed ax (for felling trees) behind. Farther to the right are a saw, shovel, and an adze. (Courtesy of GEM/Ferris Album.)

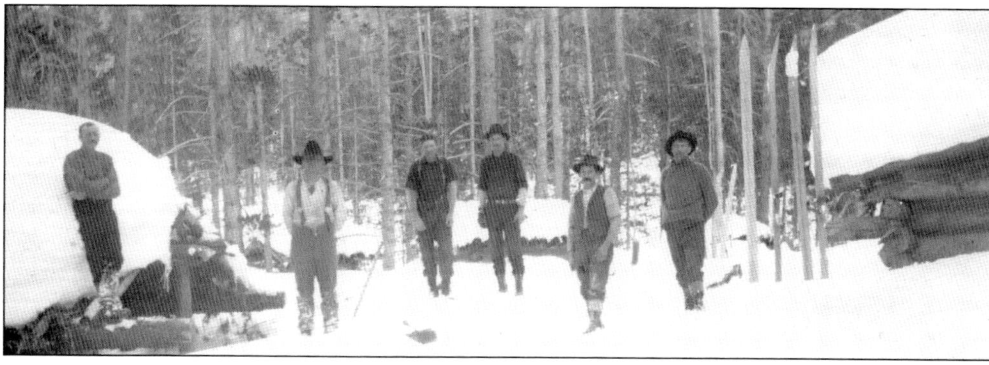

Above, the deep snows of winter are evident in this image from the Hog Park tie camp. Difficulties in getting around on horseback encouraged many tie hacks to ski. Below, Joe Johnston (left) and others drive ties on Billy Creek. Sylvia Ethell later wrote, "It is a thrilling sight to see a timber drive in full swing, with the melting snow forcing an over-flow to the banks of the river in violent torrents carrying the ties, tumbling in mass over each other as they roll and dip in and out of sight, from bank to bank, until a 'jam' starts to pile. Then the men ever on the alert to prevent a 'hang-up' break it and in a violent surge of motion with a deafening noise, the moving mass gives way as it starts on its course by a frantically working crew, until normal floating is restored." (Both, courtesy of GEM.)

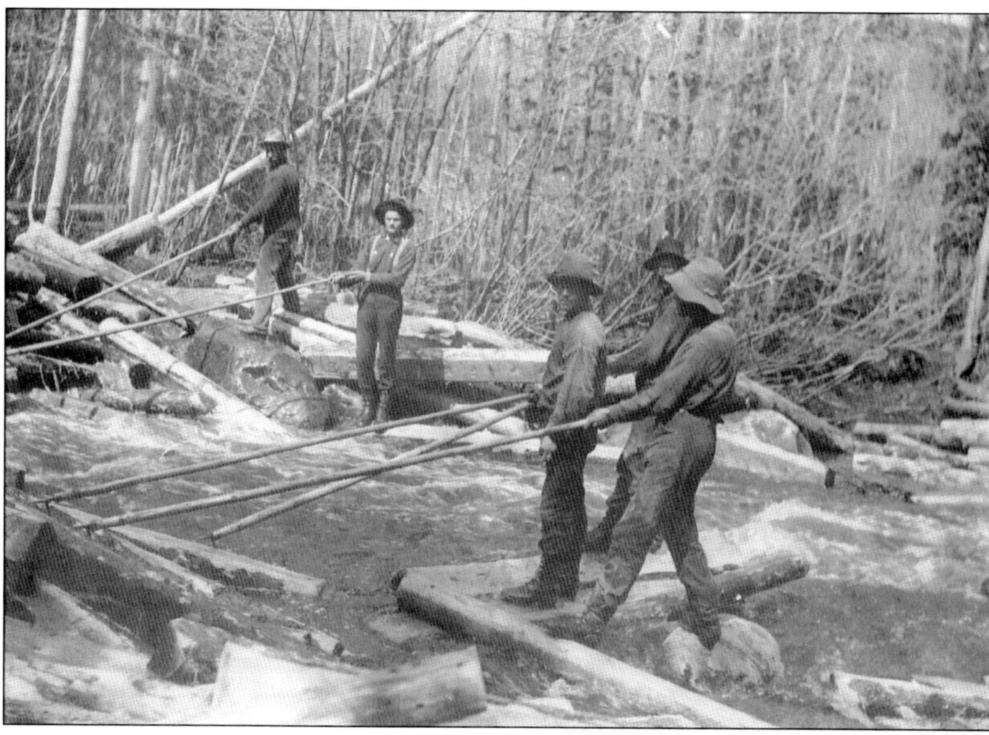

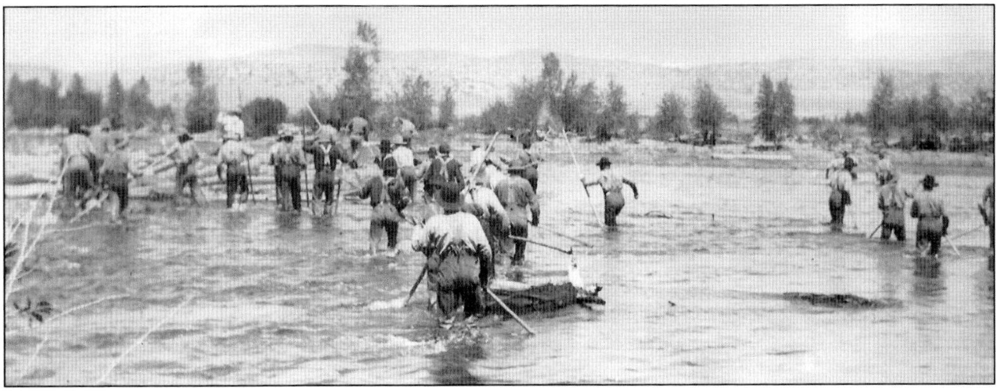

Ties from the Encampment area were gathered together and sent via the swollen streams to Fort Fred Steele. In this image, tie-drive crews carrying long pikes hasten to work ties in the North Platte River. Once at Fort Fred Steele, the ties were loaded onto railroad cars and sent to the Laramie area for treatment. (Courtesy of GEM/Cecil Ryan.)

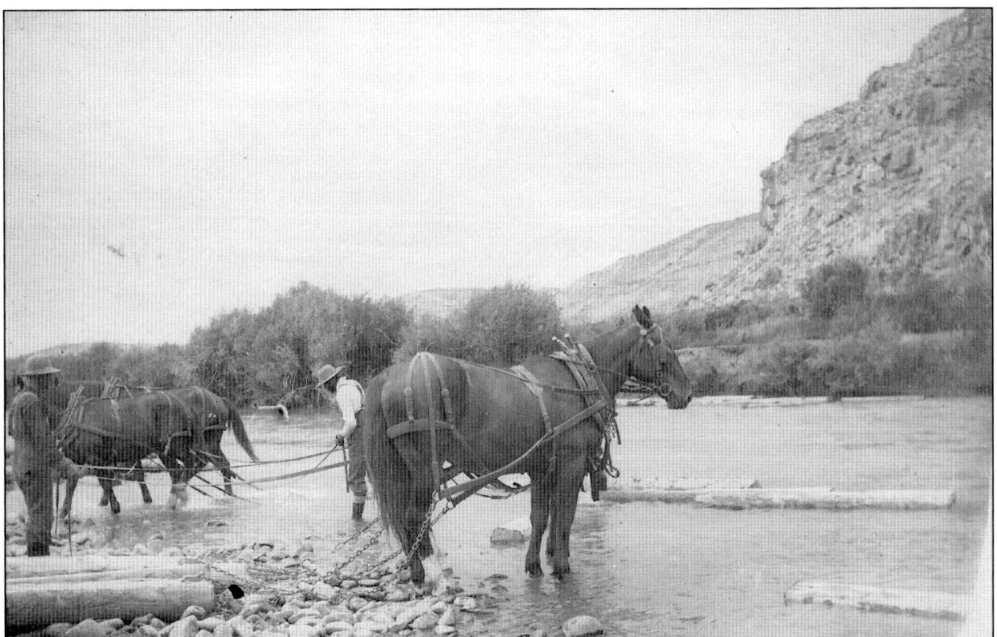

Ties that washed out of the river and onto higher ground had to be skidded back to the water during the tie drives. (Courtesy of GEM/ Ferris Album.)

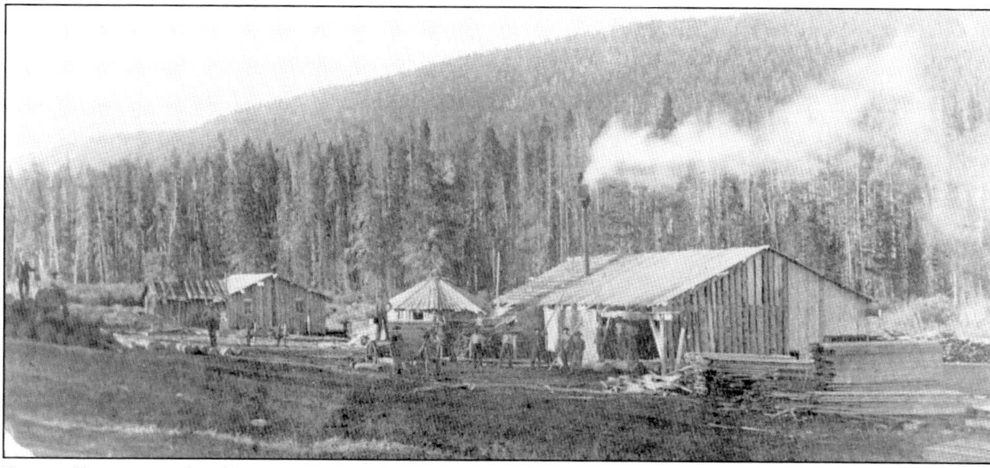

Sawmills operated in Encampment, Saratoga, Ryan Park, and at many locations within the forest where temporary mills were in use. Tom Ryan ran this sawmill in Ryan Park around 1890. R.L. "Mike" Hammer came from a lumbering family—his father worked in the tie camps on French Creek—and he and his sons David and Tom later ran Hammer Timber and Lumber Co., the lumber mill in Encampment. (Courtesy of GEM.)

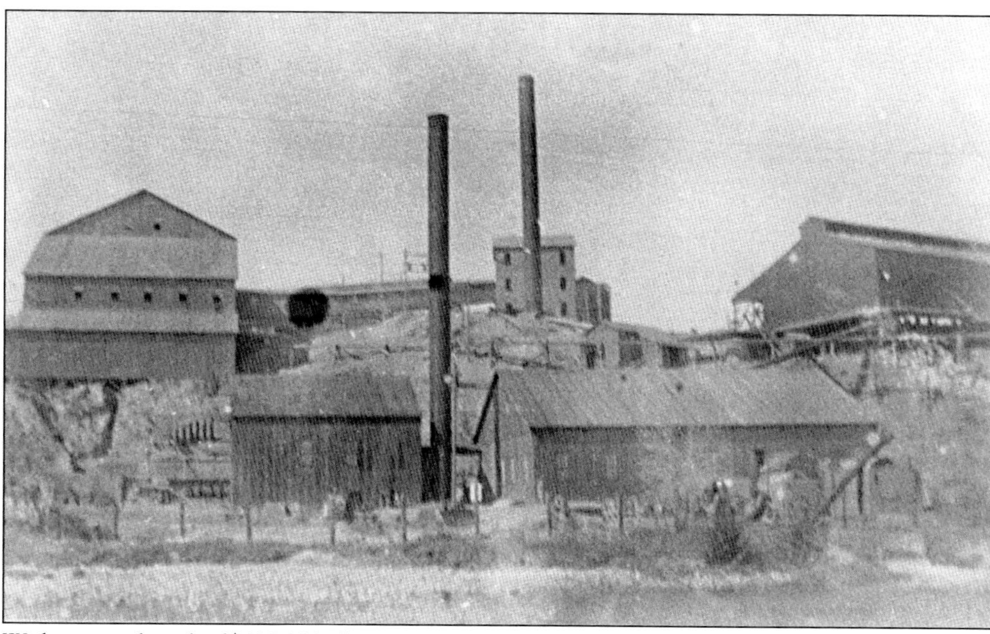

With a capital stock of $600,000, the Boston-Wyoming Smelter & Power Company was incorporated in 1900. Investors included promoter Willis George Emerson, banker W.C. Henry, sheep man and mine owner George Ferris, and Rawlins sheep man I.C. Miller. Construction of the smelter enabled raw ore to be converted to blister copper, which was easier to freight to the railroad at Walcott for sale to markets elsewhere. (Courtesy of GEM.)

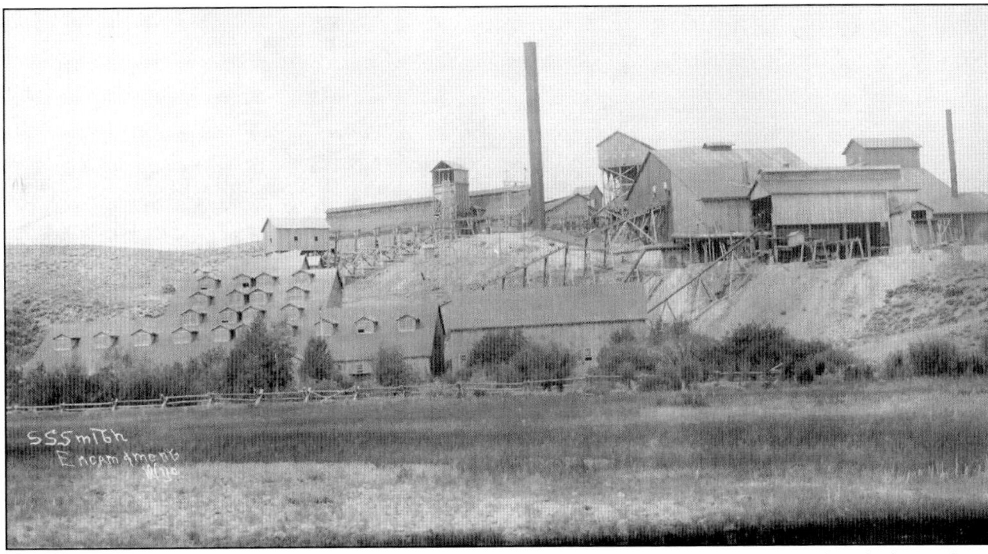

By 1901, the smelter at Grand Encampment was in production. Freighters hauled ore from operations such as the Ferris-Haggarty, Doane, Eureka, Hercules, Ledbetter, Copper King, Copper Queen, and Philadelphia Mines. The *Platte Valley Lyre* on June 7, 1900, predicted the mines in the district "can readily furnish 200 tons of ore per day." This photograph is by S.S. Smith. (Courtesy of GEM/Henry S. Granberg.)

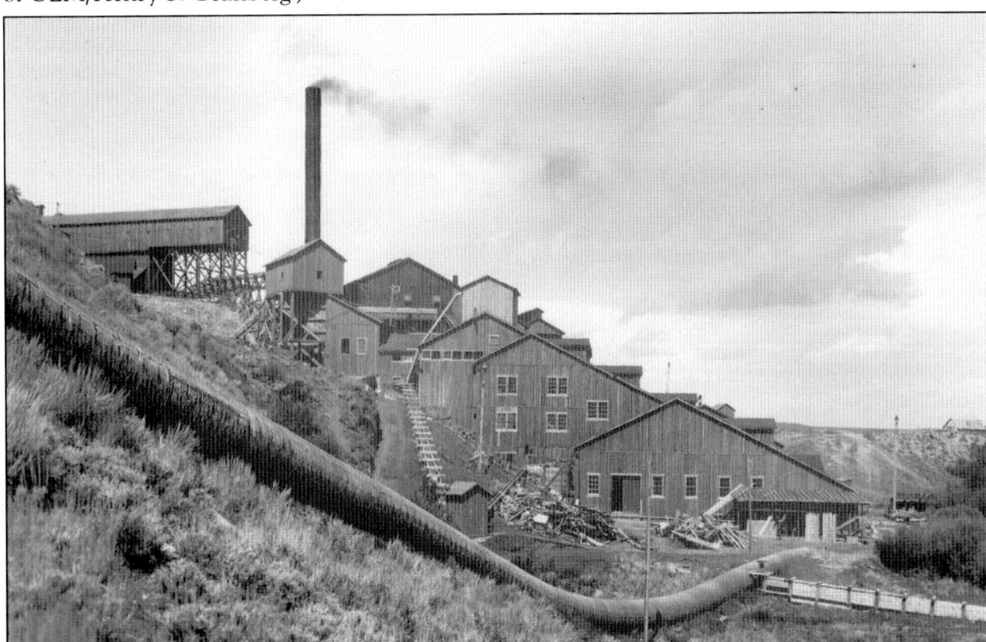

Photographer J.E. Stimson's image of the smelter clearly shows the wood-stave pipeline leading to the site. This water line, which originated on the North Fork of the Encampment River, provided the hydropower needed to operate the smelter. Boston-Wyoming Smelter & Power Company was sold in 1902 to North American Copper Company, which was sold to Penn-Wyoming Copper Company in 1904. (Courtesy of the J.E. Stimson Collection, Wyoming State Archives, Department of State Parks and Cultural Resources.)

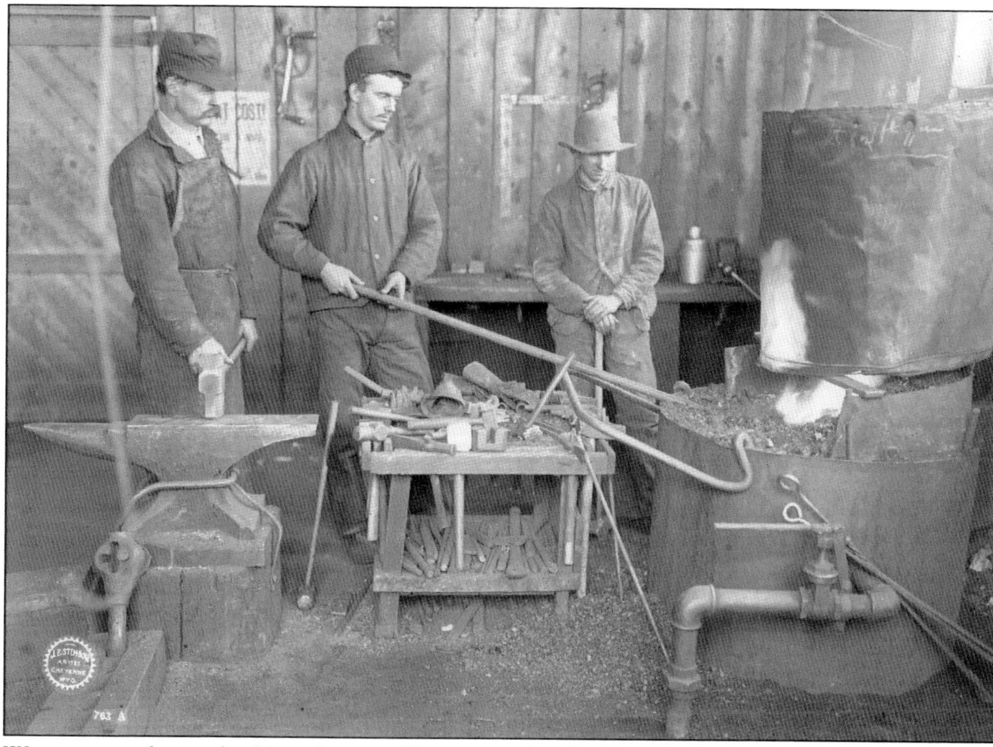

Waterpower drove the blast furnace blowers at the Boston-Wyoming Smelter. Above, these unidentified men are working in the smelter power plant and appear to be undertaking some blacksmithing. Matte, which consisted of copper, iron, gold, silver, and sulfur, was the final product at the smelter until 1903 when a converter was added that could be used to heat or "blow" the matte and produce blister copper, a high-value product that was 99 percent pure copper. The photograph below shows men blowing (or heating) copper. (Both, courtesy of the J.E. Stimson Collection, Wyoming State Archives, Department of State Parks and Cultural Resources.)

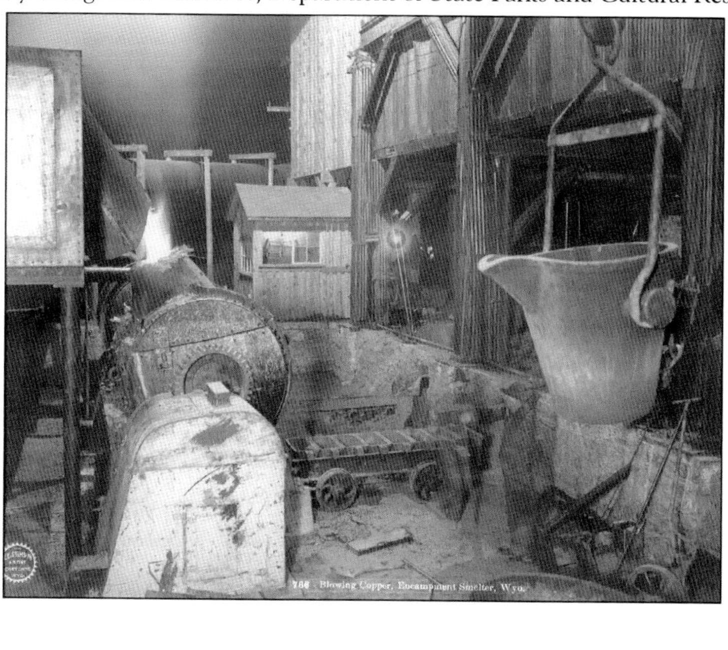

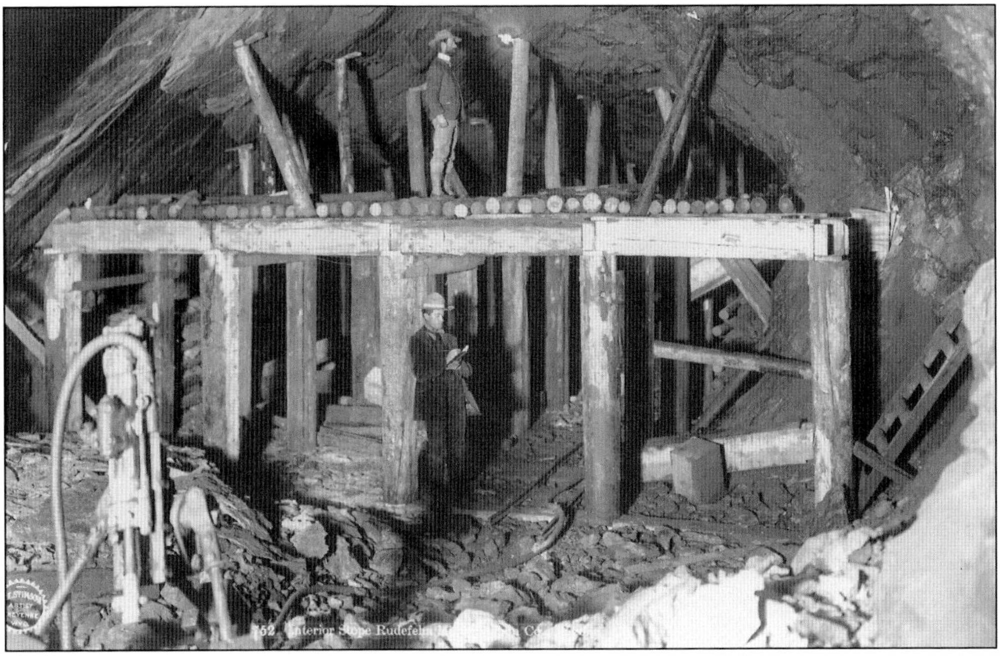

J.E. Stimson took this image of men working in the interior stope of the Ferris-Haggarty Mine when he photographed the region around Grand Encampment in 1903. The mine was the largest and most productive in the Grand Encampment Copper District. It began operations in 1897 and ceased in 1908 because of falling copper prices. (Courtesy of the J.E. Stimson Collection, Wyoming State Archives, Department of State Parks and Cultural Resources.)

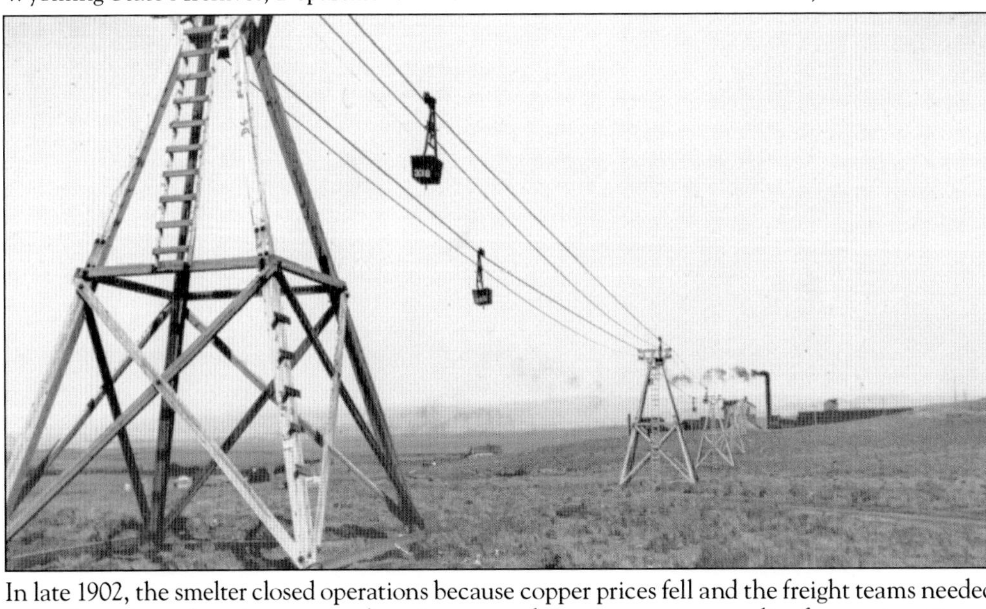

In late 1902, the smelter closed operations because copper prices fell and the freight teams needed to haul ore from the mines were otherwise engaged in transporting supplies for construction of the Southern Wyoming Tramway. When the tramway began operating in June 1903, the smelter reopened. From then until 1908, there was a steady stream of ore buckets on the tramway cables moving ore from the Ferris-Haggarty Mine to the smelter. (Courtesy of the J. E. Stimson Collection, Wyoming State Archives, Department of State Parks and Cultural Resources.)

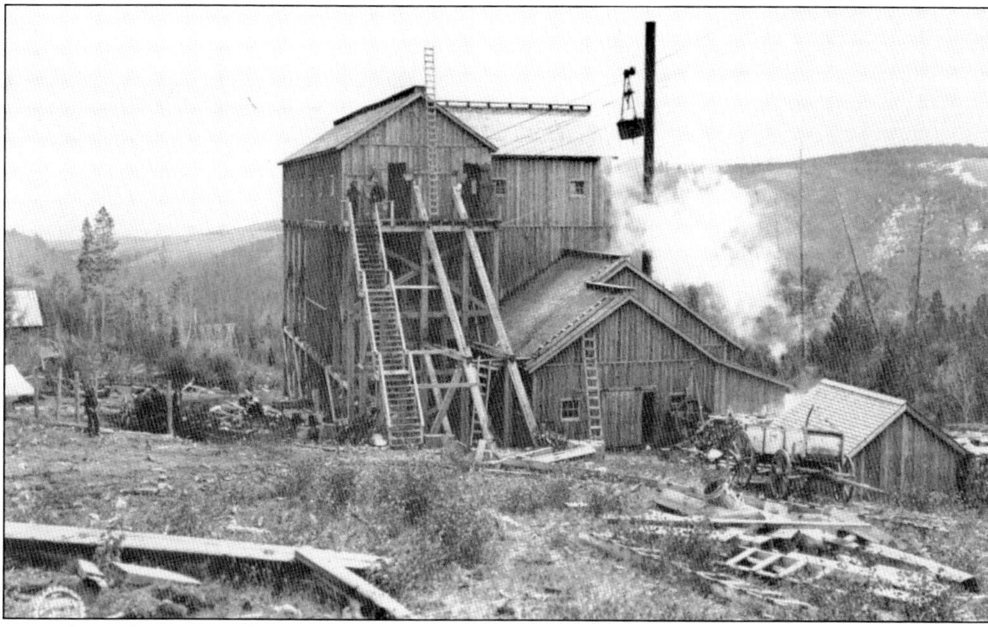

In mid-April 1902, workers established Tramway Camp No. 2 at Cow Creek where they built Tramway Power Plant No. 2. Not far away, at a location between Teddy Creek and Cow Creek, a sawmill operation was in place to cut timbers needed for building the 370 wooden tramway towers. (Courtesy of the J.E. Stimson Collection, Wyoming State Archives, Department of State Parks and Cultural Resources.)

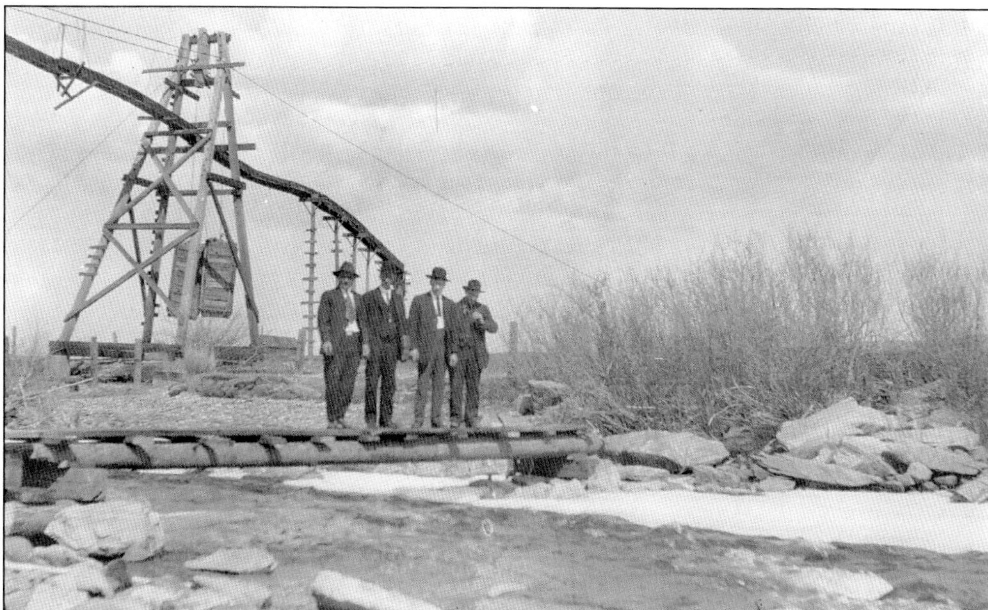

These men are standing in front of a flume that was put in to carry tailings from the mill across the river from the smelter. The flume was installed after residents protested that the tailings were killing the fish in the Encampment River. This image was taken in 1918, about 10 years after the smelter closed. Decades later, the Environmental Protection Agency undertook a major cleanup of the tailings site. (Courtesy of GEM.)

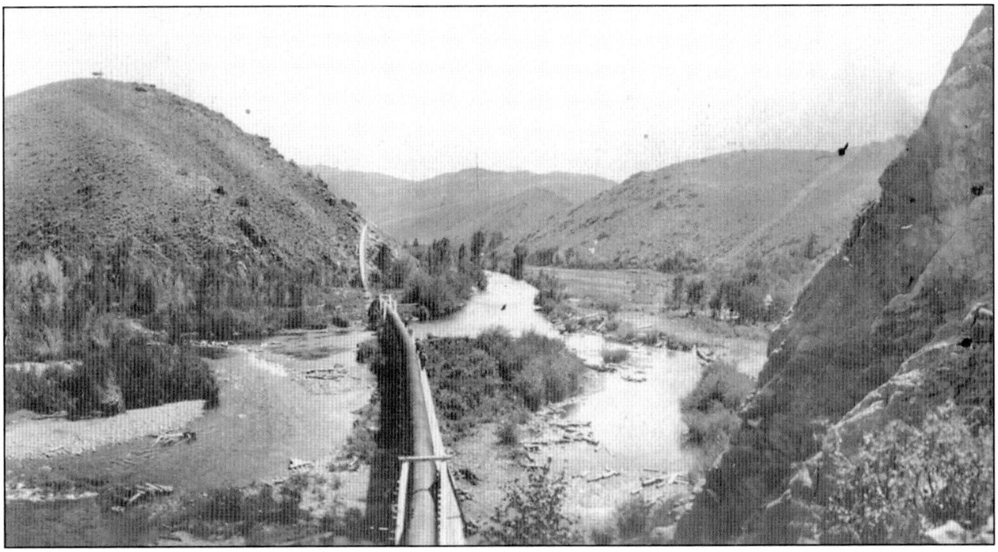

This postcard showing the pipeline that powered the smelter where it crossed the Encampment River was sent by Kate (last name unknown) to Mrs. Frank Cook on August 5, 1907. On the postcard, she wrote, "Hello. Here is some more of the pretty places up here you must come up for 28 & 29 of August going to be a Celebration at Saratoga Kate." (Courtesy of GEM.)

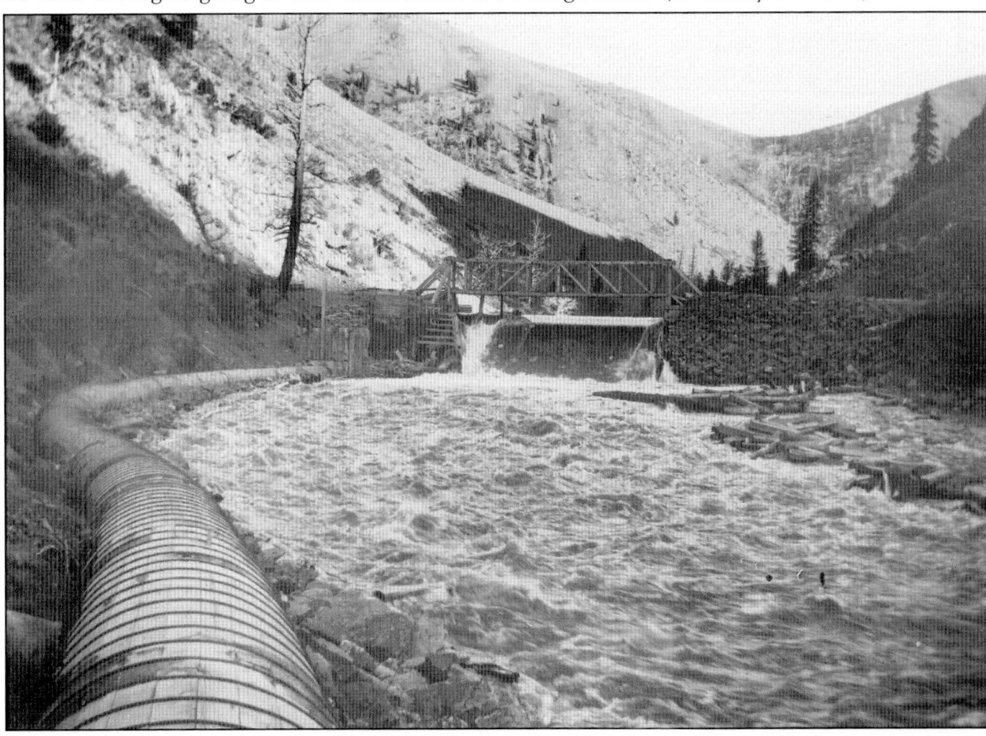

A dam constructed on the North Fork of the Encampment River allowed for diversion of water into the pipeline that provided power for the smelter operation. The hydropower generated not only supplied the smelter, but also the town of Grand Encampment, which had electric lights and even a 75-foot-high water fountain. When the smelter closed, the power generation ceased. Encampment was without electricity until the 1920s. (Courtesy of GEM.)

Four

The Good, the Bad, and the Friendly

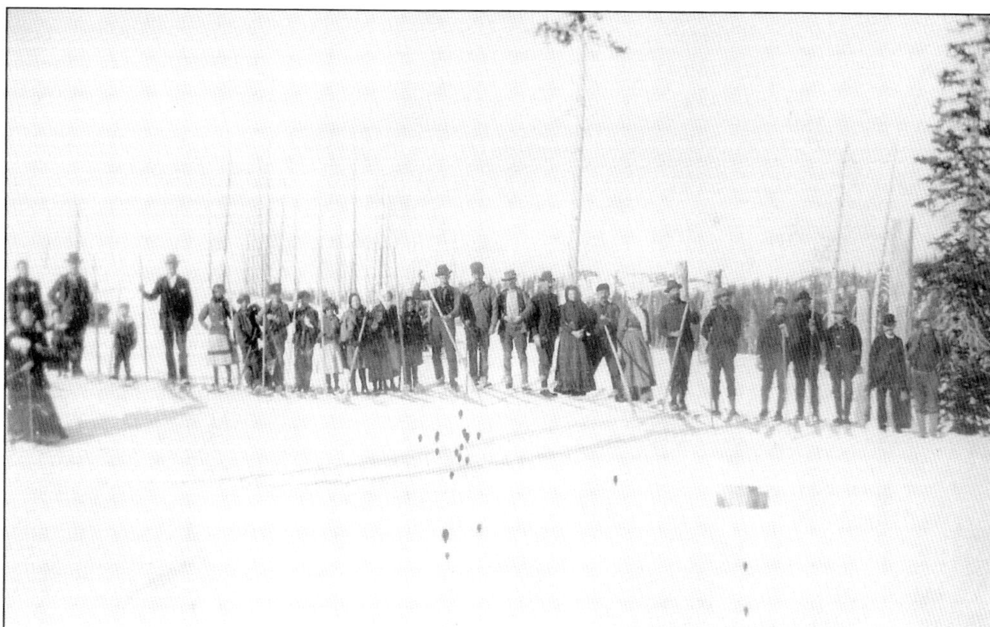

Near the Continental Divide, where snow flies in October and remains on the ground in the mountains well into June, early residents found skis to be a good form of transportation. The Swedish and Norwegian tie hacks brought their long cross-country skis to this country and found them useful. Other residents soon had fashioned their own long skis. As this photograph shows, men, women, and children living in Battle all had them. The area remains popular for cross-country skiing with a series of trails established at Bottle Creek in the Medicine Bow–Routt National Forest some six miles west of Encampment. Those trails are groomed during the winter season. (Courtesy of Jack Ledbetter Photograph Collection.)

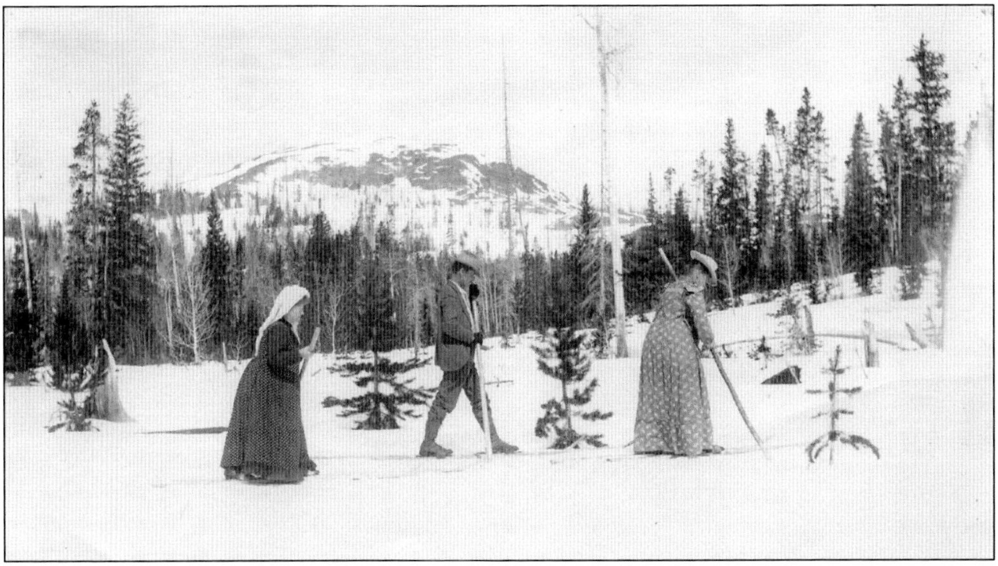

With snow piled high, skis were the best form of transportation in the Grand Encampment Mining District. Judging by the clothing of the two women and a man skiing near Battle, the photograph above was probably taken during late spring or early summer. The Battle resident below also had on his skis and was using a rather stout staff for guidance and stability. Notable is the deep snow near the roof eve of the smaller cabin. In winter, snow at Battle can be anywhere from 12 to 25 feet deep, which made life there quite challenging. To deal with the significant snowpack, residents in the mountains constructed two-story outhouses. They used the lower floor during better weather but took care of business from the second story in winter when snow literally buried the lower facilities. A replica of a two-story outhouse stands at the Grand Encampment Museum, built as a project for the American bicentennial in 1976. (Both, courtesy of GEM/Ferris Album.)

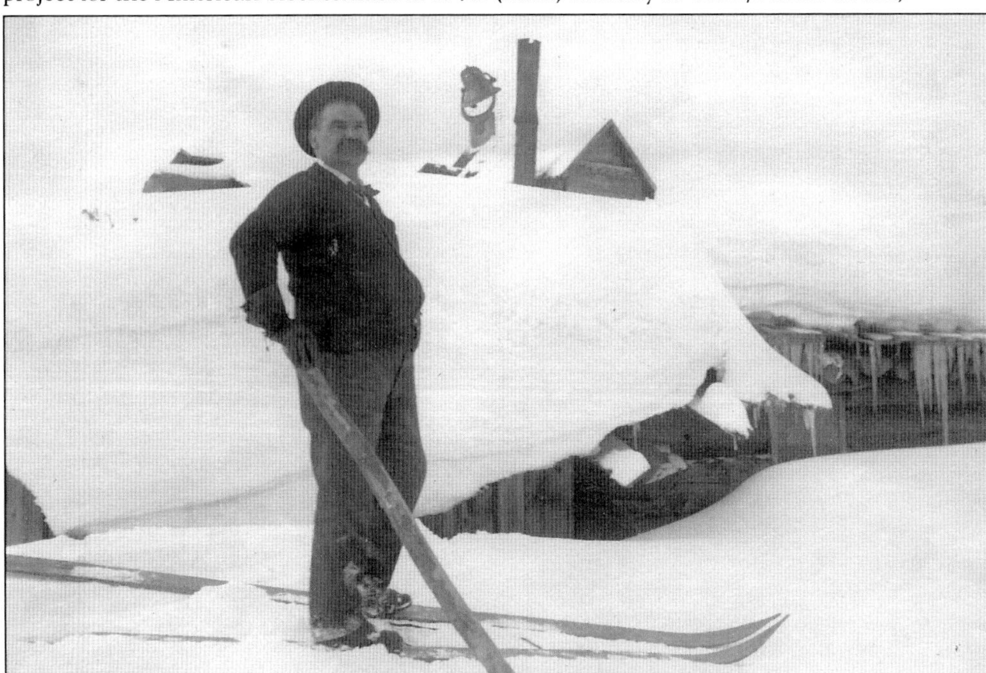

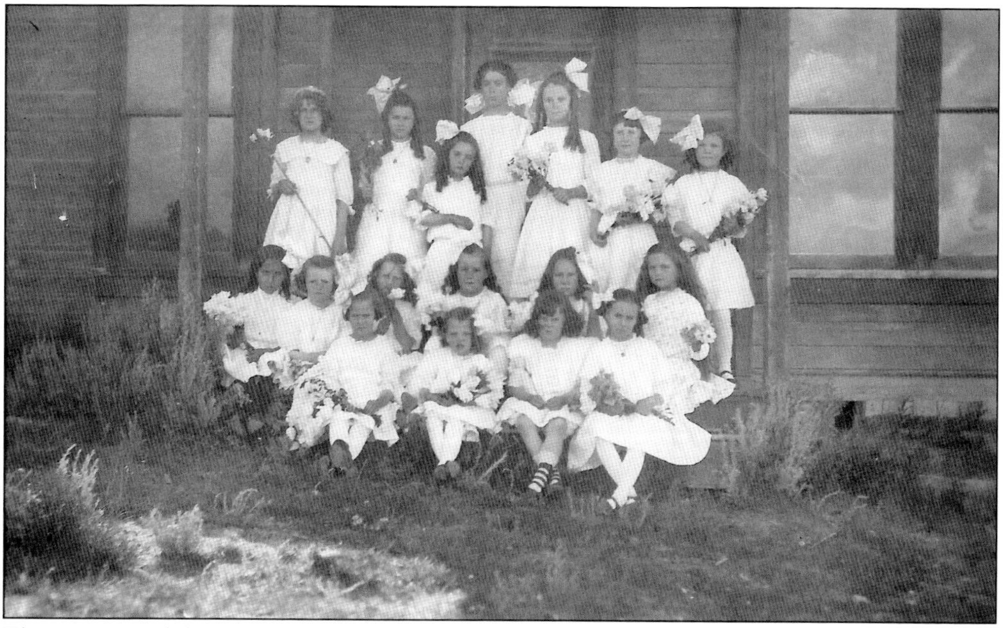

These young girls had their photograph taken at the William and Grace Kuntzman home following Sunday school. Because each is attired rather formally in a white dress, many with bows in their hair, the girls may have been involved in a special program, but judging from the expressions on their faces—not one of them is smiling—there must been some challenges for the young ladies that day. (Courtesy of GEM/Grace Kuntzman Healey.)

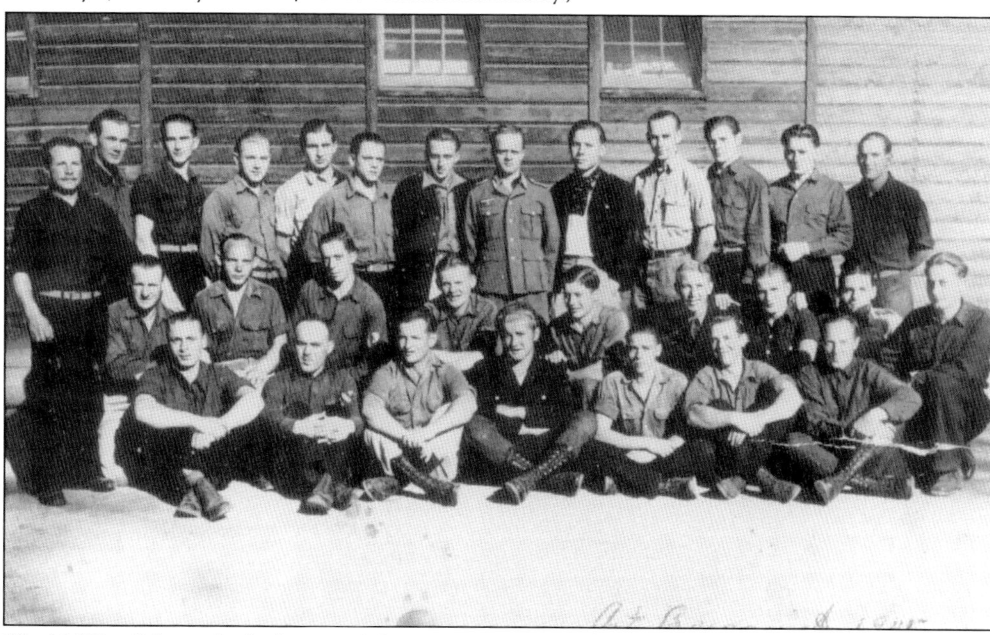

World War II brought Italian and German prisoners of war to an old Civilian Conservation Corps camp at Ryan Park in 1945. Up to 200 POWs were at the camp, and many of them logged for R.R. Crow and Company from 1943 to 1945, solving the difficult issue of having enough manpower to run the sawmill when local men were serving in the military. (Courtesy of GEM/Art Bergquist.)

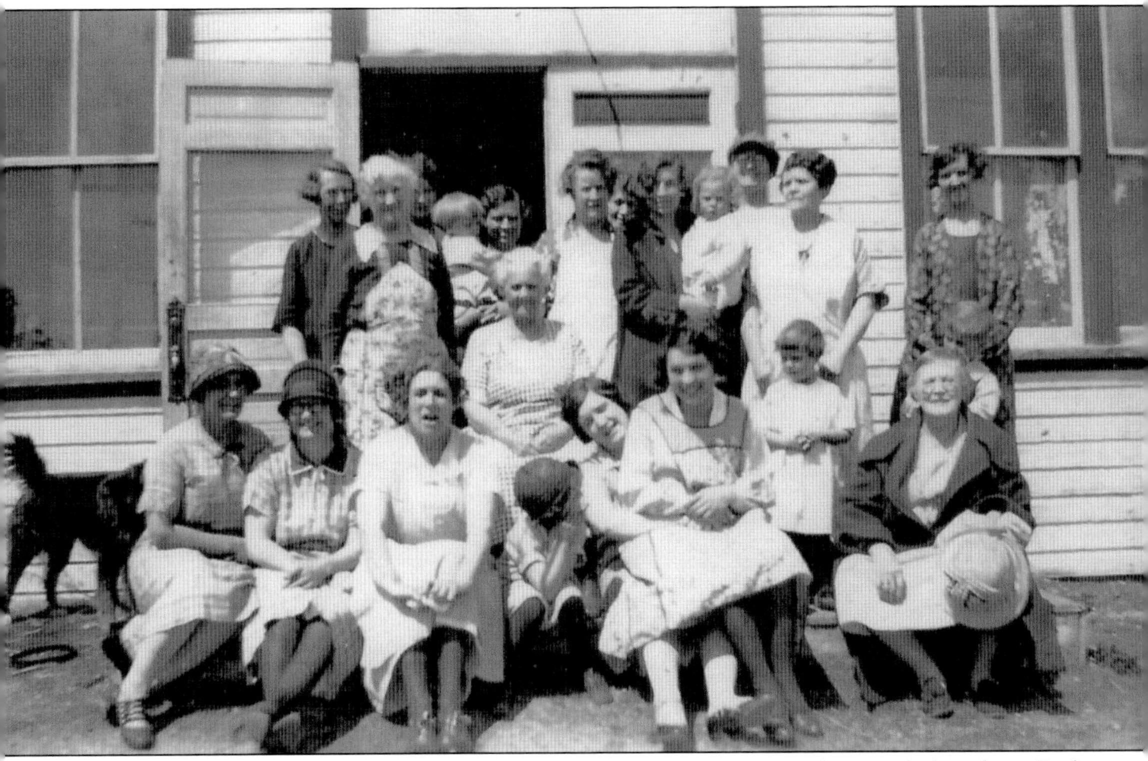

Civic organizations have played a vital role in Encampment since the town's founding. Early on, they provided entertainment in performances at the Encampment Opera House (which was restored in 2011 and is the location of productions by the Grand Encampment Opera Club). Groups, like the Encampment-Riverside Lions Club, Beta Sigma Phi Sorority, Dirt Diggers Garden Club, the Chug and Tug Tractor Club, and Grand Encampment Cowboy Gathering Outfit, sponsor events and activities and hold meetings that are social as well as business-oriented. Some formerly active organizations, including the Masonic Lodge No. 43, Order of Eastern Star Lodge No. 17, Sunshine Rebekahs, Independent Order of Odd Fellows No. 34, and Encampment Homemakers, no longer exist in the community; some have merged with Saratoga's associated organizations. The Women's Civic Club shown here held a Cemetery Day on April 21, 1927. The women include Anna Montgomery, Ellen Anderson, Ida Nickell, Alice Bashore, Ida Ashley, Susie Corlett, Ada Carver, May Ferry, Mrs. Delaney, Margaret Fisher, and Mrs. Charles Bower. (Courtesy of GEM/ Gladys and Ellis Herring Family Collection.)

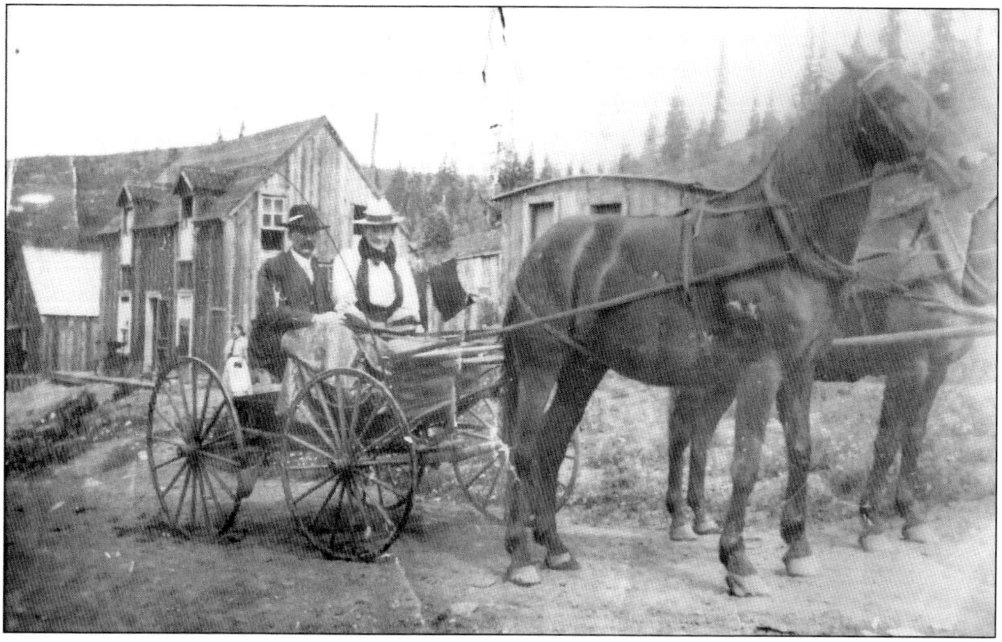

The mountain country west of Grand Encampment was sometimes difficult to traverse, but Milt and Carrie Ames (above) managed to get around just fine in their spring wagon at Battle. Carl Ashley (below) used a pack string to transport supplies through the mountains. (Above, courtesy of GEM/Charles W. Fletcher; below, courtesy of GEM.)

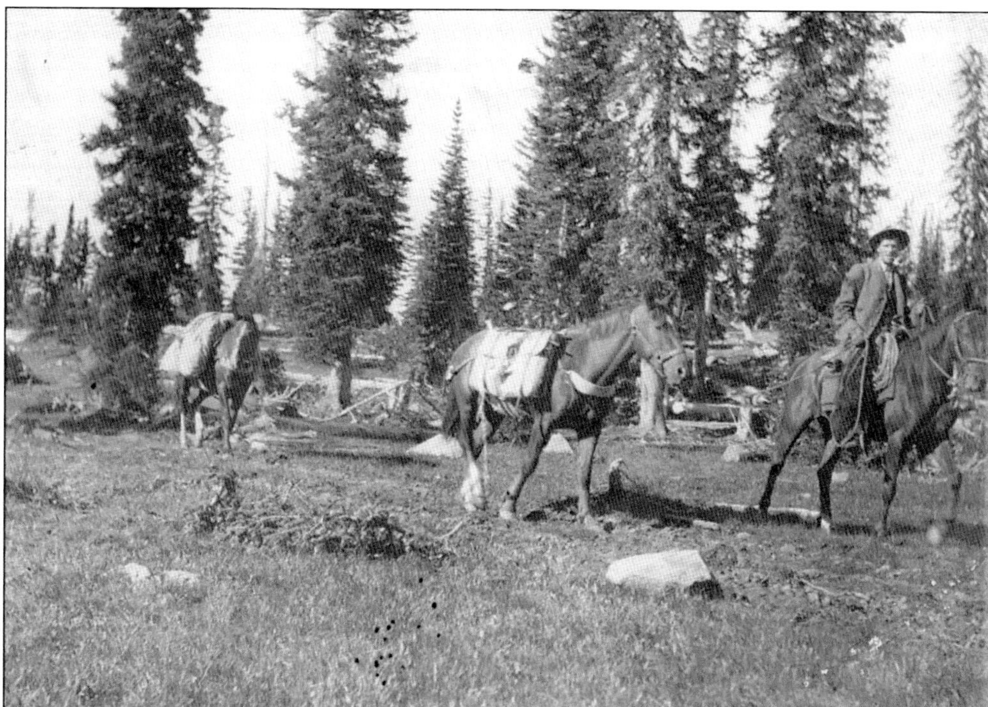

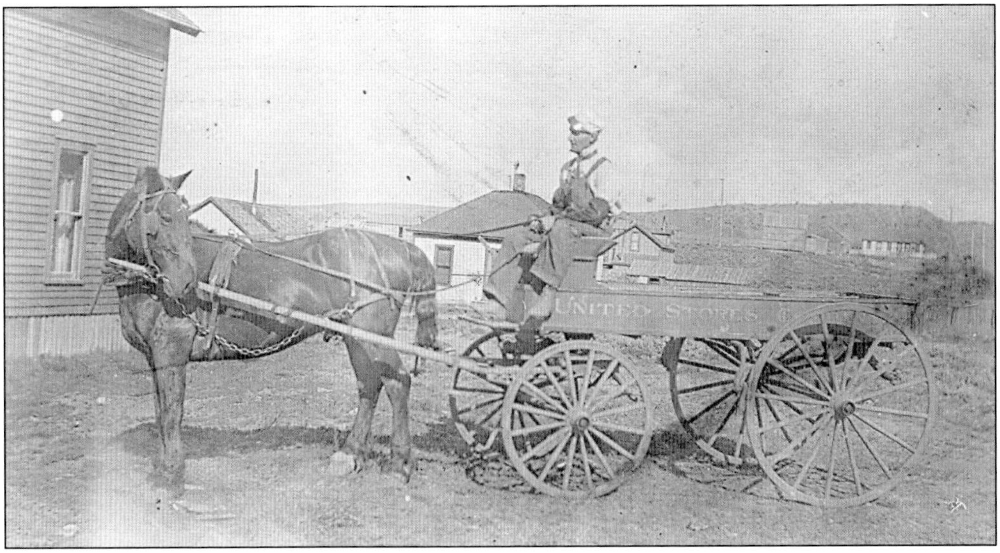

Carl Ashley (above) drives a United Stores spring wagon in Grand Encampment. This pioneer resident was a fine singer and actor, often performing in plays at the Grand Encampment Opera House. He sometimes dressed in various costumes for the productions. He and his wife, Ida Nickell Ashley, ran the C&I Gift Shop and operated the Sugar Bowl, a store that served ice cream sodas and other confections along with general goods. Carl's father, Hank Ashley (below), is standing in front of the counter in one of the 13 bars once operating in Grand Encampment. The other individual is unidentified. (Both, courtesy of GEM/Willis Collection.)

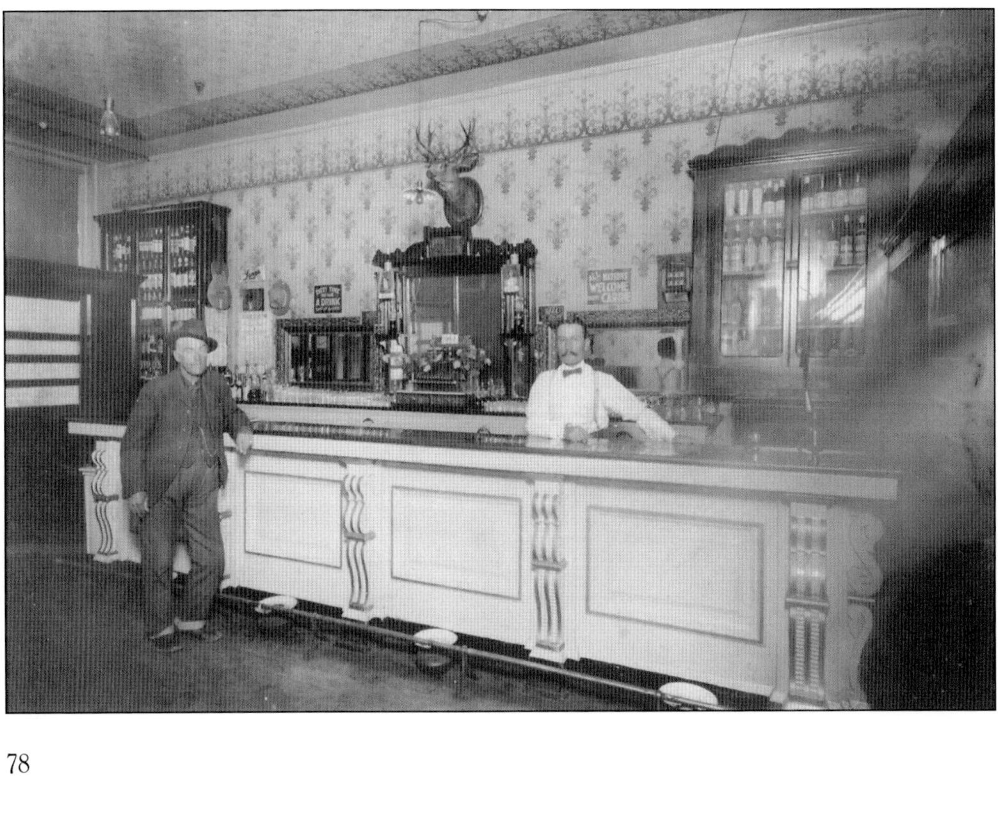

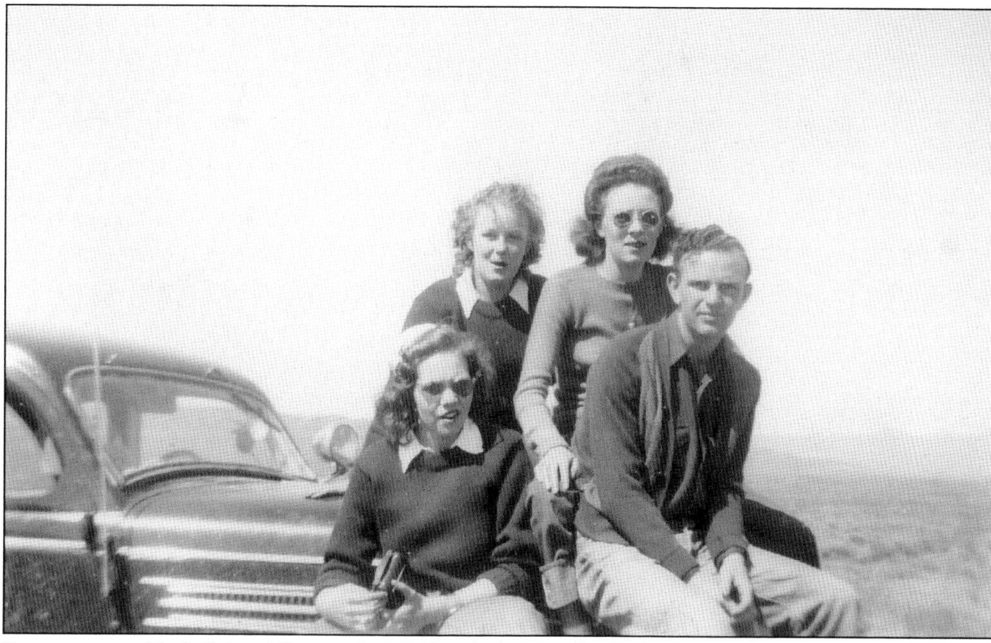

Encampment High School Senior Sneak Day (a day in which the students skipped school) in 1947 involved, from left to right, senior Betty Herring, junior Mabel McDowell, Nona Bensen (who had already graduated from high school), and junior Chuck Severns. The other two seniors that year, Charles Bixler and Kermit Platt, did not take part in this Sneak Day. (Courtesy of Betty Herring Vyvey Collection.)

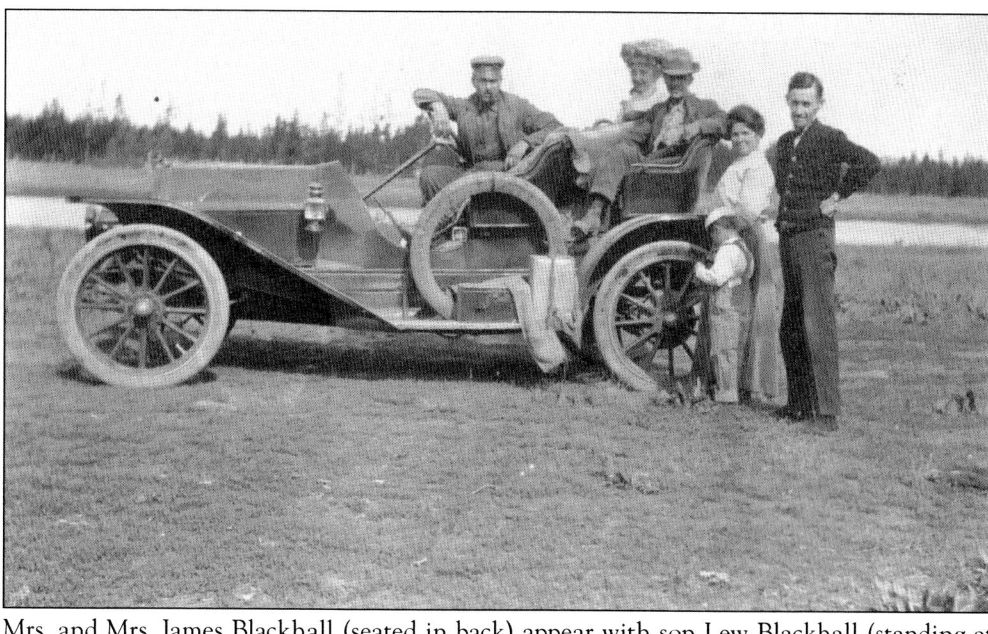

Mrs. and Mrs. James Blackhall (seated in back) appear with son Lew Blackhall (standing at right). The other people are unidentified. James Blackhall was the first Hayden National Forest supervisor, and Blackhall Mountain is named for him. The Hayden National Forest became the Medicine Bow–Routt National Forest. (Courtesy of GEM/ Lew Blackhall.)

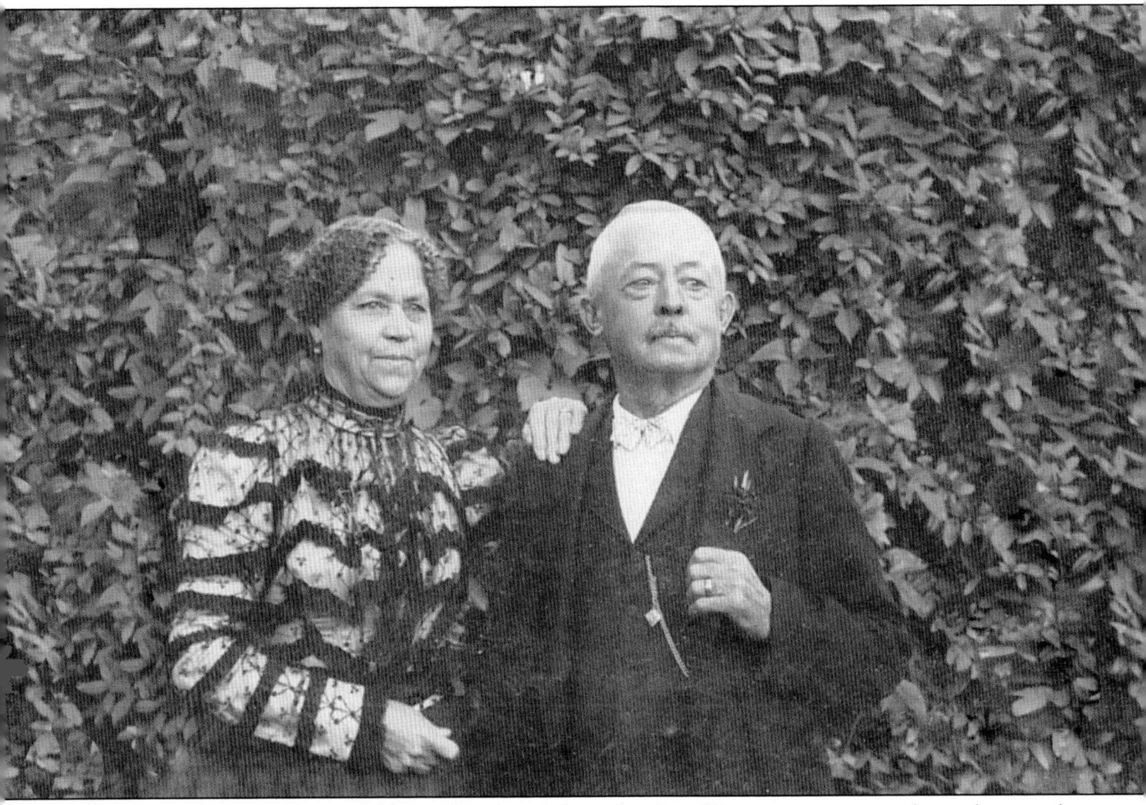

Amos and Miriam Baggott (shown here) and their daughter Emma were among the earliest settlers in the Encampment Valley, arriving in 1879. There was cause for concern about hostilities, and at times when there were Indian scares in the valley, Miriam and Emma hid in the brush by the river until they felt it was safe to return home. The Baggotts imported dairy cattle, and Miriam soon had a steady business making and selling butter. She was an able midwife who became known as "Dr. Baggott." The rock outcrop north of their log home became known as Baggott Rocks. (Courtesy of GEM.)

Shown here in his uniform, Earl Boyd served during World War I. Also answering the call of duty in that war was Wilbur Toothaker, a Beaver Creek rancher's son, who fought in the Meuse-Argonne offensive in Belgium. When Toothaker returned home after the war, he arrived in Encampment and went to the Bohn Hotel where Mary Bohn broke into tears at seeing him safely returned. (Courtesy of GEM.)

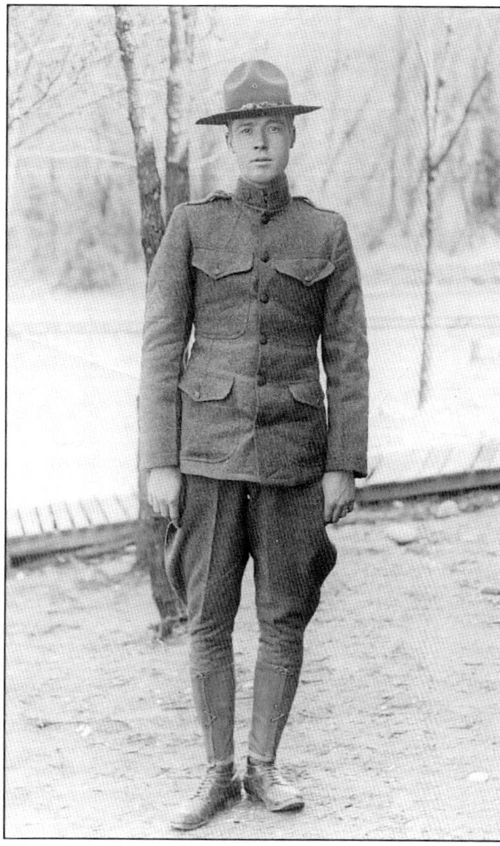

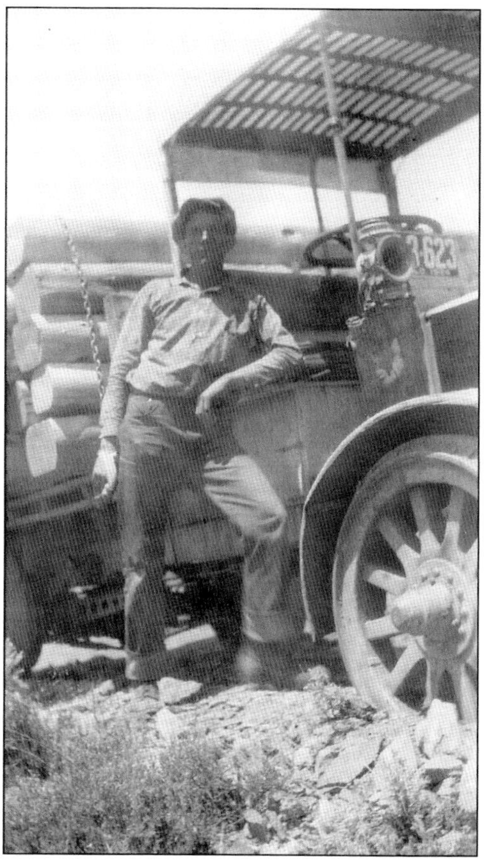

Frank Bridges operated a lumber mill at Downington, a ranch community located 10 miles southeast of Encampment near Beaver Creek. He has a load of ties on his truck in this c. 1920 image. (Courtesy of GEM.)

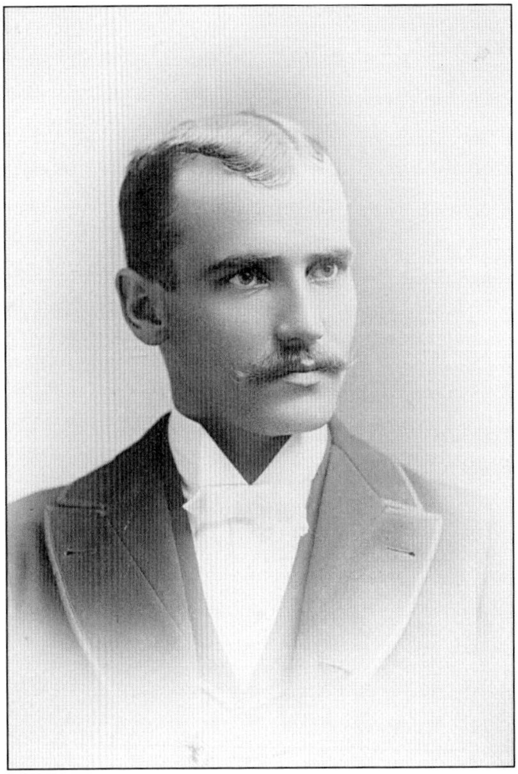

George E. Brown (left) was the son of George R. Brown who ranched on Indian Creek. Evelyn Connerly (below) came to Encampment in 1925 when her father, Dave, got a job on the Huston Ranch. She attended Encampment schools, graduating in 1940. She married R.L. "Mike" Hammer. He was a timberman all his life and ultimately owned and operated the R.L. Hammer Timber and Lumber Company. As they wrote in a history of the area, "Many changes have taken place during Mike's time. Hand saws, pickeroons, and axes have been replaced by chain saws and big tree shears. Horses and sleds have gone to big diesel 4x4 skidders, tree length diesel trucks, and hydraulic loaders. Oiled highways transport the timber instead of the rivers, wagons, sleds, and teams." Mike had been around to see all those changes. (Both, courtesy of GEM.)

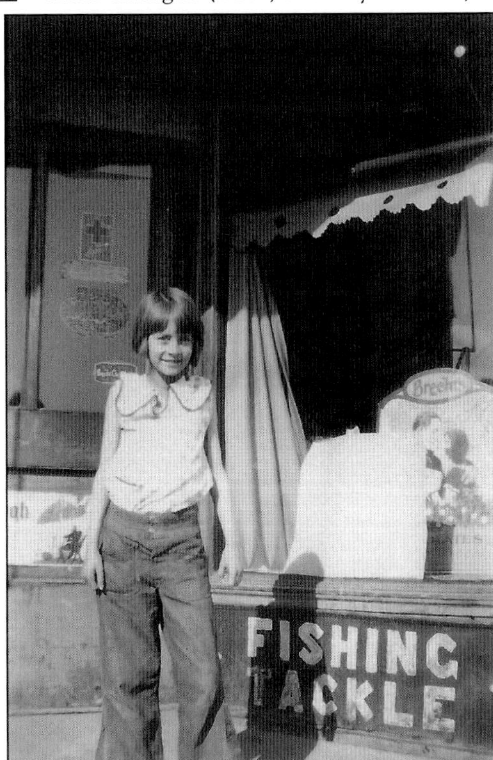

Etta Crank handles the rifle while Indian Creek rancher George R. Brown peers at a point, perhaps to see if she hits the target at which she is aiming. He was the grandfather of Mamie and Jeanette "Nettie" Culleton. (Courtesy of Mamie Brown.)

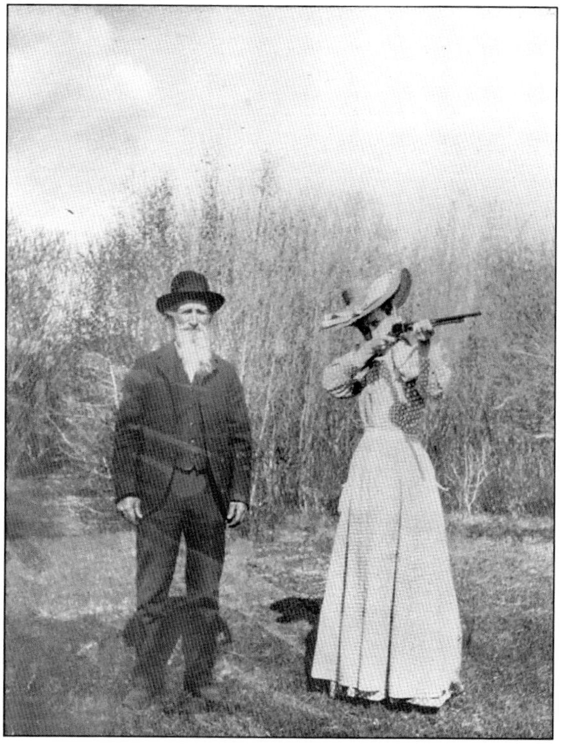

As shown in this image taken around 1890, hunting was necessary for men to put meat on the table. These men are, from left to right, Pitt Thornkey, unidentified, A.H. Huston, Doc Culleton, and Ben Culleton. Huston Park was named for Huston, a well-known hunter, and the area is now the Huston Park Wilderness Area, one of two federally designated wildernesses in the Sierra Madre (the other is the Encampment River Wilderness Area). (Courtesy of GEM.)

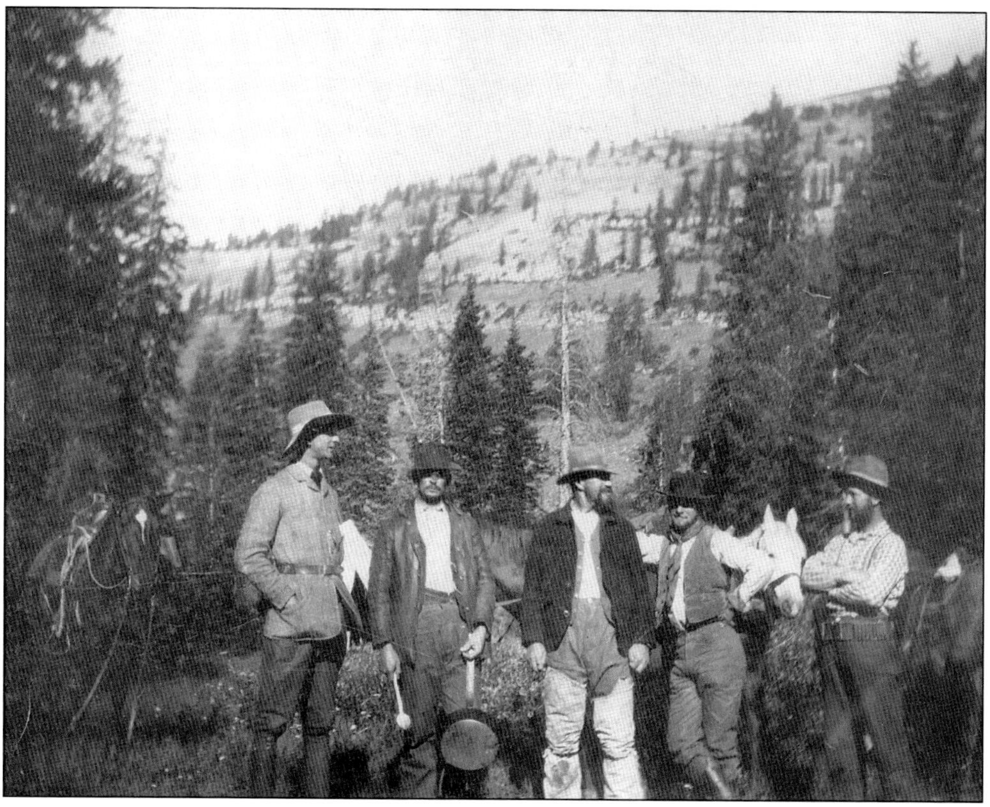

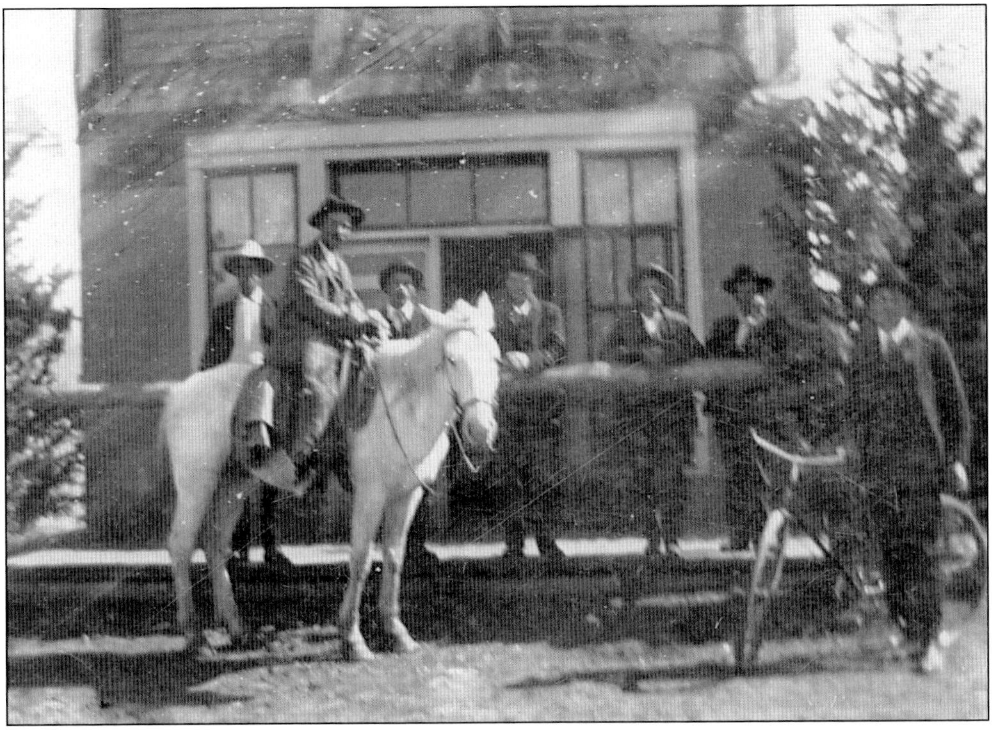

Henry P. "Doc" Culleton (shown above on his horse and below at right with Omar Dunbar) came to Encampment with his family in 1879. Henry married Lizzie May Brown in 1895 and claimed a homestead that he sold for a townsite where the town of Riverside now stands. He worked at the Ferris-Haggarty Mine and later became a saloon keeper. A niece wrote that he would stand at the bar and chant, "I'm Doctor Brown, and talk of the town, ask me again and I'll knock you down." He became Doc Culleton. He worked for the A Bar A Ranch from 1932 to 1939. A Bar A Ranch owner Andrew Anderson thought so highly of Culleton that he donated stock valued at $12,000 to the Grand Encampment Museum with the proviso that the new facility be named the Doc Culleton Interpretive Center. (Both, courtesy of GEM/ Mamie Culleton Marshall.)

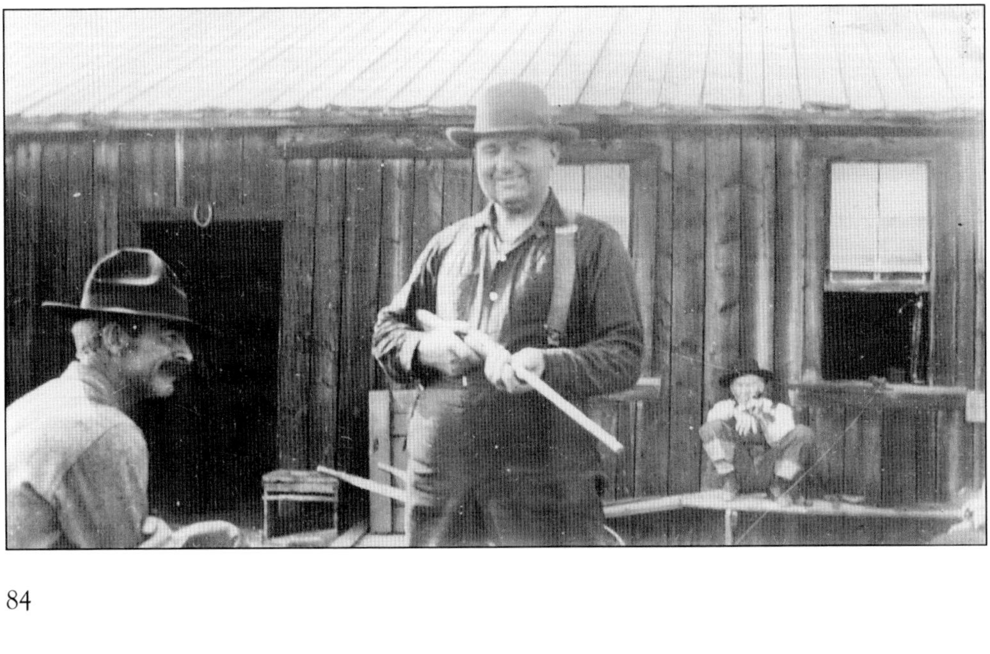

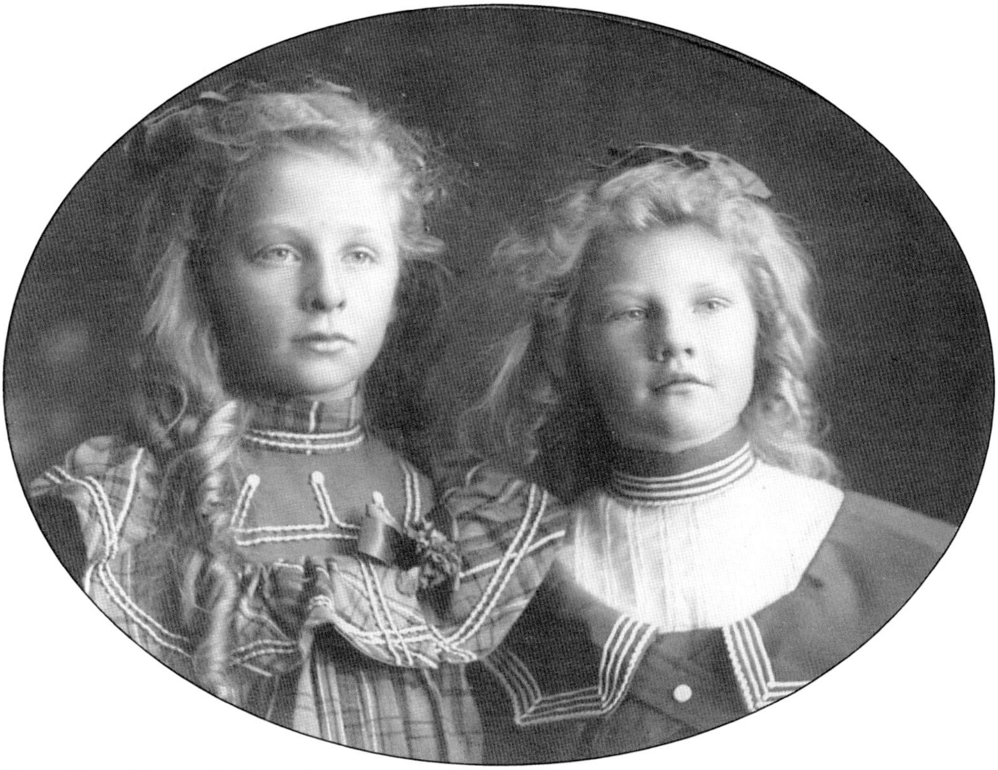

Henry P. and Lizzie Culleton had two daughters, Jeanette "Nettie" and Mamie. The little girls' grandparents were among the earliest settlers in the Encampment Valley. Their mother's family homesteaded on Indian Creek, and their father's mother, whose first husband died, had married Guy Nichols in 1879, a homesteader who operated the store at Swan located a mile north of present Riverside. (Courtesy of GEM/Mamie Marshall.)

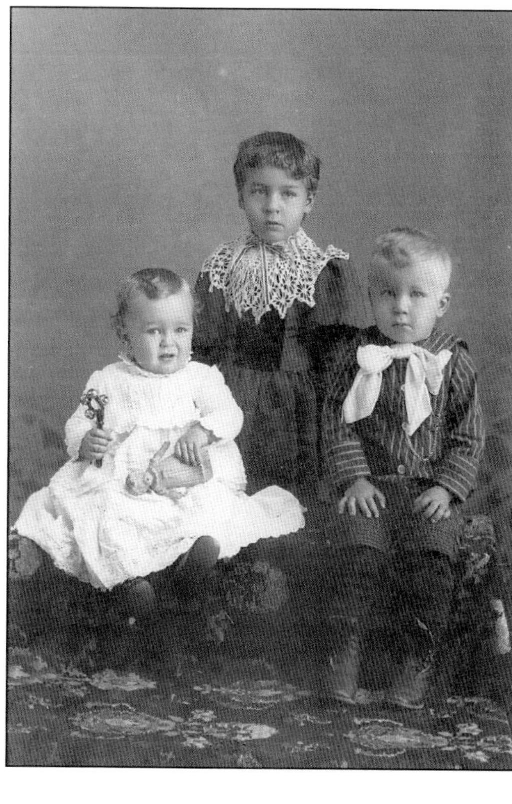

Margaret Mamie Culleton (aged four years, nine months), Johnny Edward Culleton (aged two years, ten months), and David Otto Culleton (aged one year) were the children of Ben Culleton, who along with Al Huston discovered gold in Purgatory Gulch in 1896. This was the first major mineral strike in the Grand Encampment Mining District. Ben contracted pneumonia and died that October, not long after finding the gold. This photograph is by Baker Studios in Carbon, Wyoming. (Courtesy of GEM.)

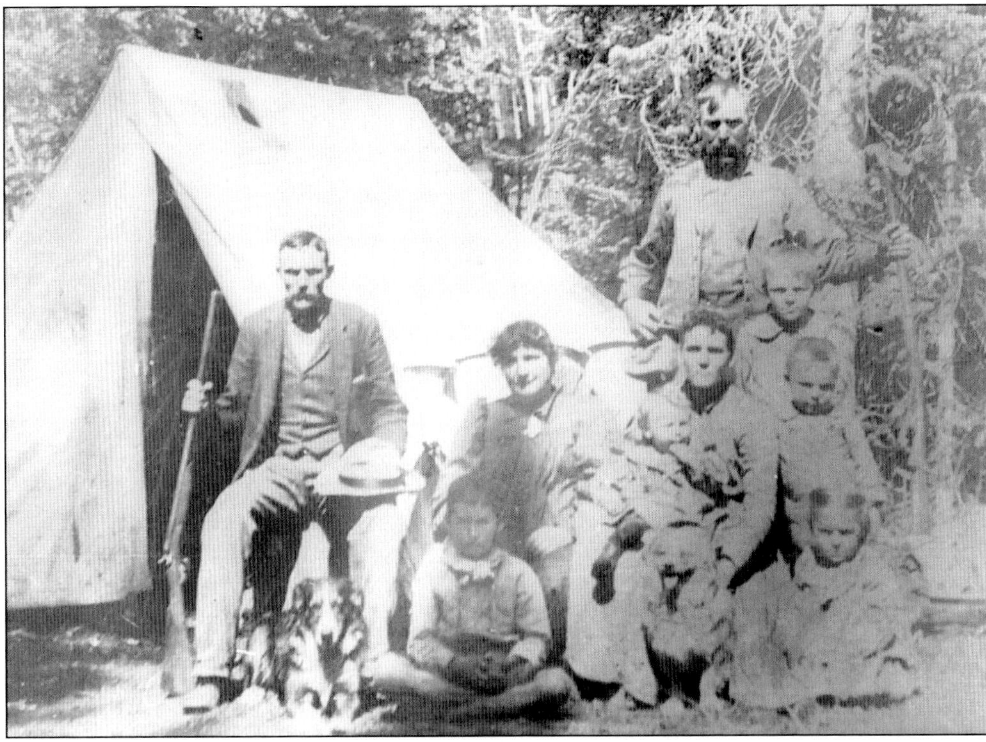

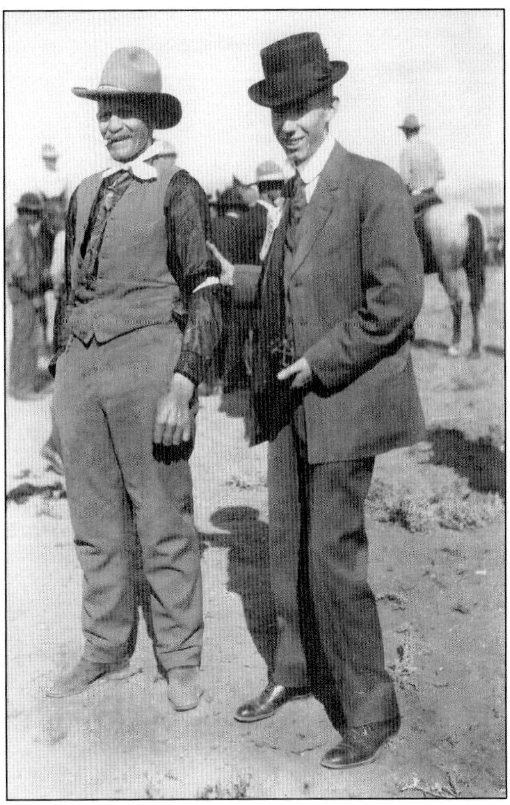

Robert Deal was one of the men who backed Edward Haggarty in the early discovery and beginning of the Rudefeha Mine. This photograph is of the Deal family and shows, from left to right, (first row) Johnnie Sullivan (in shadow) and Nida Deal; (second row) Mike Sullivan, Mrs. Sullivan, Luella Ganson Deal holding Edith Deal, and Bill Deal; (third row) Robert L. Deal and Oscar Deal. (Courtesy of GEM.)

Jim Dettinger's family came to the Encampment area with other members of the German Baptist Brethren and established homestead ranches in the 1880s. Here, he is shown with an unidentified banker in Encampment in 1916. (Courtesy of GEM/Cecil Ryan.)

W. Milton Englehart operated a hardware store and delivery service in Colbran, Colorado, and a similar enterprise in Cripple Creek, Colorado. Hearing reports of rich mineral strikes in the Grand Encampment District, he headed north in 1899. At the time, Ed Parkison was a partner of Englehart, so their first joint business venture was called Parkison's. Later, Englehart also came to Encampment where he opened the Englehart Hardware. (Courtesy of GEM/Dorothy Painter.)

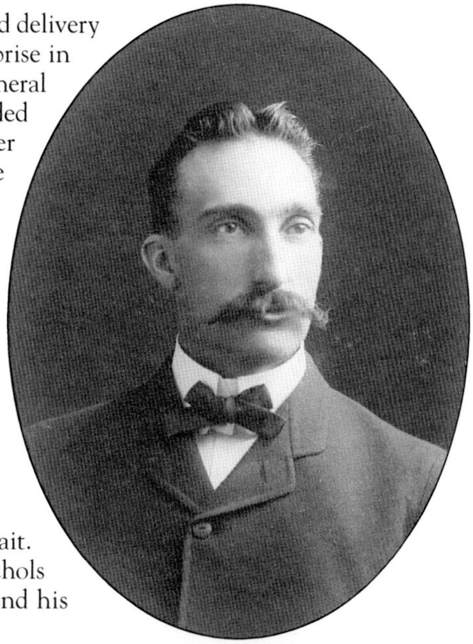

This image shows the happy family of Charley Fait. Seated next to Charley is his first wife, Lizzie Nichols Fait. The other two women may be his mother and his sister. (Courtesy of Lora Nichols Collection.)

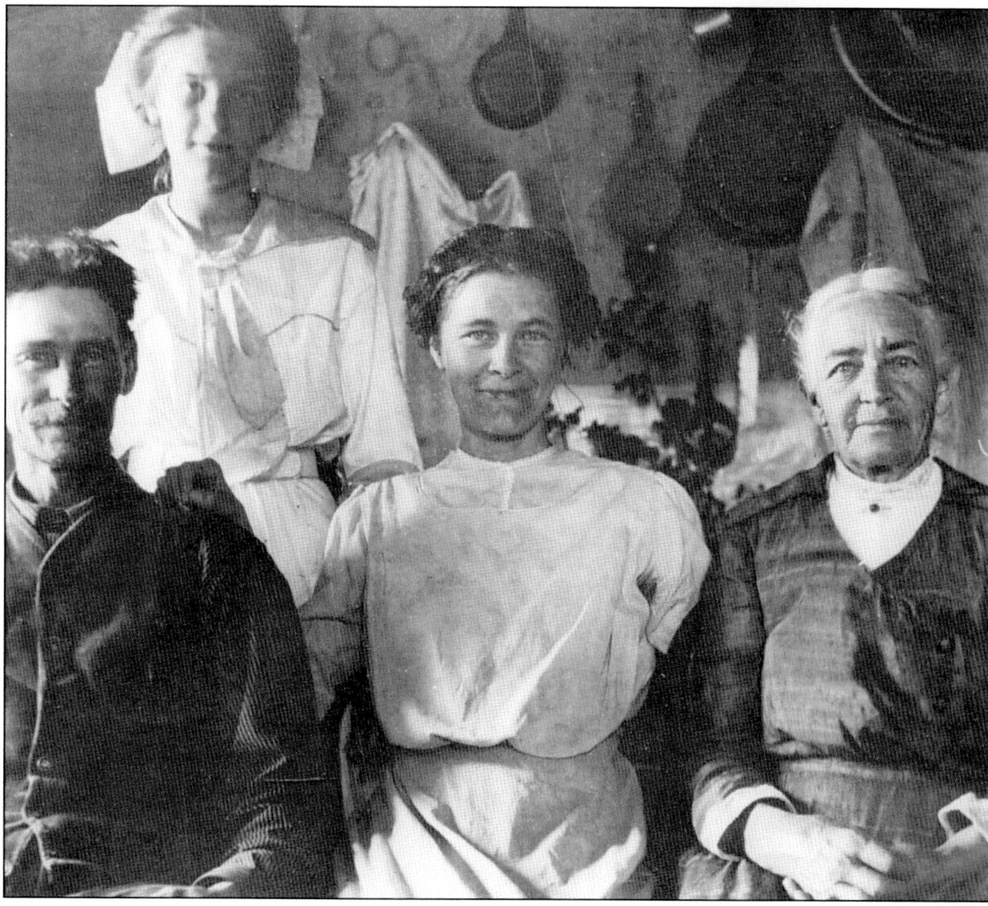

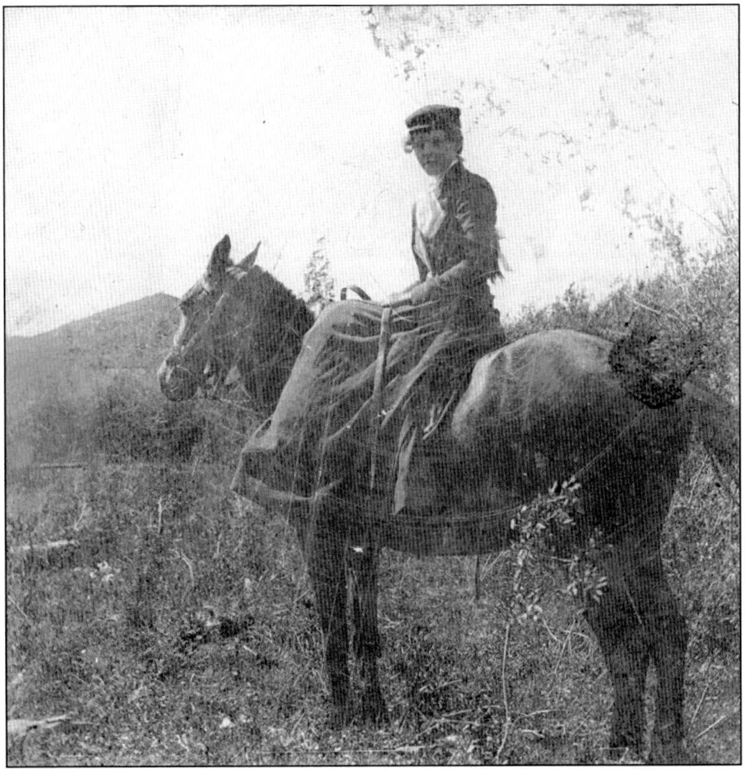

Lizzie Nichols married Charley Fait on December 6, 1898. The 17-year-old bride had needed a crutch to get around on her wedding day. Charley and Lizzie lived two miles north of Encampment on the Spring Ranch. Some years later, Lizzie was captured in this image riding sidesaddle. (Courtesy of GEM.)

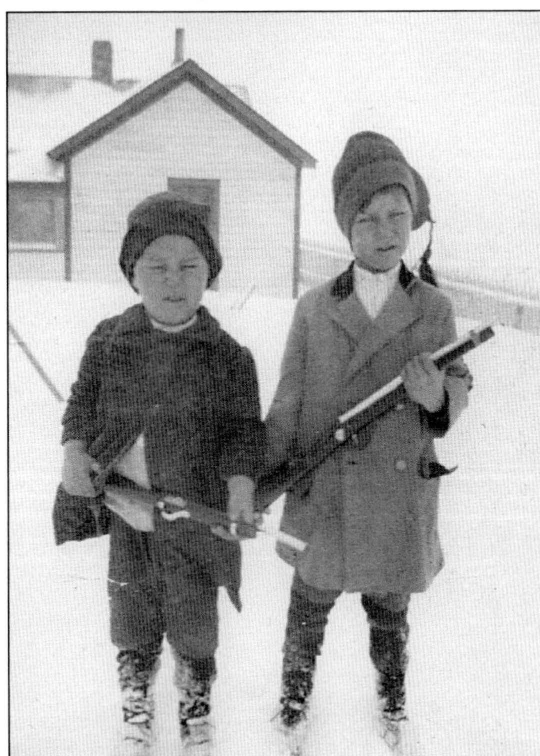

Chester (left) and Travis Ferry, the children of Mae and Art Ferry, hold their toy guns. These two little boys drowned along with two other boys in the city reservoir on April 16, 1910. Not just personal tragedies for the families involved, the loss of so many children in a single accident shook the Encampment Valley dwellers to the core. Two of the boys were seven, and two were five years of age. The bodies were recovered by draining the reservoir. (Courtesy of GEM.)

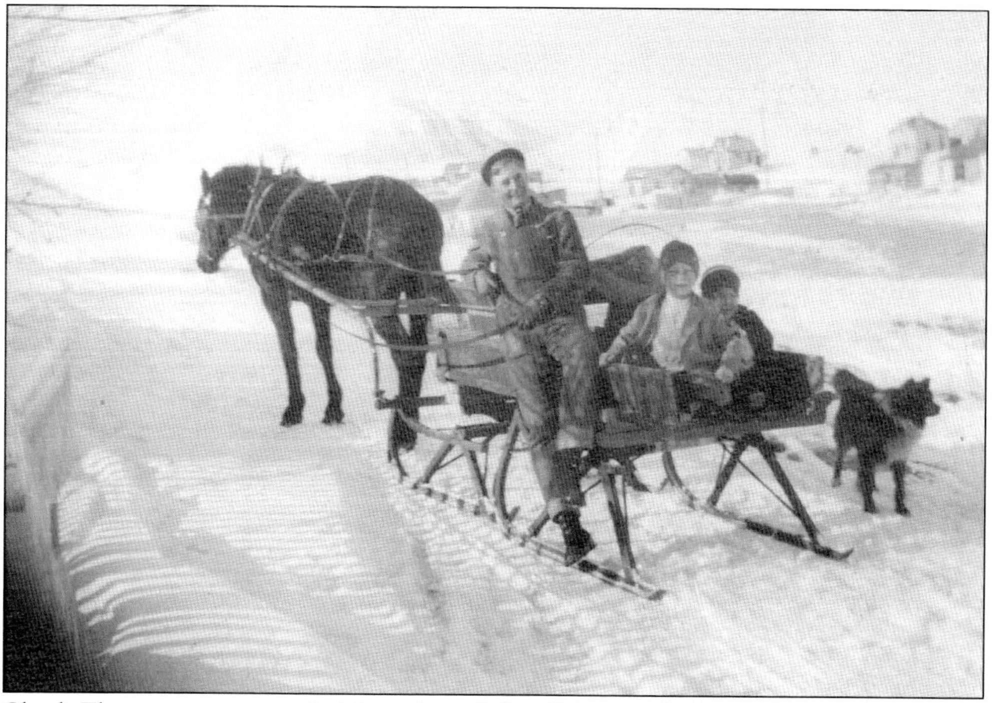

Claude Thompson appears with delivery horse Bill and Travis and Chester, the two ill-fated Ferry children. The winter wonderland of the Encampment Valley is brightened by the smiles of all as they share the simple pleasures of a sleigh ride. Below is an image of the funeral of the four boys who drowned in the city reservoir in 1910. The children were Travis and Chester Ferry, sons of Art and Mae Ferry, and the two sons (Teddy and Tommy) of Pearl Madden. The funeral was attended by the whole town and took place in city hall. An excerpt from the commemorative poem by HSP in the *Grand Encampment Herald* of April 22, 1910, reads, "Whisper softly—Heaven is near, / God hath called the children home. / Could they longer tarry here, / When their Father bade them come?" (Both, courtesy of GEM/Gladys and Ellis Herring Family Collection.)

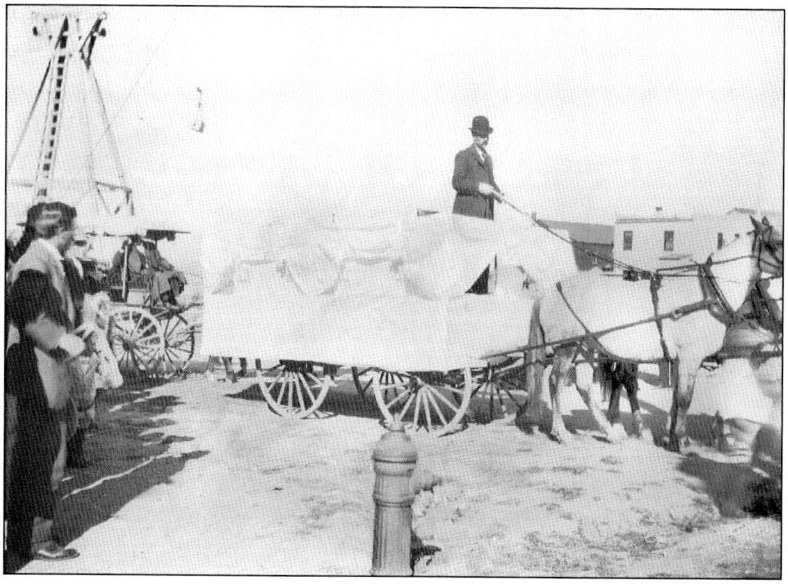

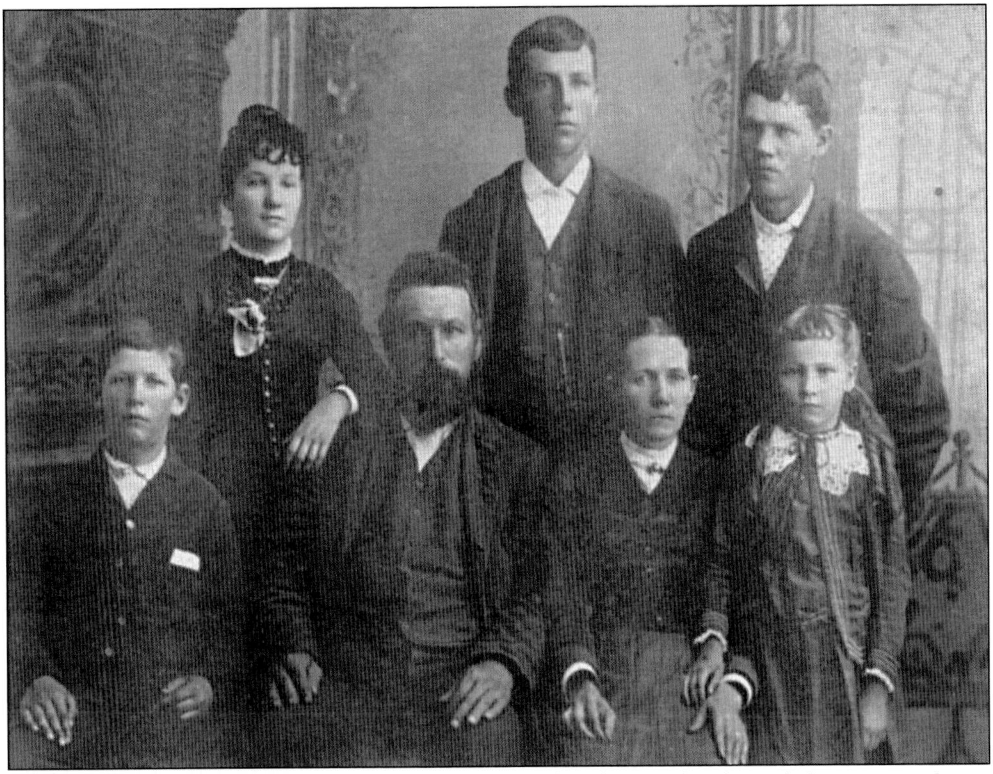

The Fleming family settled just west of Encampment and across the road from the prominent Nichols family. From left to right are (first row) Gene, George, Rebekah, and Annie; (second row) Malinda, Jim, and Delbert Fleming. Malinda later married George Herring while Annie married Charles C. Hickok. (Courtesy of Candy Vyvey Moulton Collection.)

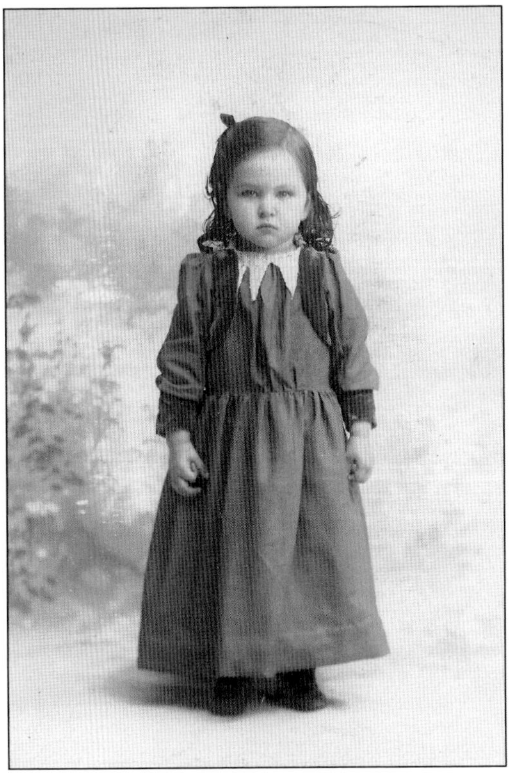

Hester Margaret Kepner was born into a well-to-do family in Effingham, Kansas, and spent her childhood there. As an adult, she married Joseph Fisher, and they came to Grand Encampment with the beginning of the copper mining boom, living in the town the remainder of their lives. (Courtesy of Betty Herring Vyvey Collection.)

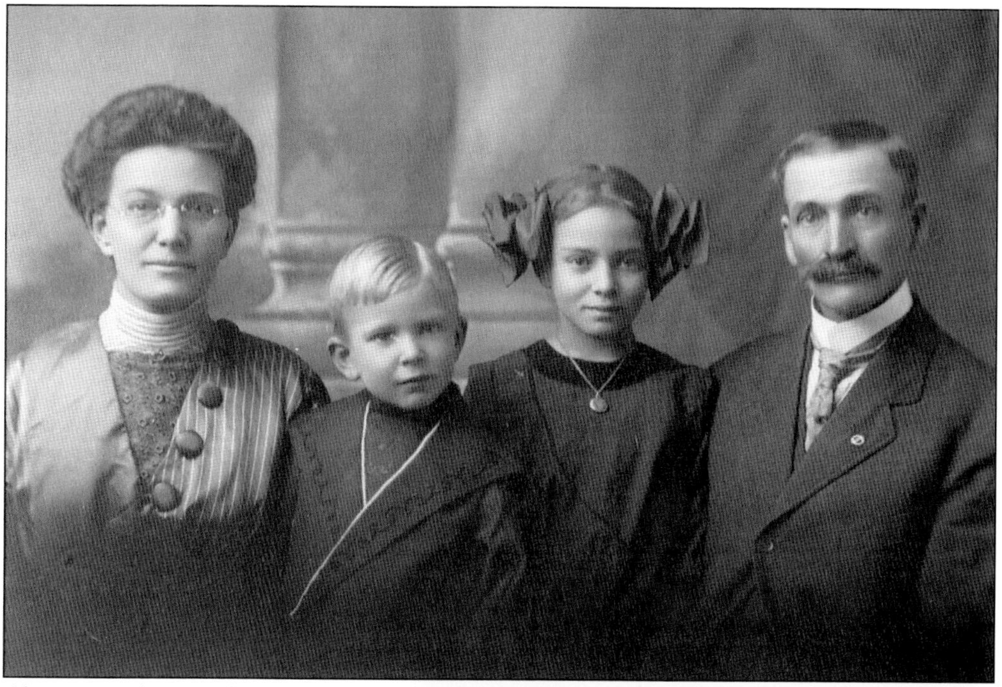

Above, Joseph W. and Margaret Fisher appear with two of their children, Harry Milton and Gladys Louise. At right is a photograph of Harry, who was born February 6, 1908, in Grand Encampment. The Fishers also had Vlasta, a younger daughter. Joseph Fisher was an active carpenter, building a fine home for himself at the corner of Ninth and Rankin Streets (which is now owned by his grandchildren John W. and Jan Herring). He also assisted in construction of the Parkison House (now on the grounds of the Grand Encampment Museum), the Ferris Hotel in Rawlins, the Virginian Hotel in Medicine Bow, and the Plains Hotel in Cheyenne. Joseph invested in the local copper mines and lost a fortune when the industry collapsed as a result of over speculation and falling prices. (Both, courtesy of Betty Herring Vyvey Collection.)

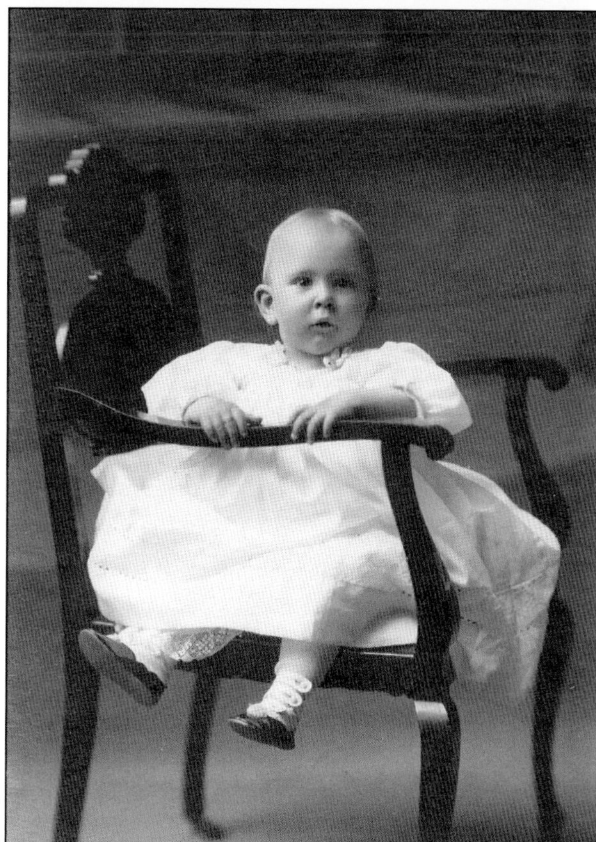

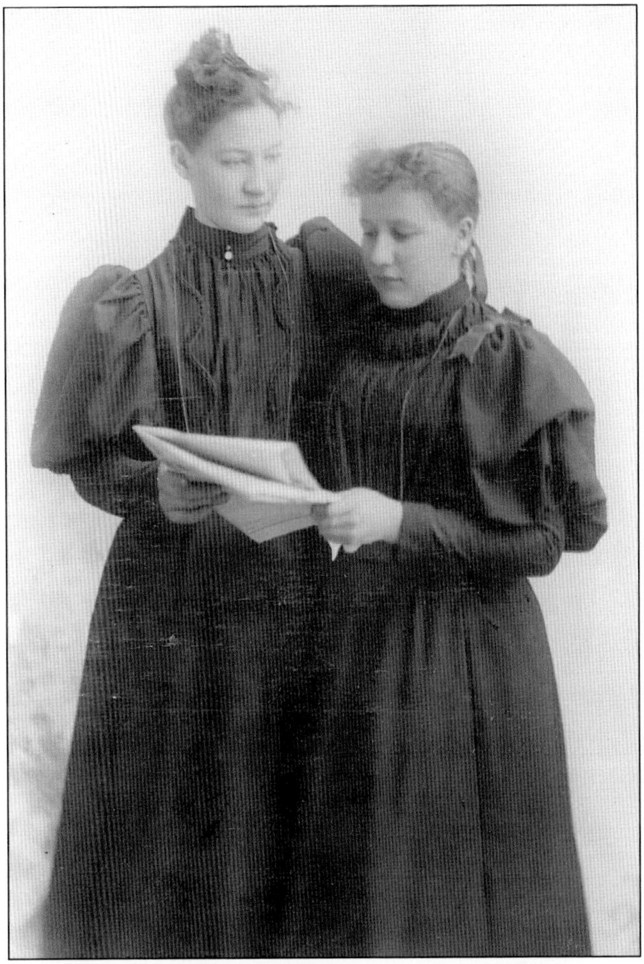

Pictured are Margaret Andrews (left) and Annie Fleming. Annie was the daughter of Dell and Rebakah Fleming. Annie later married Charles C. Hickok (a great-nephew of James Butler "Wild Bill" Hickok) and had one daughter, Mallie, who married Harry Fisher. (Courtesy of GEM/ Mamie Marshall.)

This is the 1932 Encampment High School basketball team. From left to right are (first row) David Peryam, Horace Carpenter, Carlton Ashley, John Peryam, and Robert Severns; (second row) David Garrett, Coach Garrett, and Ezra Nichols. The photograph was taken on the steps in front of the school. Behind the team, people are looking through the windows of the doors. (Courtesy of Betty Herring Vyvey Collection.)

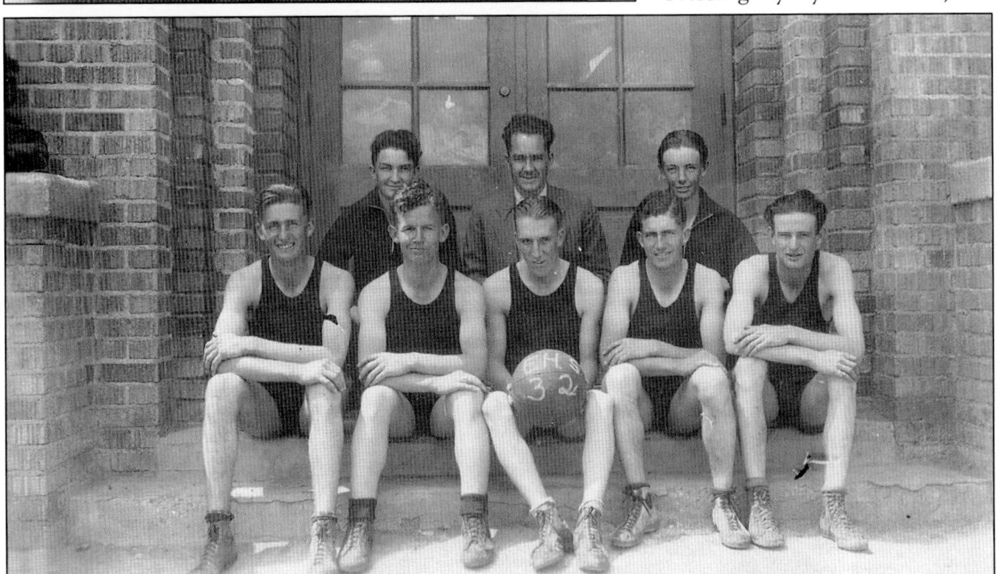

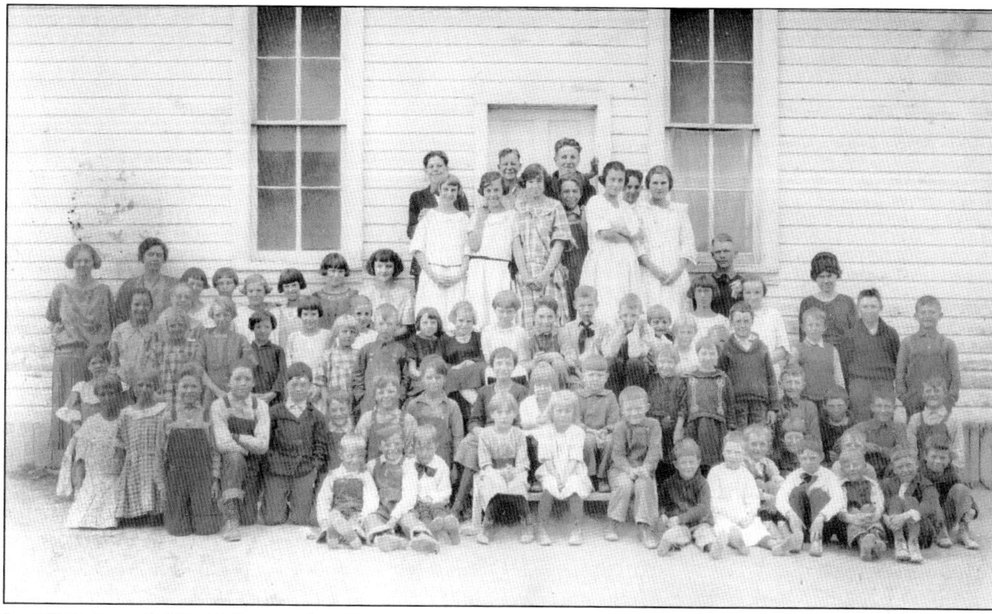

In 1909, Joseph W. Fisher took this photograph of the students at Encampment School. This was taken at the first Encampment schoolhouse, which was located at the corner of Lomax Avenue and Fifth Street. The building still stands and is in private ownership. (Courtesy of Betty Herring Vyvey Collection.)

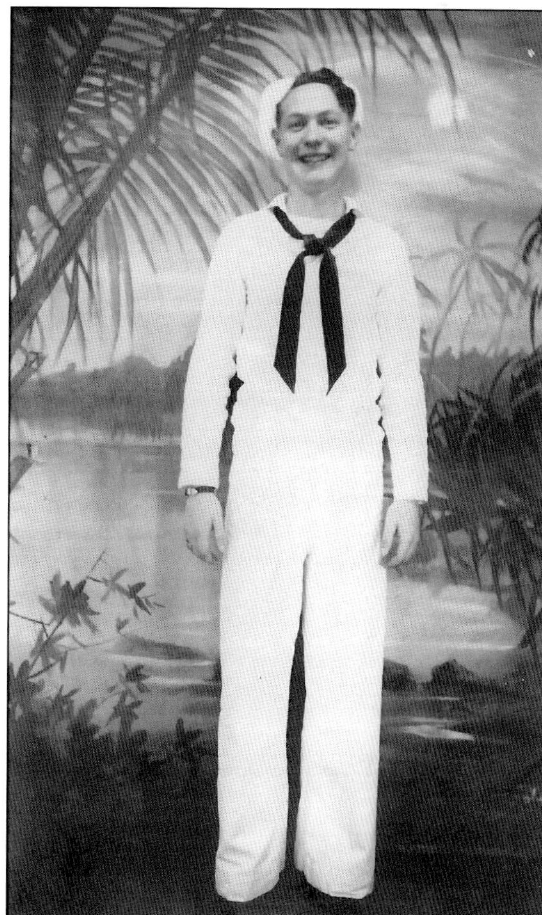

Like many other local men, Jack Gray joined the Navy during World War II. He was later stationed at Pearl Harbor. There, he had an opportunity to go on liberty with Harry Robert Herring, who along with his future wife, Barbara, had been at Pearl Harbor when the Japanese attacked the American fleet on December 7, 1941. Another Encampment man was killed during that battle when the USS *Arizona*, on which he served, was sunk. (Courtesy of GEM.)

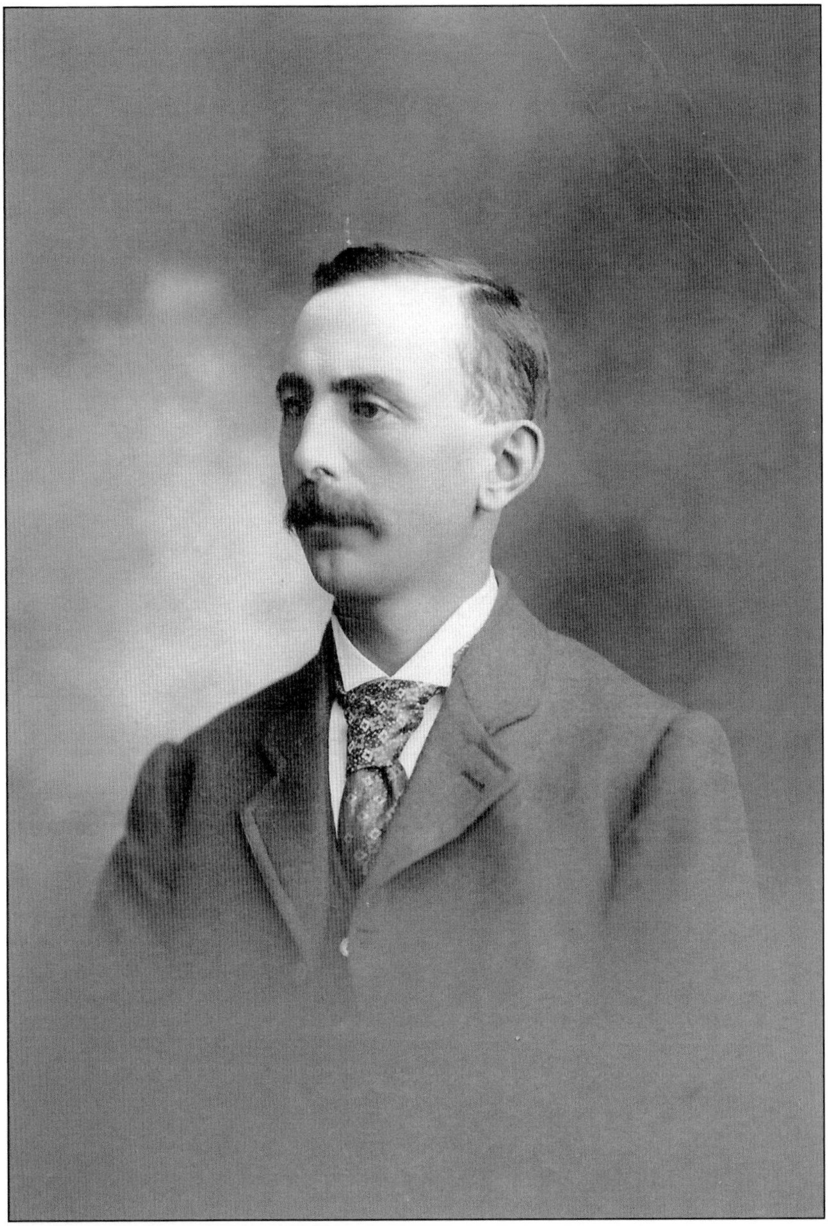

Edward Haggarty located the ore that was developed as the Rudefeha (later Ferris-Haggarty) Mine. Haggarty was born at Stonefolds Hesket, Kirkoswald, Cumberland County, England, on December 6, 1866, the son of Thomas and Hannah Thompson Haggarty. He had been living in Carbon County. He worked as a sheepherder and prospected, looking for the gossan that revealed a rich ore deposit. He struck pay dirt in 1896 with exploration of the quartzite dyke that spilled from the mountain where the Rudefeha Mine went into production in 1897. The mine name came from the men who grubstaked (sponsored) him and his own name: James Rumsey, Robert Deal, George Ferris, and Haggarty. Both Rumsey and Deal quickly sold their interests; Ferris was killed in an accident in 1899, and Haggarty sold out that year for $30,000. He sailed back to England with a comfortable amount of money in his pocket but later returned to Encampment. (Courtesy of GEM/Edna and Ida Haggarty.)

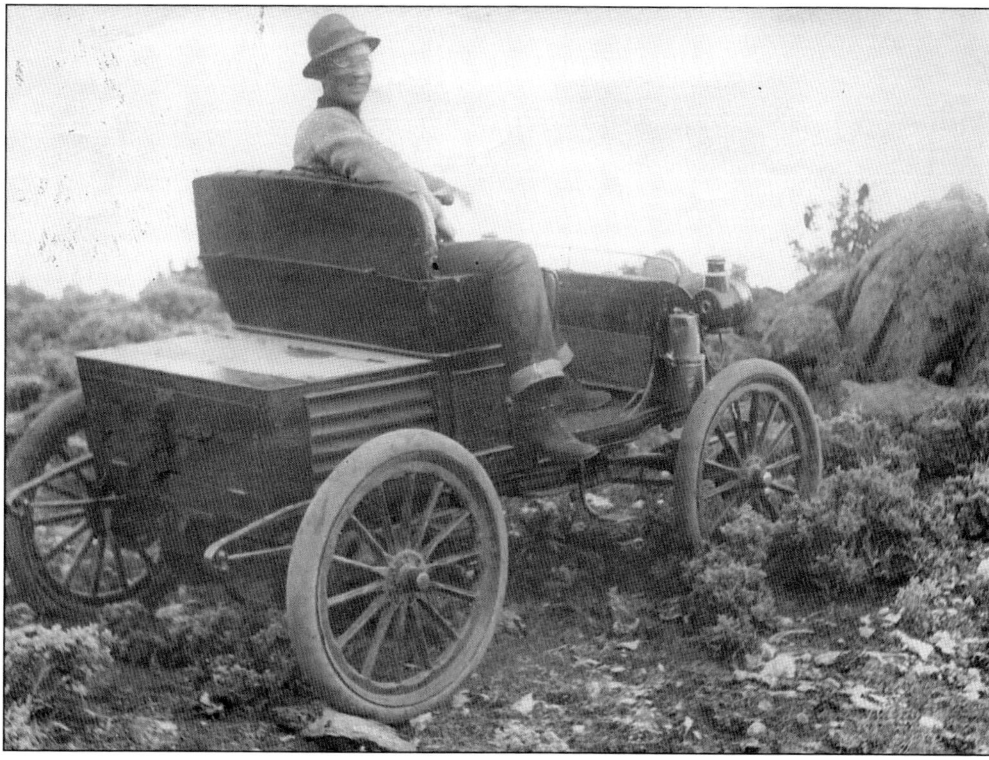

Everett Gross (above) has driven his horseless carriage to the end of the road—if there even was a road. Below, Charles and Grace Hunter Herring pose at the Continental Divide with their 1926 Chevrolet Sport Roadster. (Above, courtesy of GEM/Cecil Ryan; below, courtesy of GEM/Gladys and Ellis Herring Family Collection.)

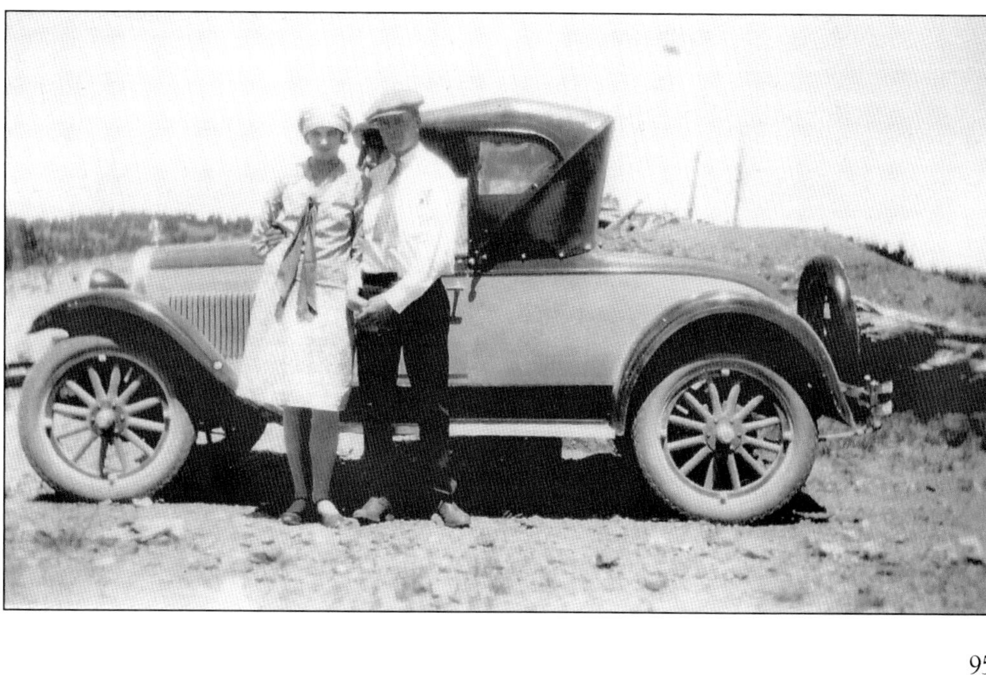

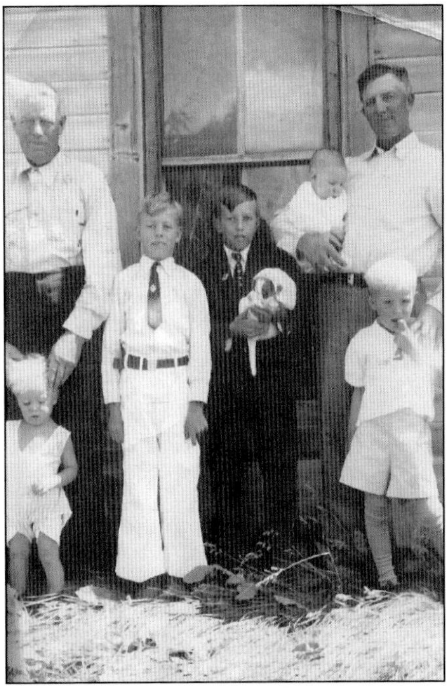

George Herring (left) and his son Ellis (right) pose with some of Ellis's sons. From left to right are Lloyd Wayne, Harry Robert, George (holding the family puppy), Orville (baby), and Earl. Shortly after this photograph was taken, the Ellis Herring family home burned. In the fire, two of the children perished, including Lloyd Wayne and Kenneth (not pictured). (Courtesy of Betty Herring Vyvey Collection.)

George and Malinda Fleming Herring were early settlers in Grand Encampment where their family included sons, from left to right, Ellis, William "Shorty," Garry, Henry "Bill," and Clarence "Breezy" Herring. All of these boys, except William, spent their entire lives in the Encampment area where they reared large families, many of whom continue to live and work in the area in ranching, mining, and timbering—the longstanding industries of the community. (Courtesy of Betty Herring Vyvey Collection.)

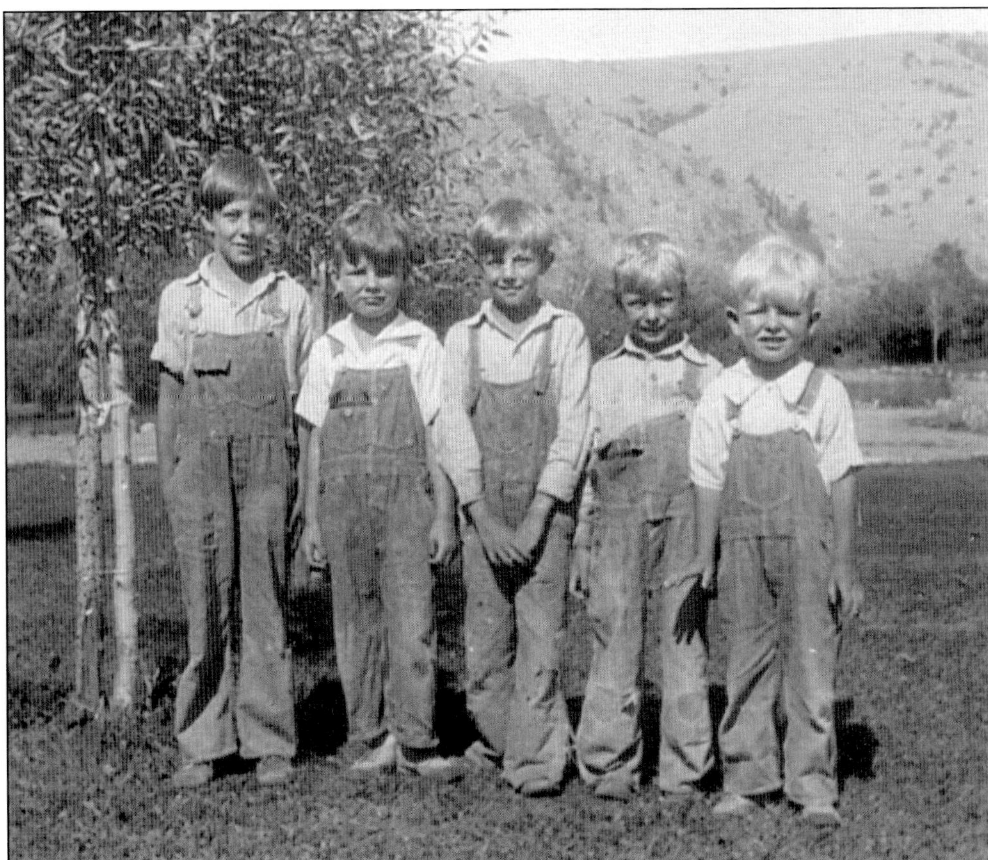

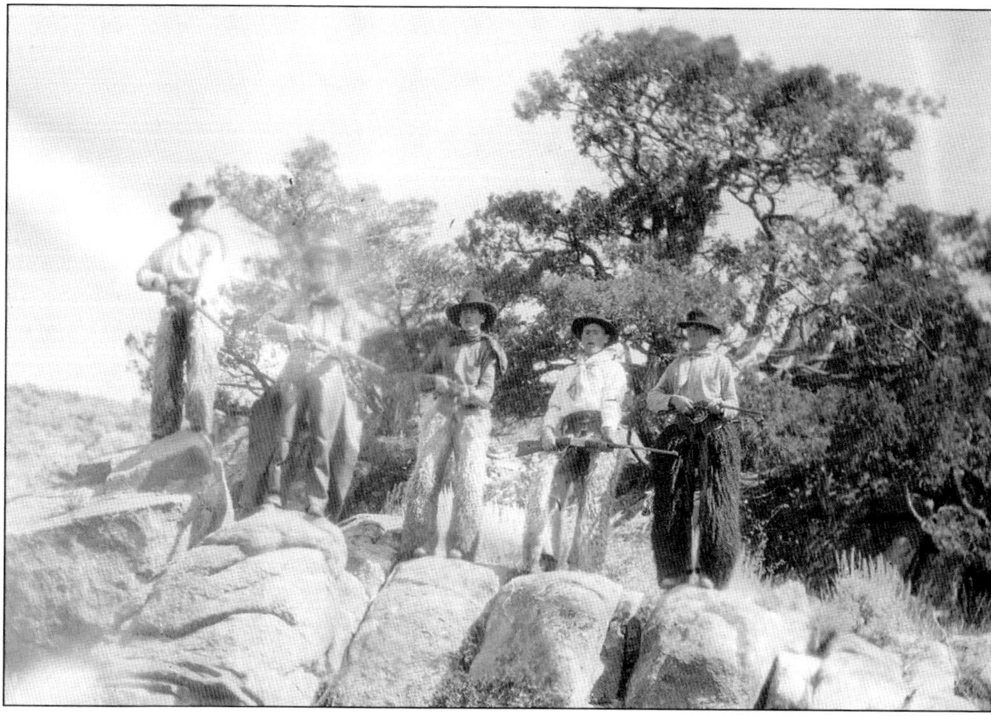

Above are the sons of George and Malinda Herring as young men. From left to right are Ellis, Garry, Henry "Bill," Clarence "Breezy," and William "Shorty. This photograph was taken on Brush Creek when the family lived and ranched in that area. Garry is wearing bat-wing chaps while the others have on wooly chaps. The photograph below shows three of them as much older men. Garry (left) has a fish while his brothers Henry "Bill" and Charles, the youngest in the family who is not shown in the two prior photographs, are yet to show success. (Both, courtesy of Candy Vyvey Moulton Collection.)

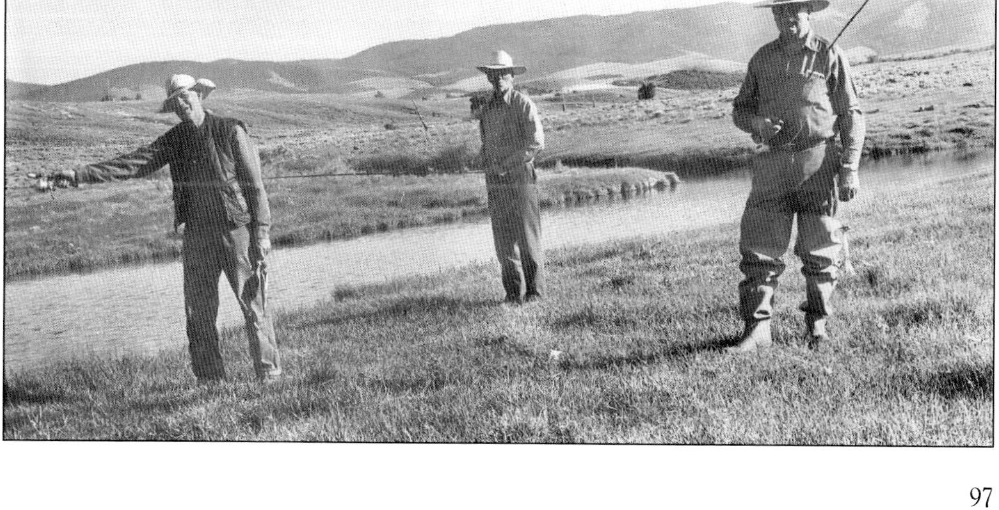

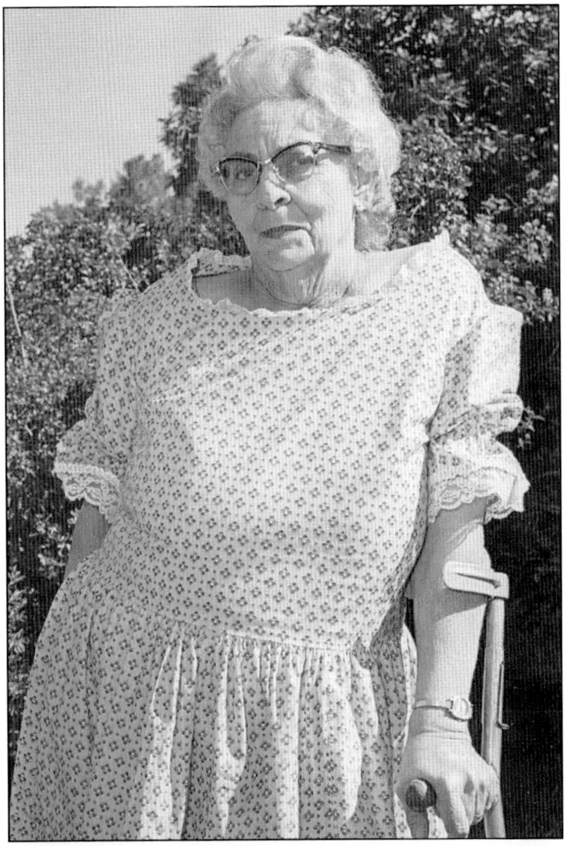

Gladys Herring (left) took part in the filming of *The Treasure of Hidden Valley*, a silent film produced in Encampment in 1975. Gladys and husband Ellis Herring reared a large family of 16 children. Sons Kenneth and Lloyd died as young children in a fire at the family home. Below, the older children are, from left to right, (first row) Patricia, Orville, Francis, and Margaret; (second row) Eugene, Harry Robert, Earl, George, and Betty. In later years, Gladys became known as the "Card Lady" because she sent hundreds of cards to people in the community for birthdays, anniversaries, and on the occasion of an illness or death. She wrote the cards both for herself and on behalf of a number of organizations to which she belonged. (Left, courtesy of Candy Vyvey Moulton; below, courtesy of Betty Herring Vyvey Collection.)

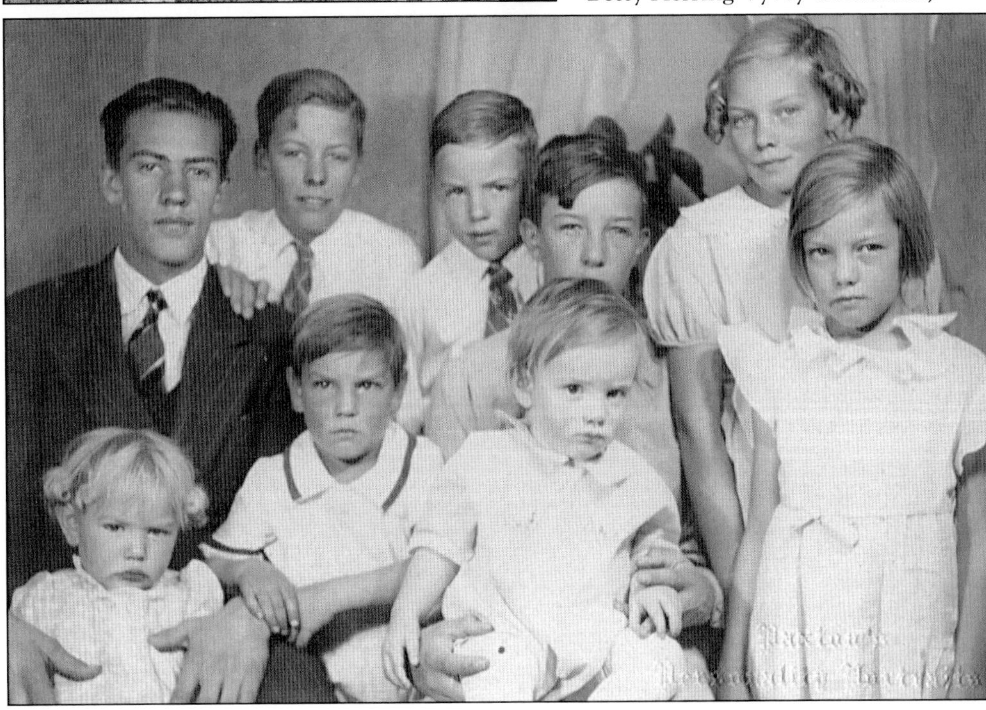

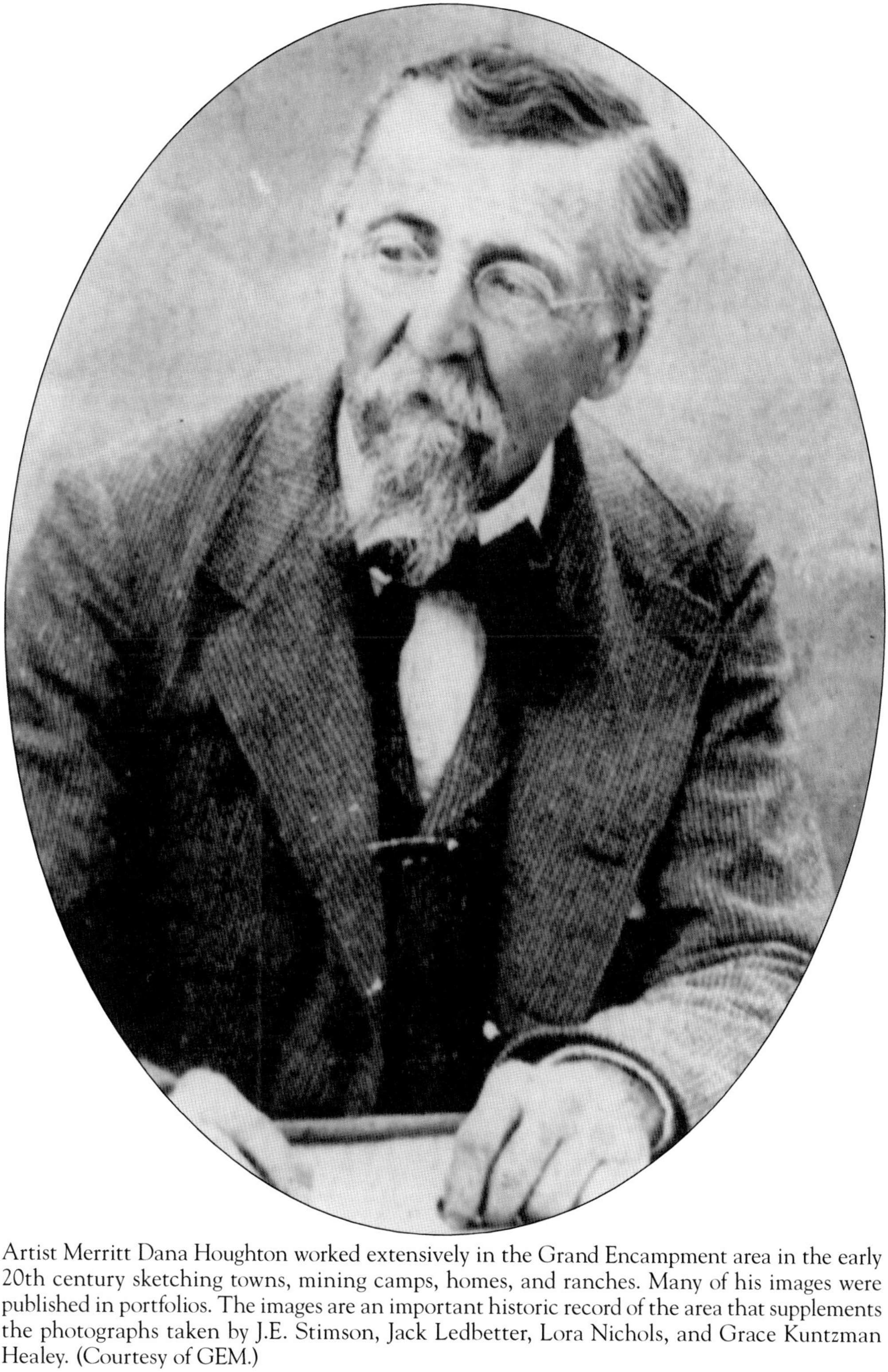

Artist Merritt Dana Houghton worked extensively in the Grand Encampment area in the early 20th century sketching towns, mining camps, homes, and ranches. Many of his images were published in portfolios. The images are an important historic record of the area that supplements the photographs taken by J.E. Stimson, Jack Ledbetter, Lora Nichols, and Grace Kuntzman Healey. (Courtesy of GEM.)

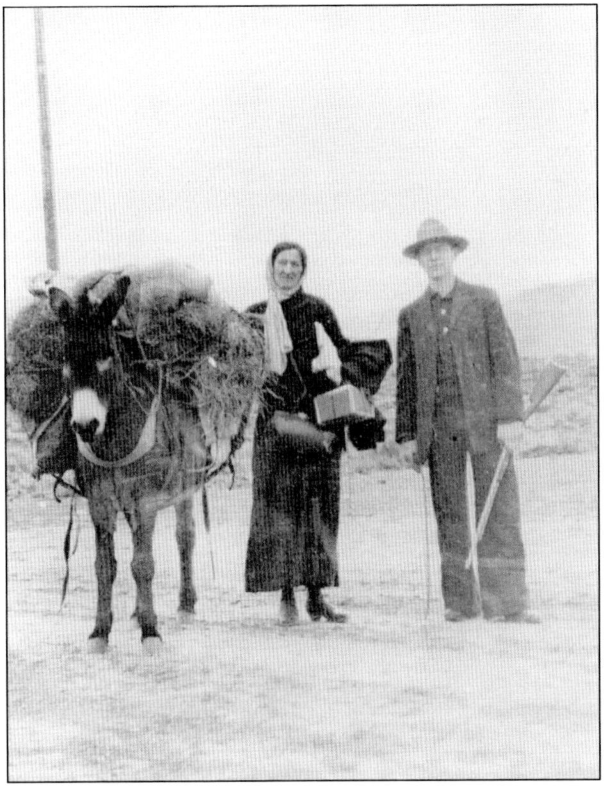

Hynda Ball and son have a full load on her burro, an animal often used—and often photographed—during the early days of Grand Encampment. Burros were widely used for packing and riding. (Courtesy of GEM/Bahs Cruse.)

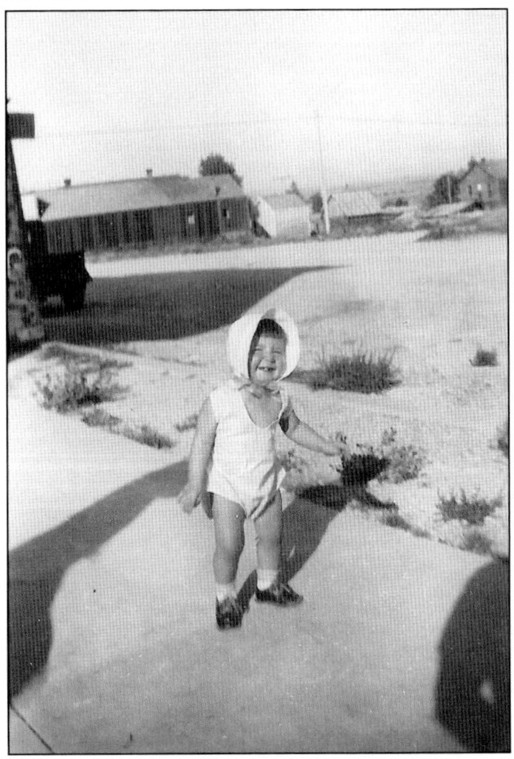

Carol Kuntzman toddles down the sidewalk in front of the E&H Building. Her parents, William and Grace Winsor Kuntzman, operated an insurance company, a music store, and later Kuntzman's Cash Store, a grocery store, in this building, which was named for its earliest owners, Willis George Emerson and W.C. Henry. After Carol's marriage to Eugene Herring, the two of them owned and operated Kuntzman's Cash Store. (Courtesy of GEM/Grace Kuntzman Healey.)

George Kuntzman rides his bike on Freeman Avenue in front of the Kuntzman Music Store and Insurance office (left). Notable is the presence of Lordier Drug Co. in the E&H Building. George was the son of William and Grace Kuntzman. (Courtesy of GEM/Grace Kuntzman Healey.)

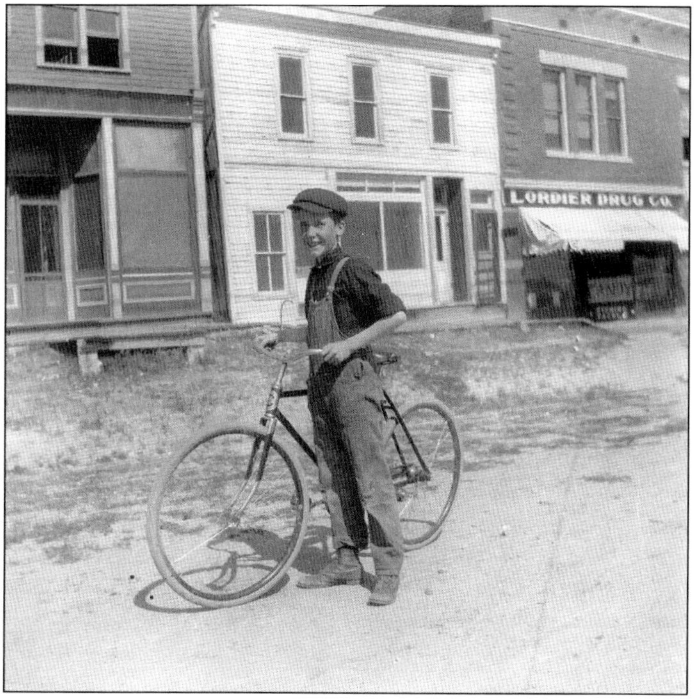

The Ledbetter brothers were among those instrumental in developing the town of Battle in 1897. Shown from left to right are Jack, Phil's son Bob, Phil, and Russ. (Courtesy of GEM/Jack Ledbetter Photograph Collection.)

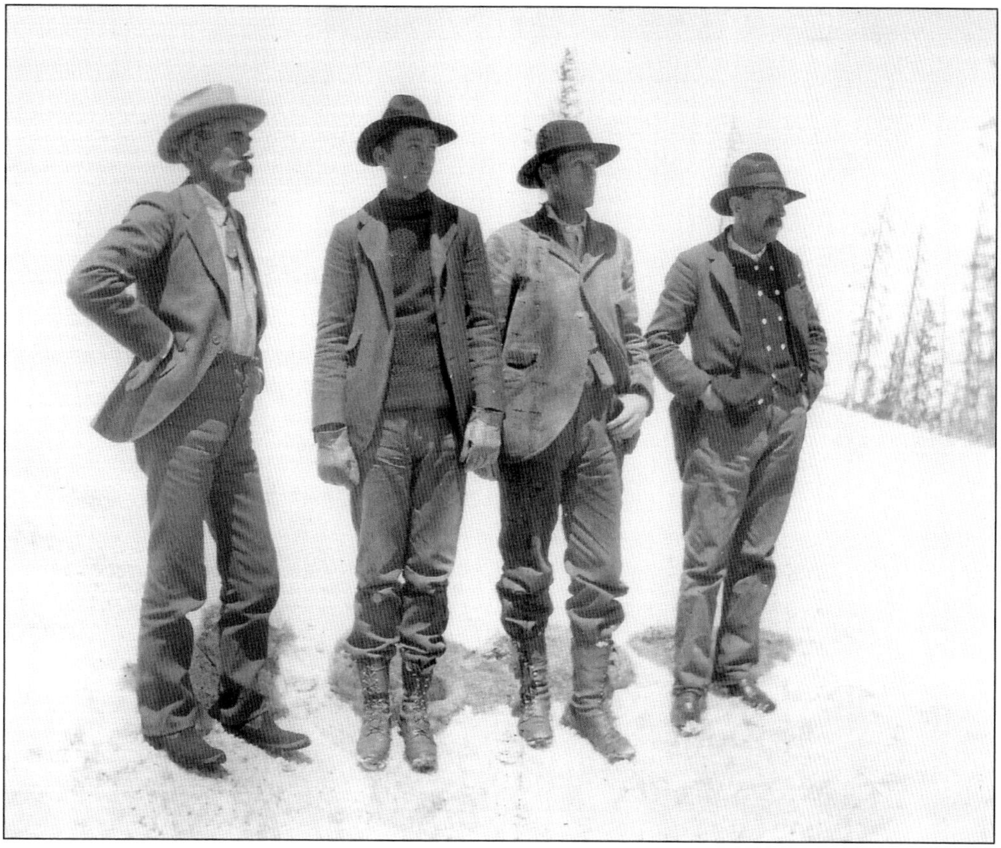

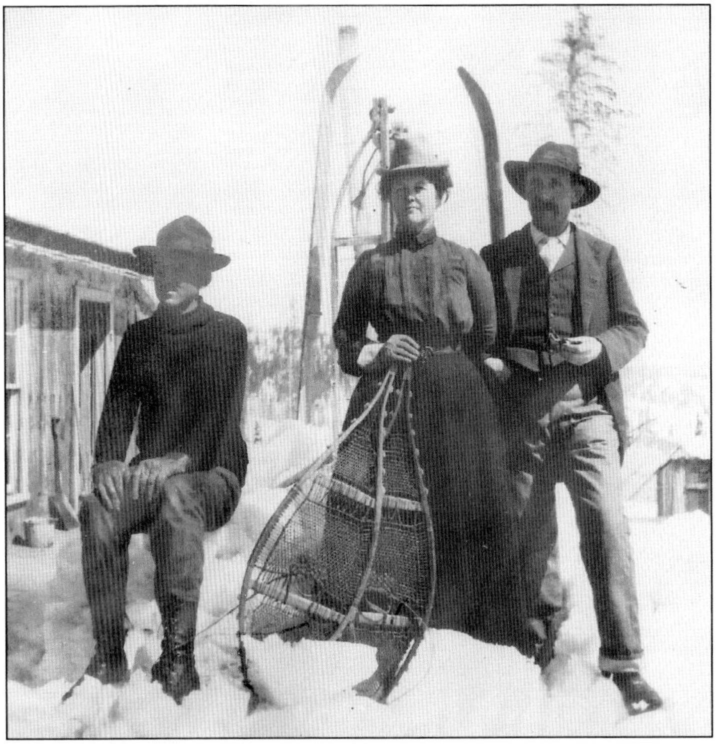

Left, Mr. and Mrs. Jack Ledbetter appear with nephew Bob Ledbetter in Battle in 1897. She holds a pair of snowshoes, and there are skis stuck into the snowbank behind her. This image probably was taken beside their cabin in Battle. In the photograph below, Mrs. Jack Ledbetter strikes a pose with the family dog Rex. (Both, courtesy of GEM/Jack Ledbetter Photograph Collection.)

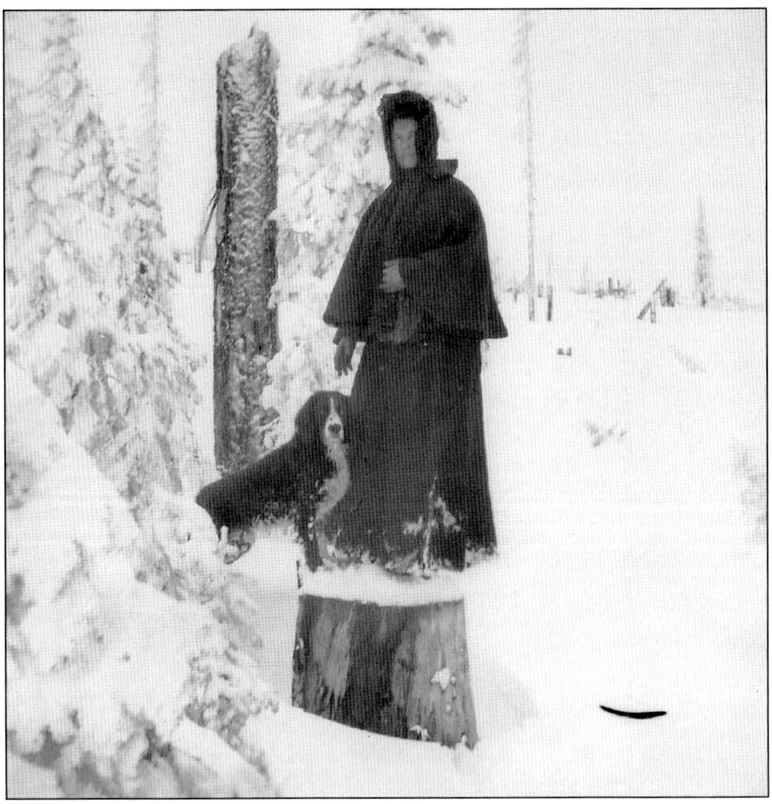

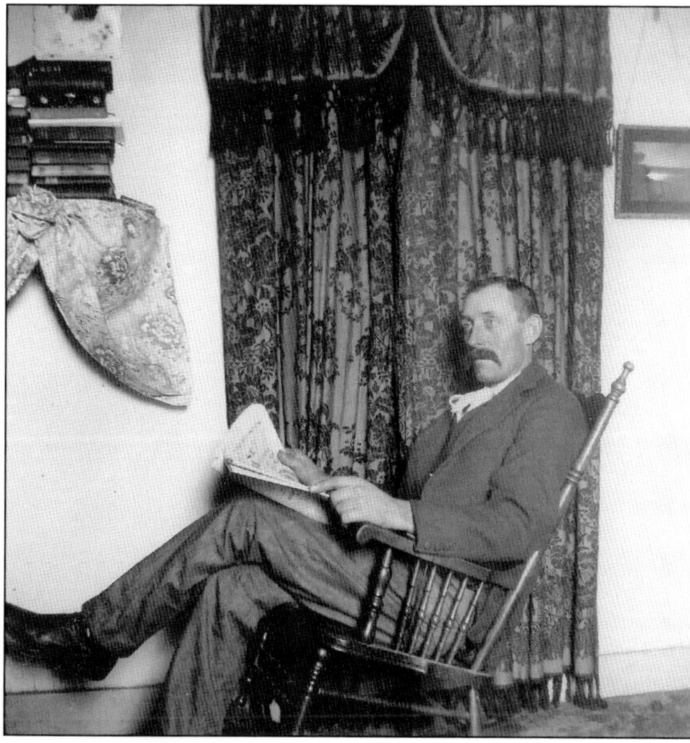

Russell Ledbetter (right) reads the paper, most likely relaxing in his cabin at Battle. He was the brother of Jack Ledbetter, who took the photograph. Davy Crockett, below, pauses with his dog at Battle. Of note are the dog's eyeglasses. The men often wore goggles to protect themselves from snow blindness during the bright days of winter, and the eye protection for the dog most likely served the same purpose. (Both, courtesy of GEM/ Charles W. Fletcher.)

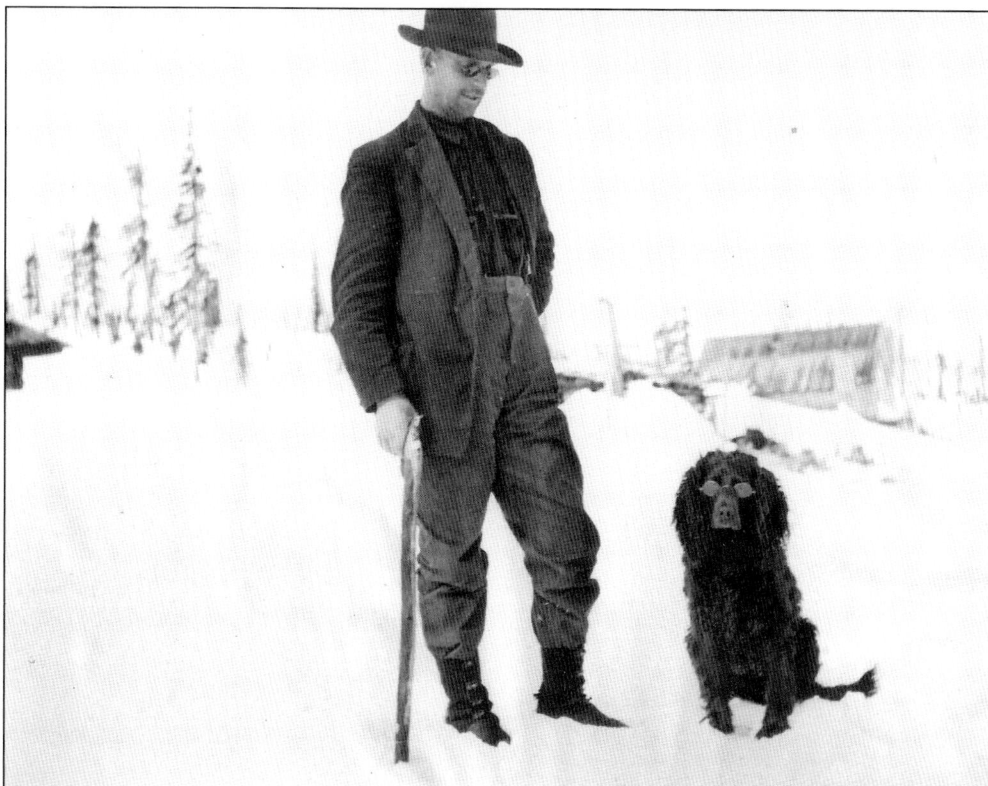

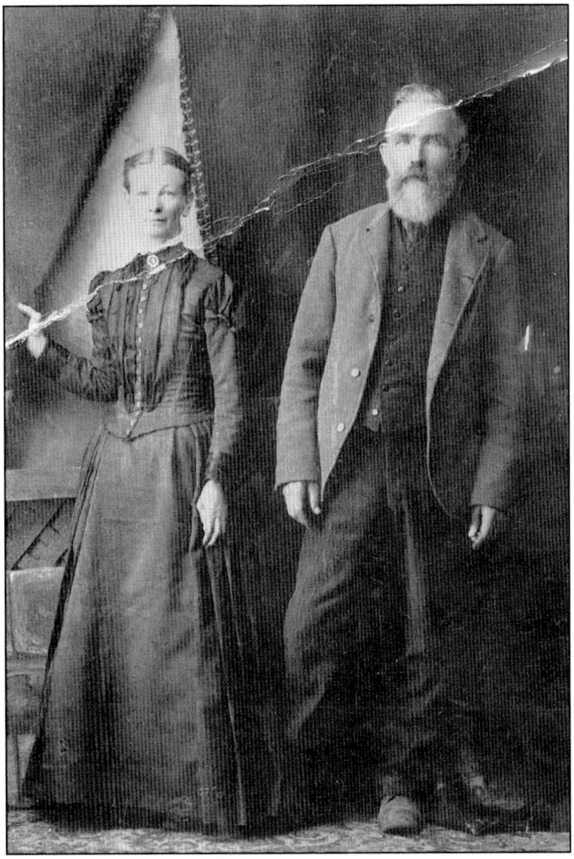

This image captures Margaret Shores Culleton, mother of H.P. "Doc" Culleton, and her second husband, Guy H. Nichols. He was one of the earliest settlers in the Encampment Valley, arriving in 1879. Guy and Margaret first lived in Swan where they operated the post office and store. (Courtesy of GEM/Mamie Brown Marshall.)

The Nichols family was one of the earliest and most prominent families in Grand Encampment. As a child, Lora Nichols began keeping a diary and taking photographs, both of which are an important part of the historic record of the valley. Her story is chronicled in the book *Lora Webb Nichols: Rancher's Daughter, Miner's Bride* by Nancy Anderson. This image is of Lora with her second husband, who was also her cousin, Guy, and her oldest son, Bert Oldman. (Courtesy of GEM/ Ledbetter Photograph Collection.)

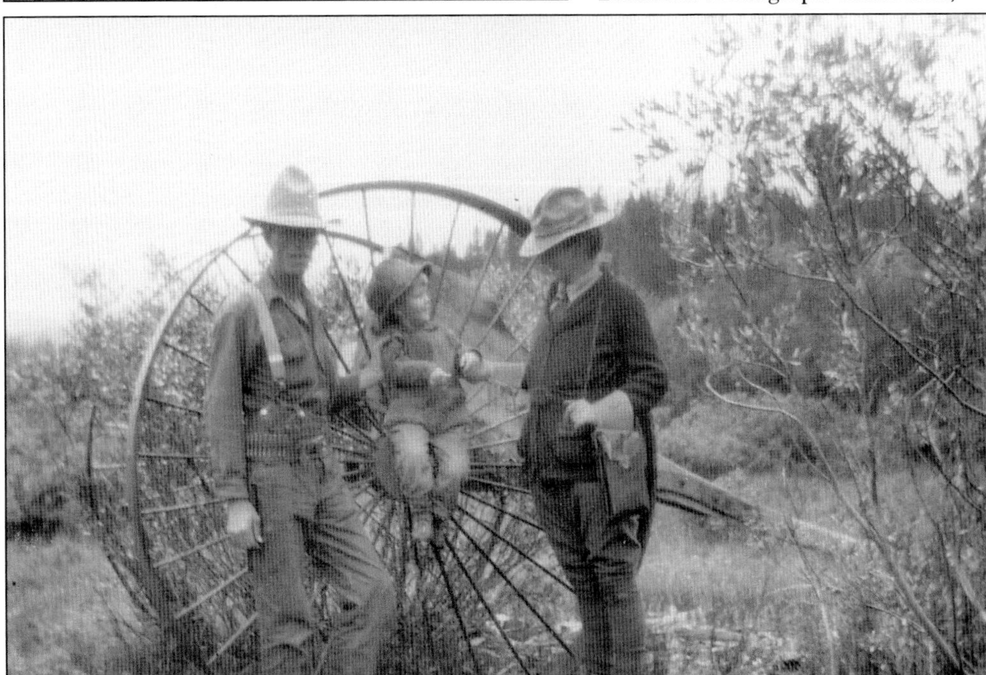

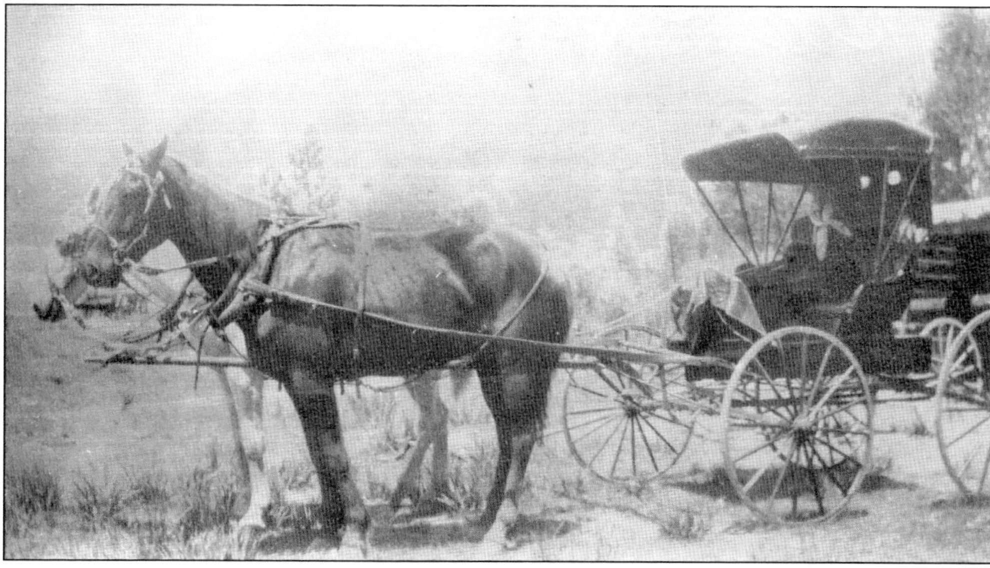

George Peck (above) takes his carriage for a drive along with his wife, Alma. The photograph at right is of Mr. Pixley, whom people called "Saxy." This photograph by Grace Kuntzman Healey comes with a story she wrote detailing how A.J. Chidester brought the ice and coal for her in-laws, Nan and George Kuntzman, delivering it to their home. Grace added, "Queer Saxy Pixley, whose skull two boys used as a ball before it reached its final resting place, cut the wood." It would be interesting to ask her some questions about Mr. Pixley's head being used as a ball. (Both, courtesy of GEM/Grace Kuntzman Healey.)

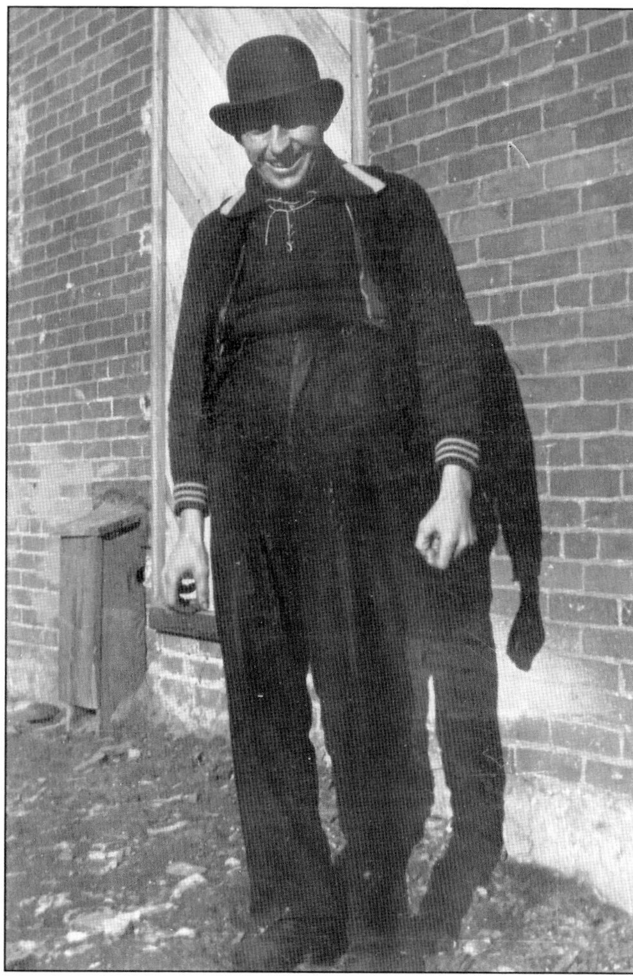

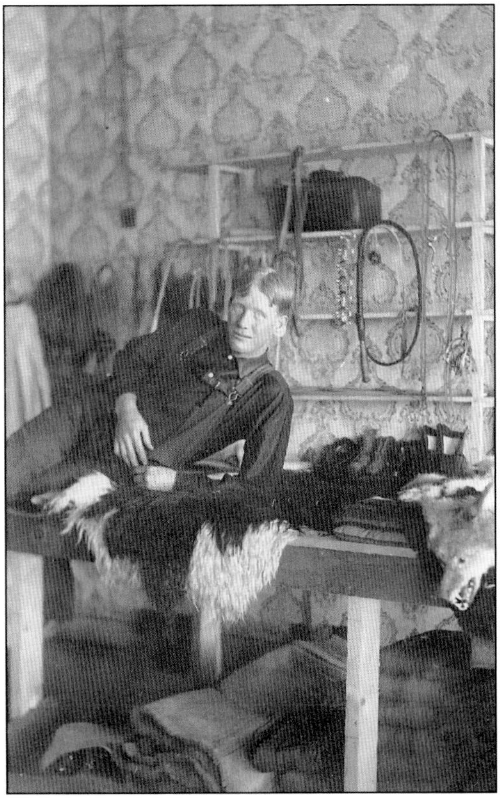

Jake Schmidt operated a saddle shop in Grand Encampment, making saddles, cowboy cuffs, belts, and other leather items, many examples of which are on display at the Grand Encampment Museum. The image at left shows Chris Schmidt in the shop. For three decades, Betty Herring Vyvey (below) did research and visited with guests at the Grand Encampment Museum, serving as one of the many volunteers who made sure the doors were open each day from Memorial Day to Labor Day. She took part in Living History activities at the museum, often dressing her grandchildren in pioneer clothing so they could take part in washing clothes at the Saratoga Cabin or tending duties at the Lake Creek Stage Station. She provided many of the photographs in this volume and is still researching and preserving Encampment-area history. (Left, courtesy of GEM; below, courtesy of Candy Vyvey Moulton.)

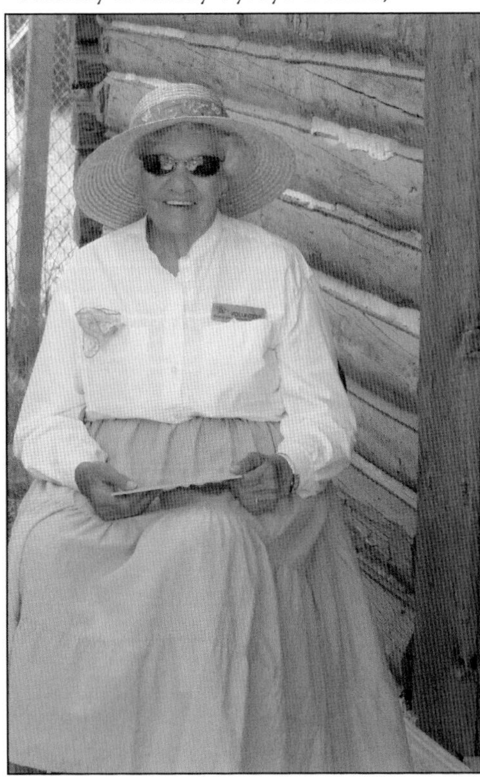

This image shows Oscar Walker working in the tie camps in 1900. (Courtesy of GEM.)

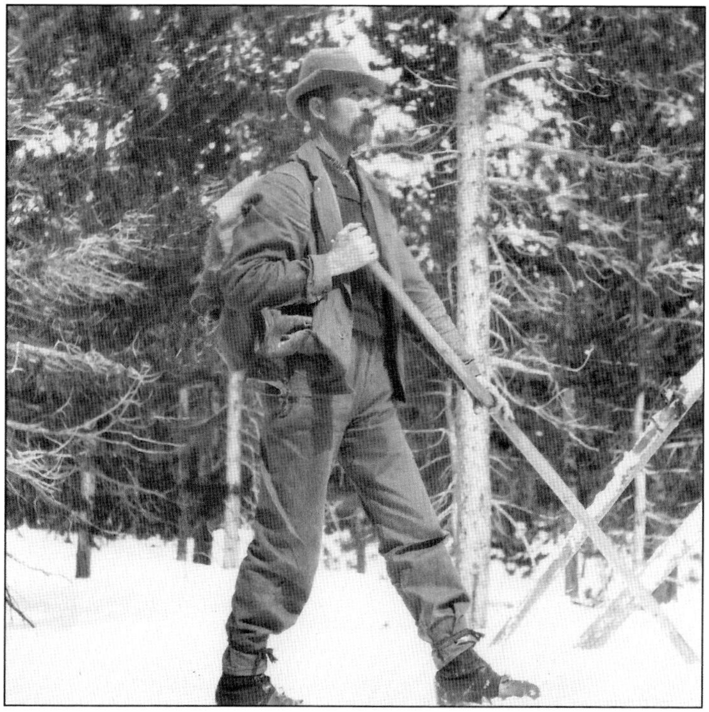

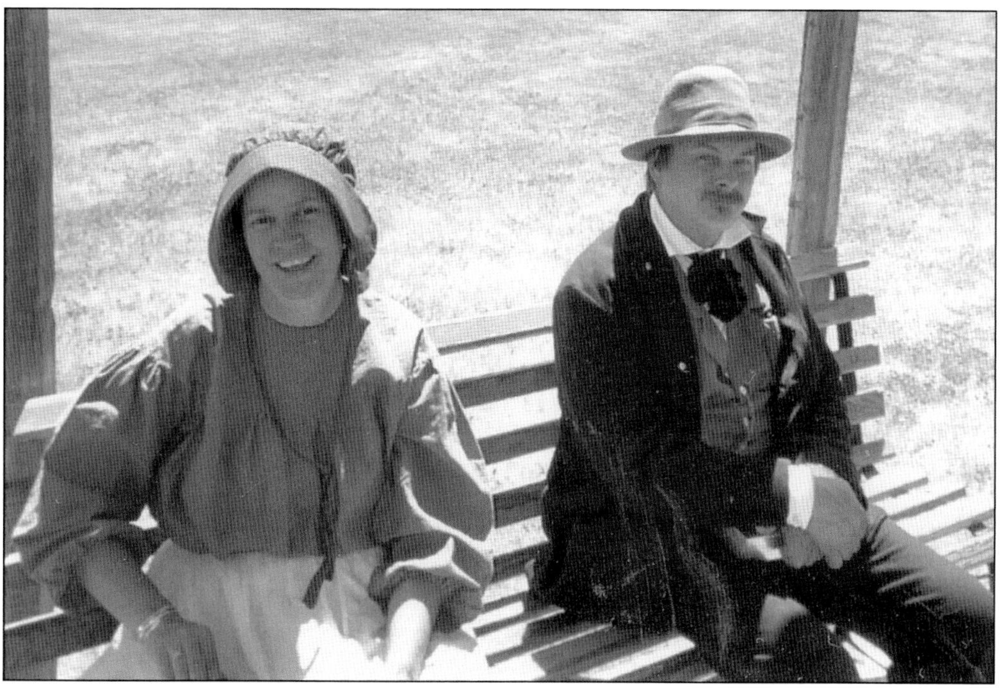

What can be said about these two characters dressed up as 19th-century pioneer immigrants and sharing their experiences of actually traveling overland by covered wagon in the 21st century? Candy Moulton (left) and Terry Del Bene, authors of this book, have been frequent presenters at Living History at the Grand Encampment Museum. They have spent their careers documenting the history of Western people and places. (Courtesy of Erin Moulton.)

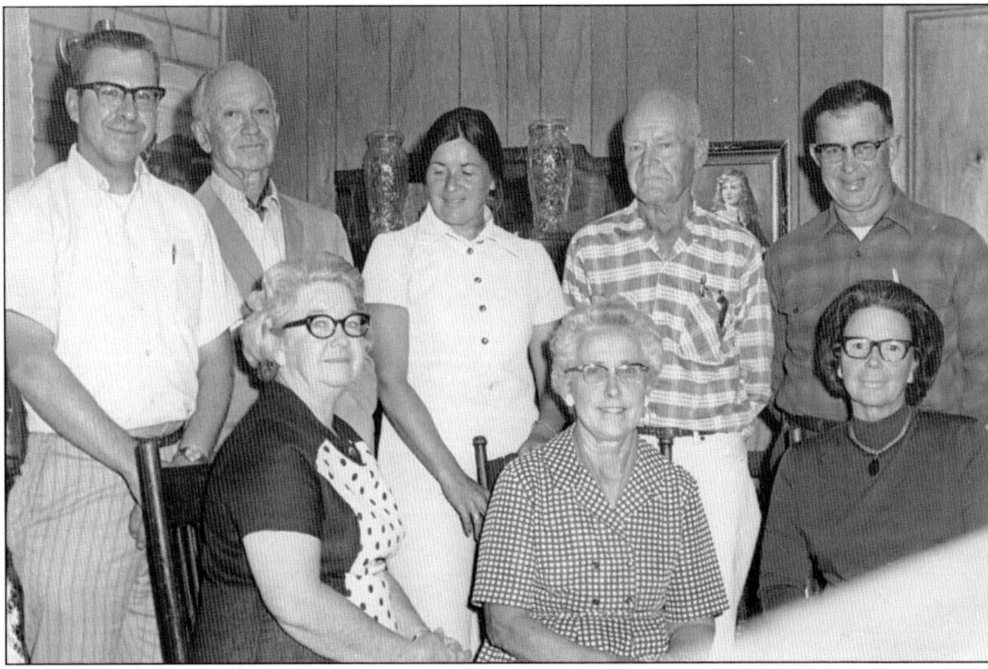

The Grand Encampment Museum Board is pictured above in 1970. From left to right are (first row) Janet Peryam, Vera Oldman, and Deborah Chastain; (second row) R. Richard Perue, Bill Sidley, Carol Kuntzman Herring, Orel Tikkaner, and Dwain Cruse. Times were tough in the early 1960s in Encampment, which prompted lumber company owner R.L. "Mike" Hammer to suggest the Encampment-Riverside Lions Club ought to put on an event that would entertain the locals and attract some visitors. Thus was born the Woodchoppers Jamboree, a woodcutting competition that involved events such as two-man hand sawing, demonstrated here by Ron Soderberg (left), a repeat winner of the All Around Championship trophy. The event expanded to include a rodeo, parade, melodrama, and other events. It takes place Father's Day weekend every June. Y'all come! (Above, courtesy of GEM/*Saratoga Sun* Photograph Collection; below, courtesy of Candy Vyvey Moulton.)

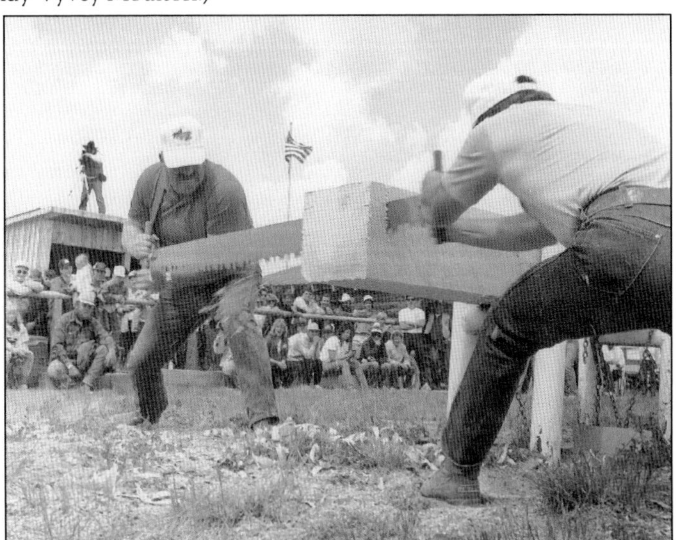

Five

The Corners of Our World

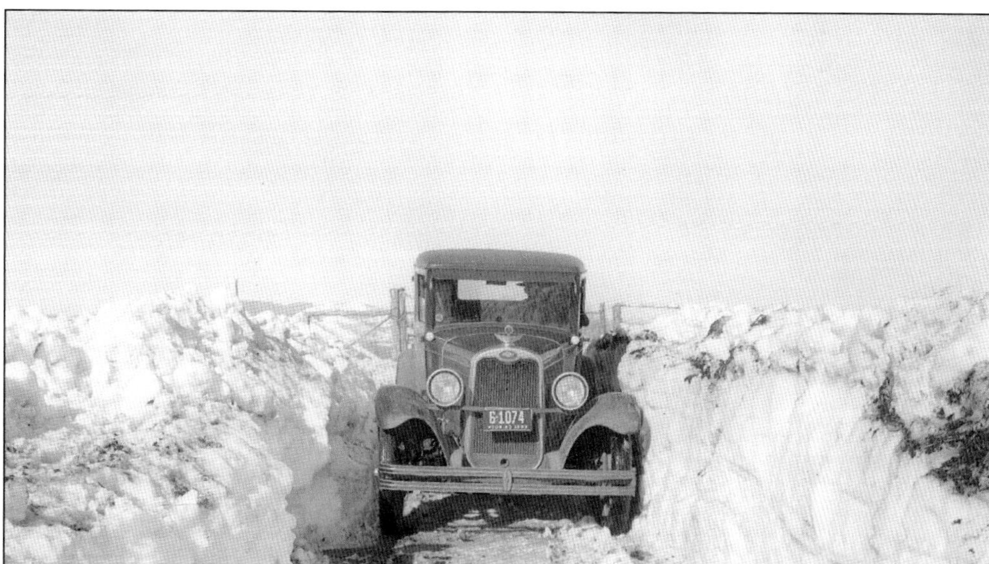

Deep snow can make it difficult to get to Encampment, as Ellis Herring found out with his 1932 Ford. (Courtesy of Candy Vyvey Moulton Collection.)

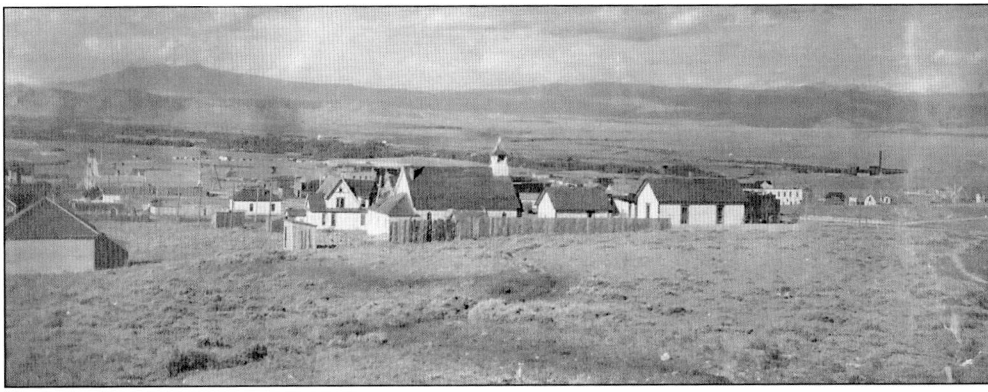

This view of Grand Encampment shows the town hall bell tower at far left, the Encampment Methodist (later Presbyterian) Church in the foreground, and the North American Copper Company Smelter to the far right. If standing in the same location today, a person might still see the bell tower and the church, but the smelter is long gone. (Courtesy of Candy Vyvey Moulton Collection.)

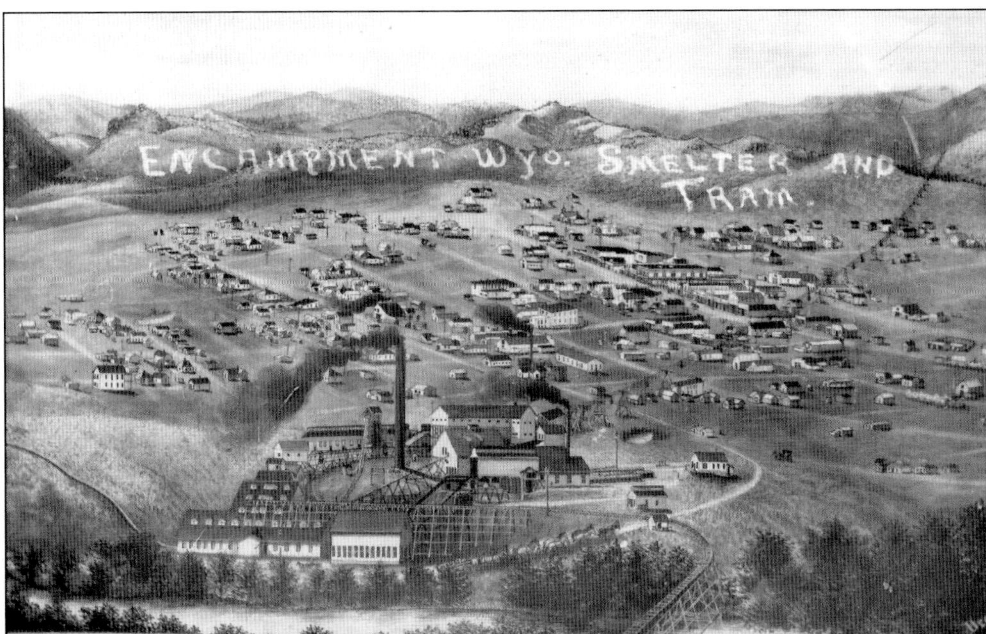

M.D. Houghton prepared this drawing of Grand Encampment in 1904. The image shows the American Copper Company Smelter, the aerial tramway, and the wooden pipeline that provided water for power at the smelter, as well as the community itself. (Courtesy of GEM.)

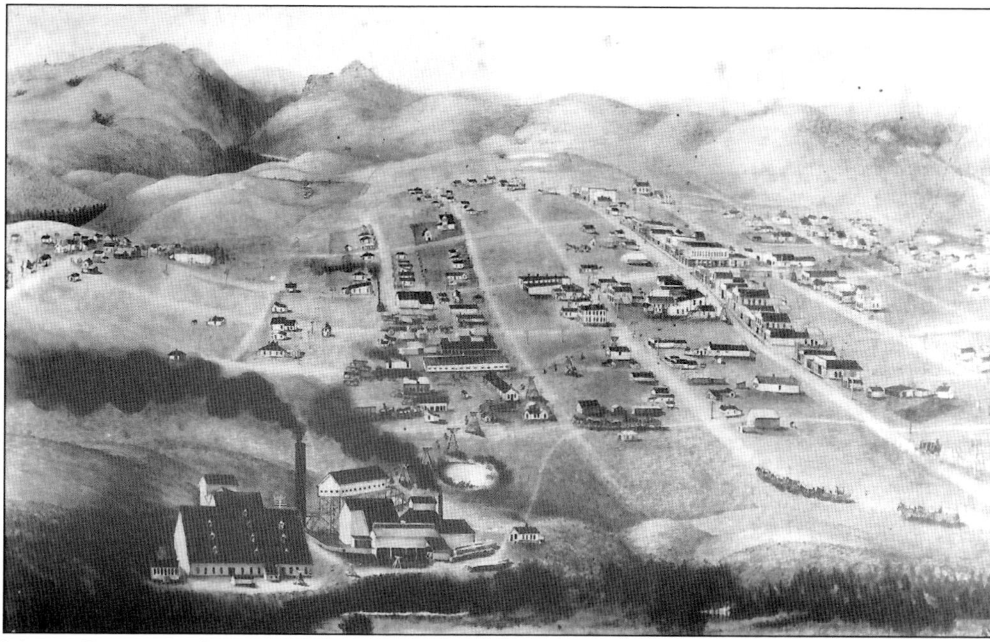

Merritt Dana Houghton created several drawings of Grand Encampment. This one dates to about 1902. (Courtesy of GEM.)

This image depicts the Bohn Hotel during a celebration, perhaps Independence Day. This building later became the Rocky Mountain Studio, owned and operated by Lora Nichols. The dog in the center of the image, apparently being scolded by a young woman, appears to be wearing some decoration as well. The poles leaning against the building are thought to be bracing for a sagging wall. (Courtesy of GEM/Grace Kuntzman Healey.)

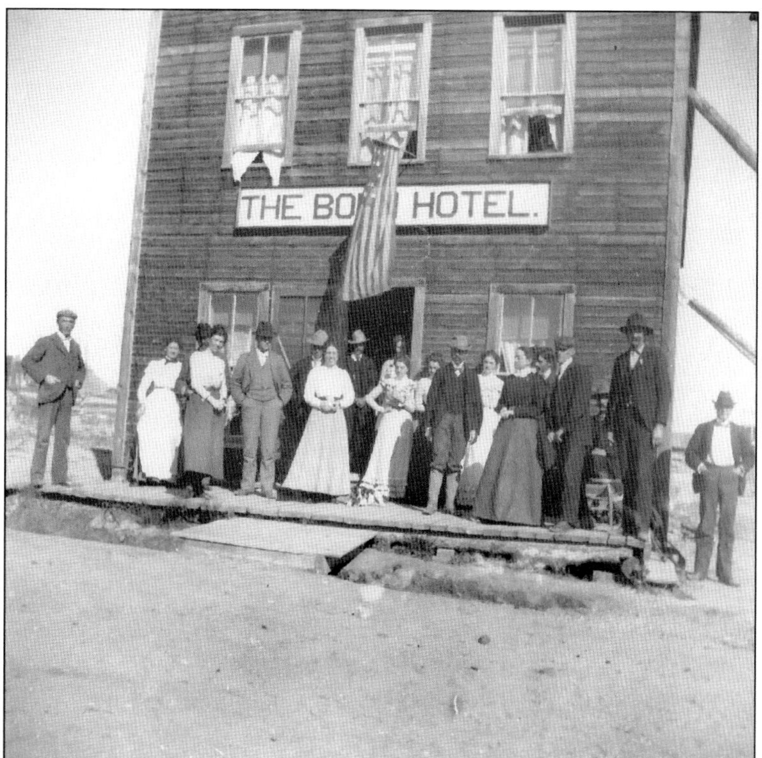

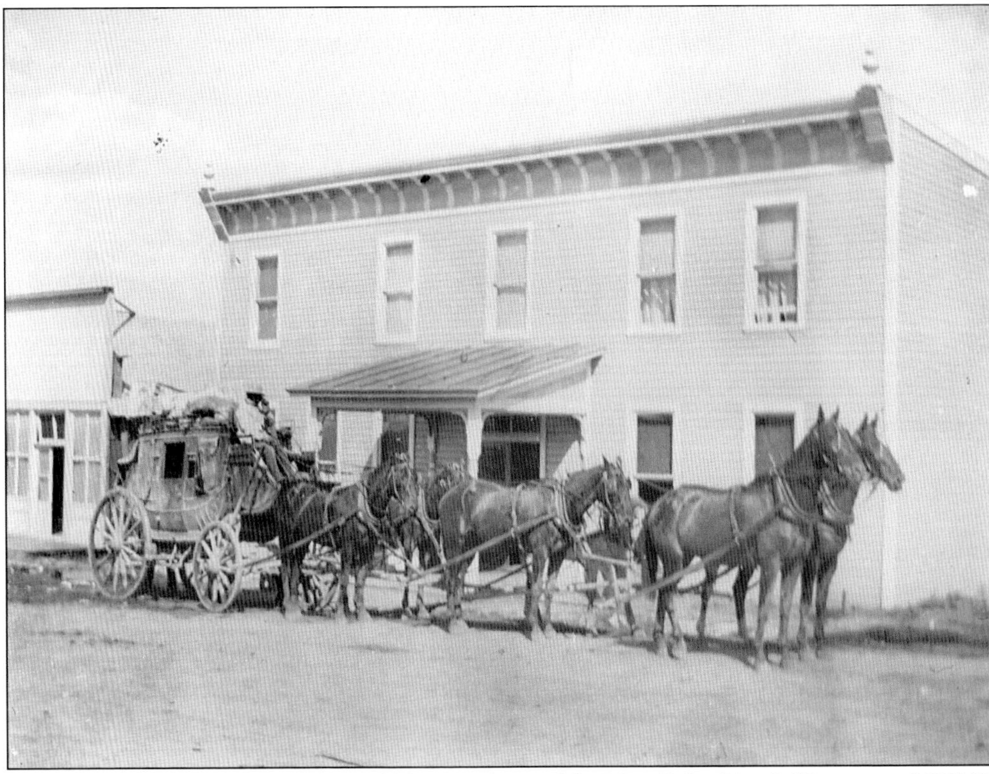

The Encampment Stage is ready to roll from in front of the New Bohn Hotel. (Courtesy of GEM.)

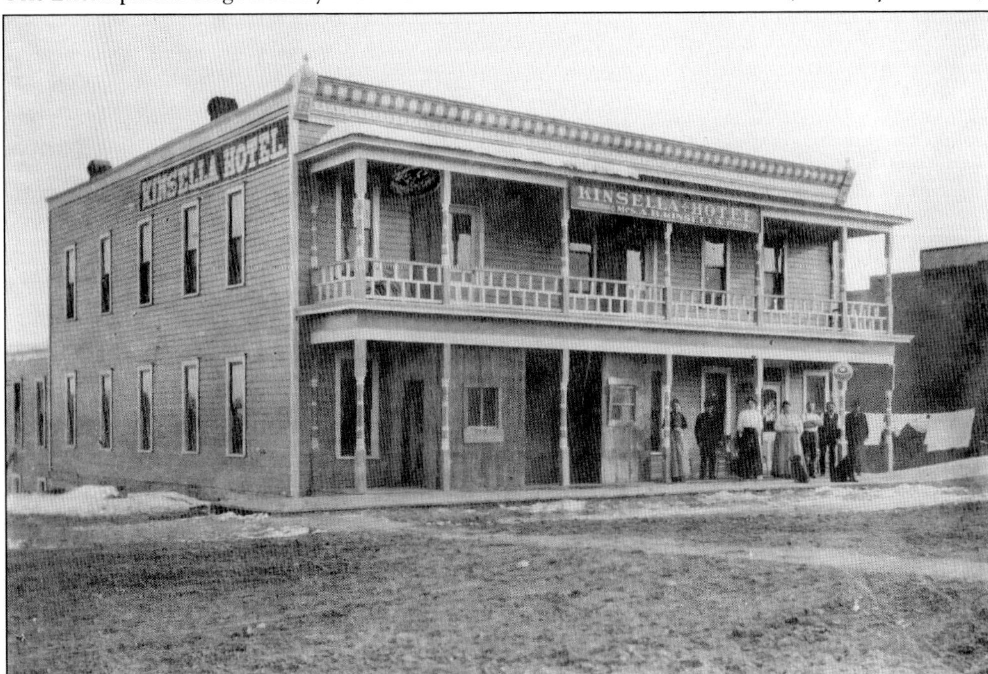

The Kinsella Hotel and Battle Rooming House was operated by Mrs. A.B. Kinsella. The two-story structure was constructed in 1900. (Courtesy of Candy Vyvey Moulton Collection.)

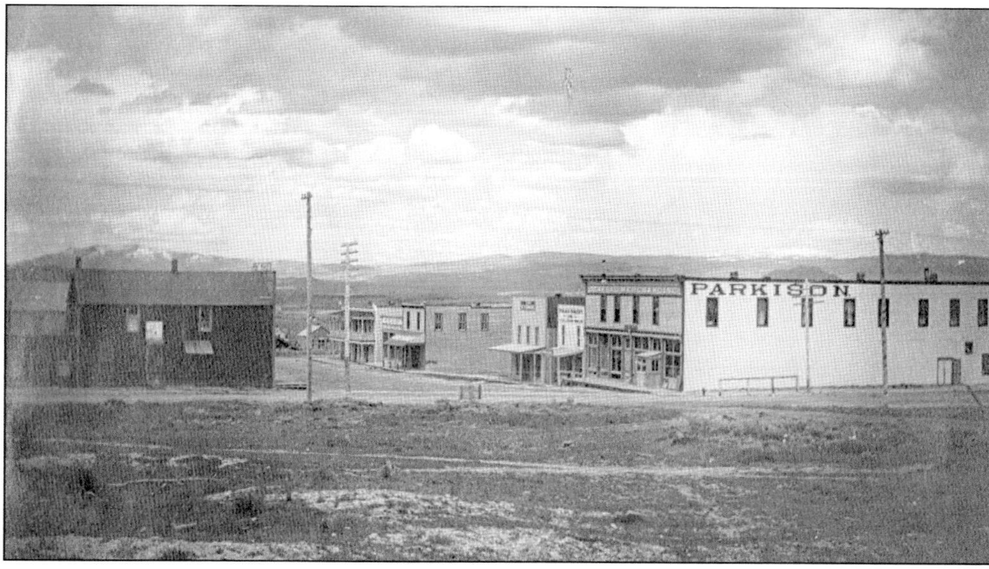

In this view of Encampment showing the Parkison Store, Palace Bakery, the Wyoming, and the Kinsella Hotel, the town appears to be deserted. However, on close examination, there are three or four people in the image. The system of fire hydrants was in place, as evidenced by a hydrant at the corner of the Parkison Store; even so, the store burned to the ground on a cold winter night in 1914 when the fire lines froze. (Courtesy of Candy Vyvey Moulton Collection.)

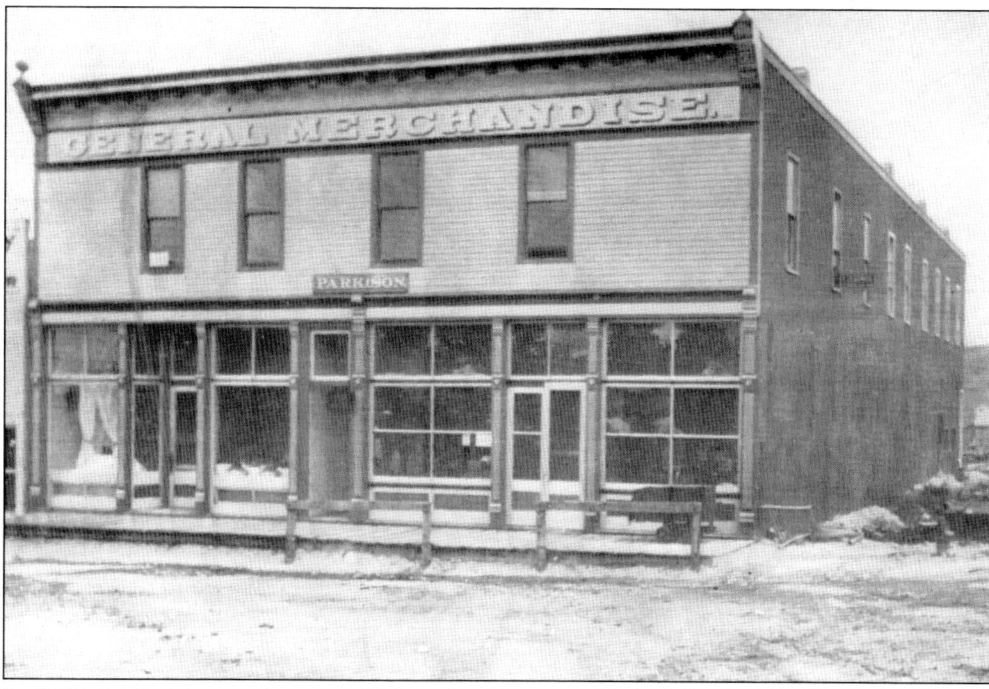

In 1900, Ed Parkison and partner Milton Englehart established the first Parkison Store at the corner of Sixth and McCaffrey Streets. The store sold hardware, dry goods, and groceries. Later, the store rented office space in the second floor. Parkison also operated a store at Rudefeha and a ranch near Antelope Creek. The second Parkison Store was built at the corner of Sixth Street and Freeman Avenue. (Courtesy of Candy Vyvey Moulton Collection.)

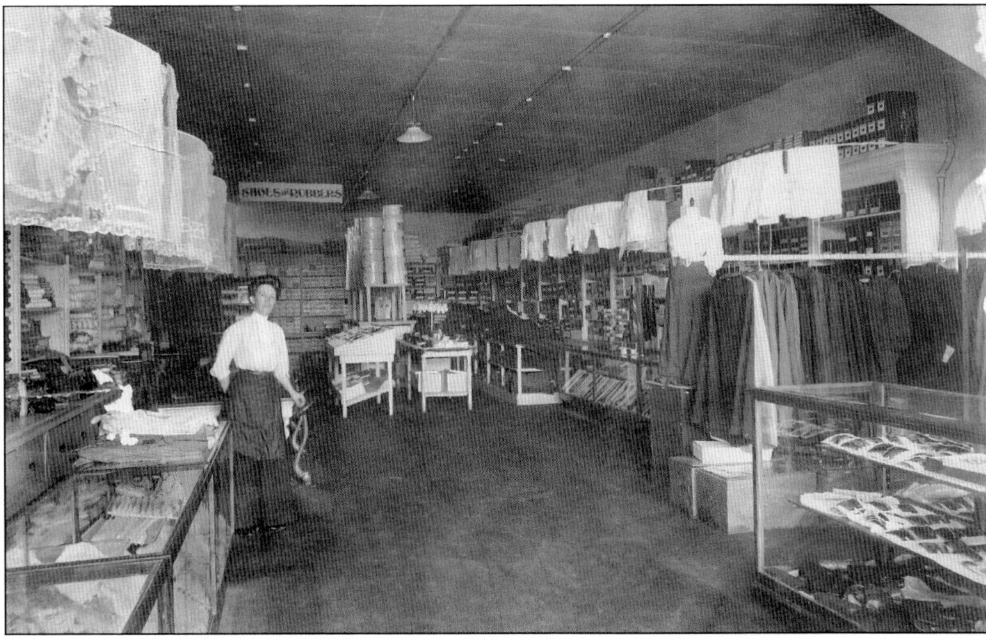

The clothing area of the Parkison Store evidences the wide range of products available in the early 20th century. The shelves are well stocked with premade "store-bought" items, such as shoes, shirts, blouses, dresses, combs, rubbers, and coats. For the more frugal shopper, there are yard goods, zippers, thread, and just about everything necessary to make a wardrobe. (Courtesy of Candy Vyvey Moulton Collection.)

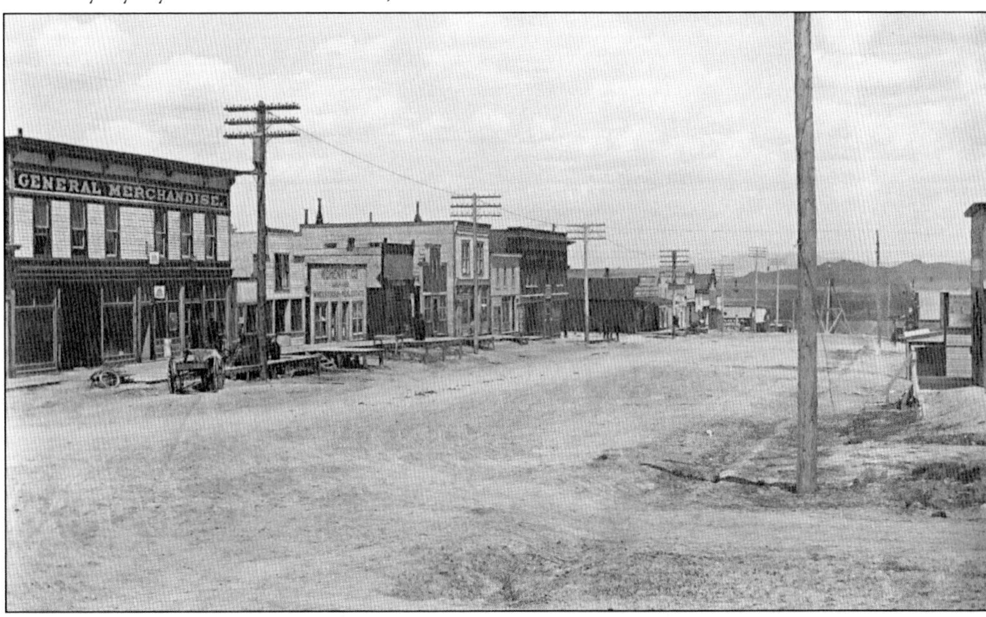

Shoppers go about their business on Freeman Avenue in Encampment. Stores include General Merchandise, W.C. Henry Co., Kuntzman Insurance, and the E&H Building on the corner. Bell Telephone and Telegraph Company has an office in the General Merchandise building. Power poles give the street a modern look, but hitching posts are still available for those with horse transport. (Courtesy of Candy Vyvey Moulton Collection.)

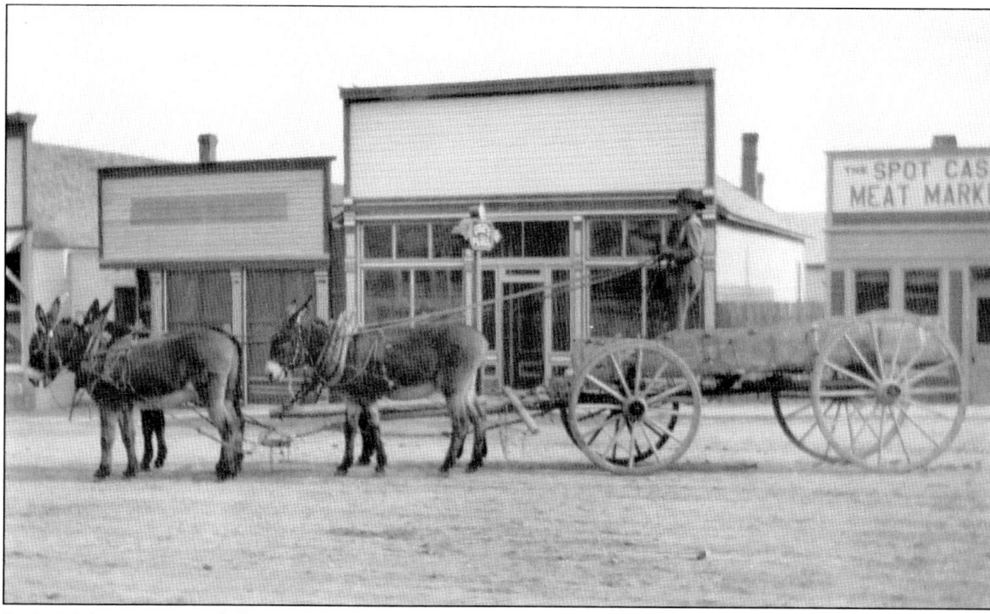

L.A. Melvin operated the Spot Cash Meat Market on Freeman Avenue. The *Grand Encampment Herald* reported on December 2, 1904, " 'Live and let life is my motto' L.A. Melvin, The Spot Cash Meat Market Man—Freeman Ave." (Courtesy of GEM/Grace Kuntzman Healey.)

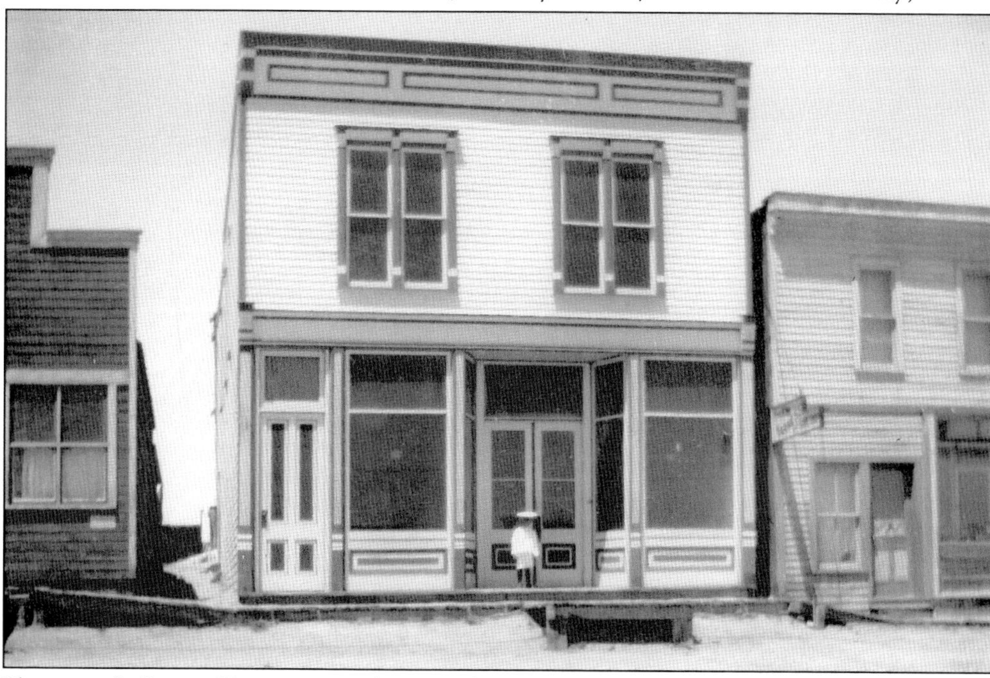

Shown with George Kuntzman on the step, the Kuntzman Music Store was located on Freeman Avenue. His grandfather, also named George Kuntzman, ran an insurance business from an enclosed cage in the front of the building. In 1908, the mines began to fail, and the smelter burned. Grandpa George held the insurance on the smelter, and it is reported that his wife, Nan, sat up with him the entire night of the conflagration trying to comfort the broken man. (Courtesy of GEM/Grace Kuntzman Healey.)

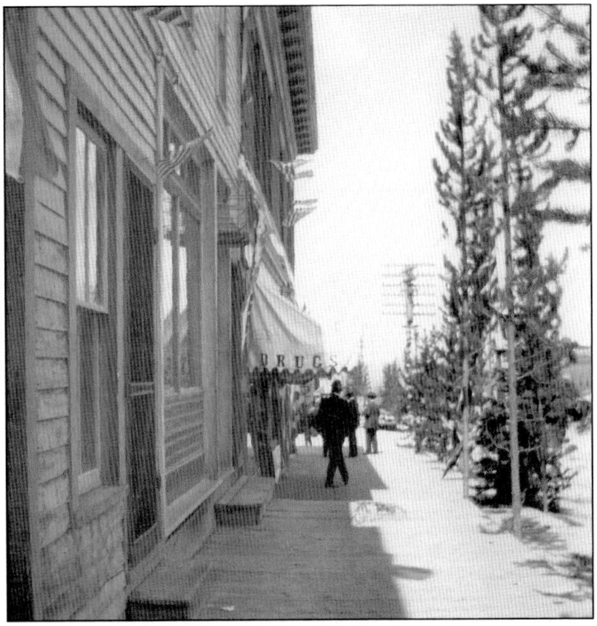

Shown on the left, the Kuntzman building, apparently decorated for the Fourth of July holiday, was located next to the E&H Building. Notable is the possible crow in a birdcage above and left of center. Below is a look into the store window of Kuntzman's music store, which clearly is catering to the Christmas season. There are three models of RCA Victrolas on sale. Based upon the costs of the various models, this image dates to roughly 1905. Customers could walk away with a phonograph for $1 a week. The reflection of George Kuntzman, the photographer, is visible in this image. He appears to be wearing a derby hat. (Both, courtesy of GEM/Grace Kuntzman Healey.)

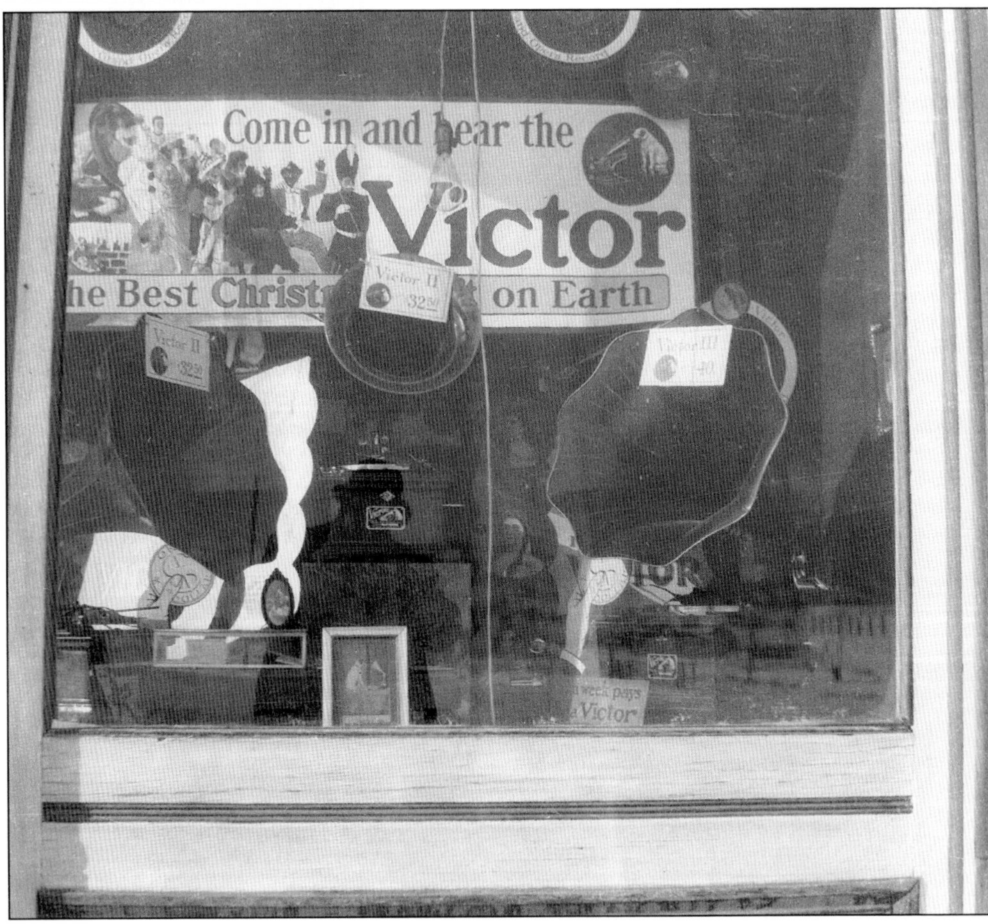

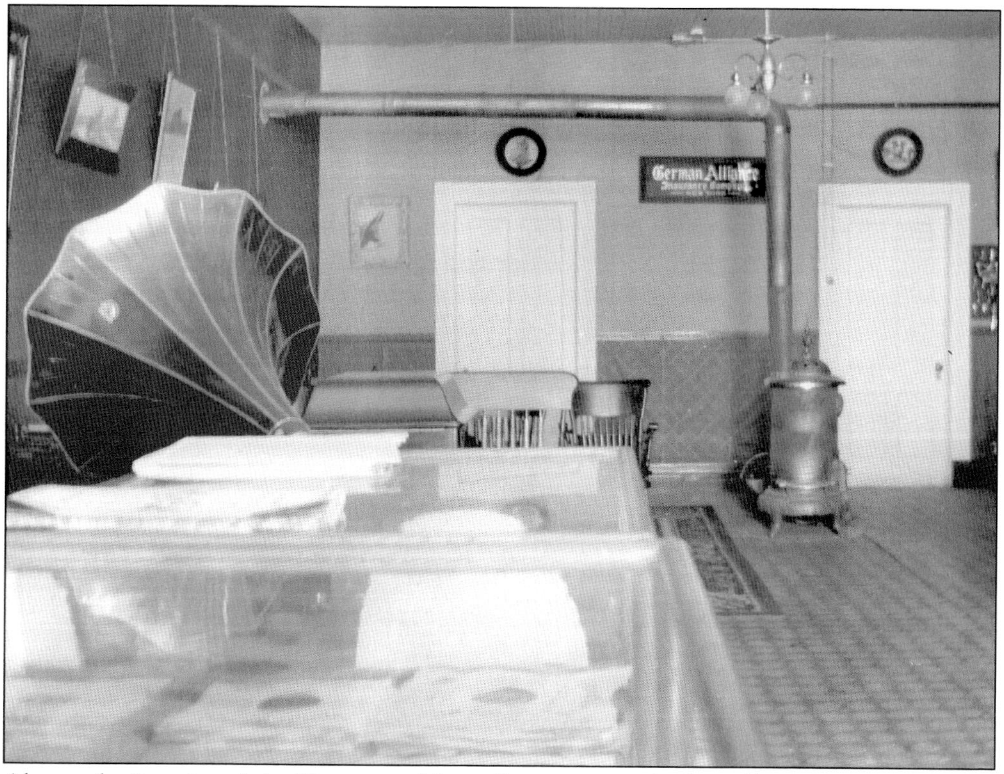

Above, the Interior of the Kuntzman Music Store is typical of a well-scrubbed store of the period. This view is toward the rear of the building. The German Alliance Insurance Company advertisement relates to a company started in the 1880s that is still in business. George Kuntzman was an insurance agent and is therefore likely to have worked for that company. (His son William also engaged in the insurance business in this building in later years.) An enclosed cage in front of the building was used for Kuntzman's insurance office. After the smelter disaster of 1908, George left to manage a hotel in New York and eventually worked the copper mines in Montana. Below, the City Express offered transportation in Grand Encampment. The woman holding the pan is Nan Kuntzman, the supportive wife of George. (Both, courtesy of GEM/Grace Kuntzman Healey.)

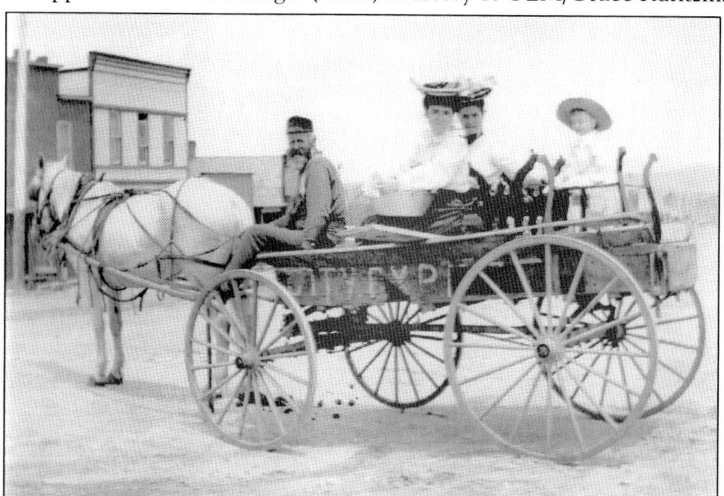

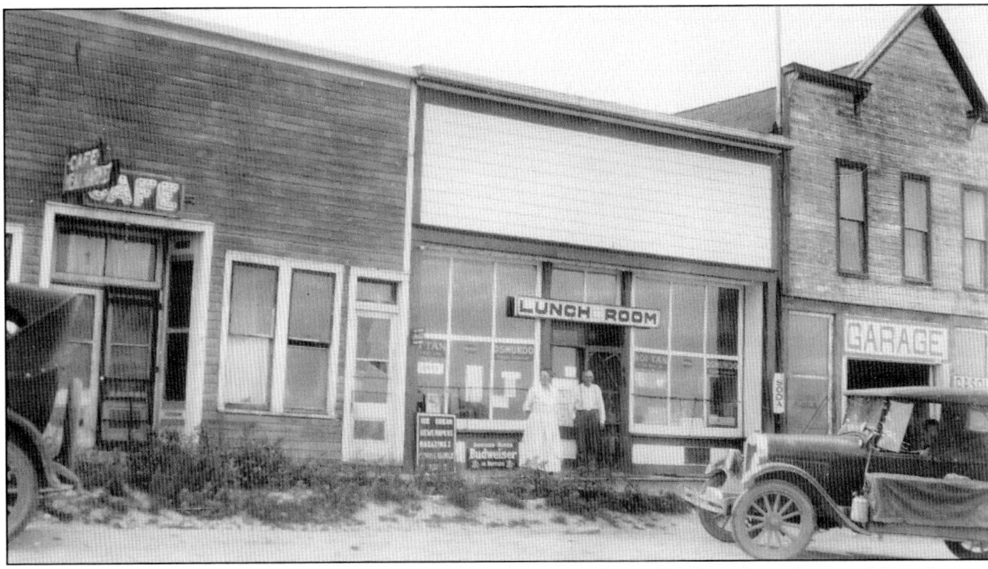

This business-district image includes the Plummer Building, Barbars hot dog and hamburger cafe, Baker's Place (the Double O Bar), and the R.M. Garage. (Courtesy of Candy Vyvey Moulton Collection.)

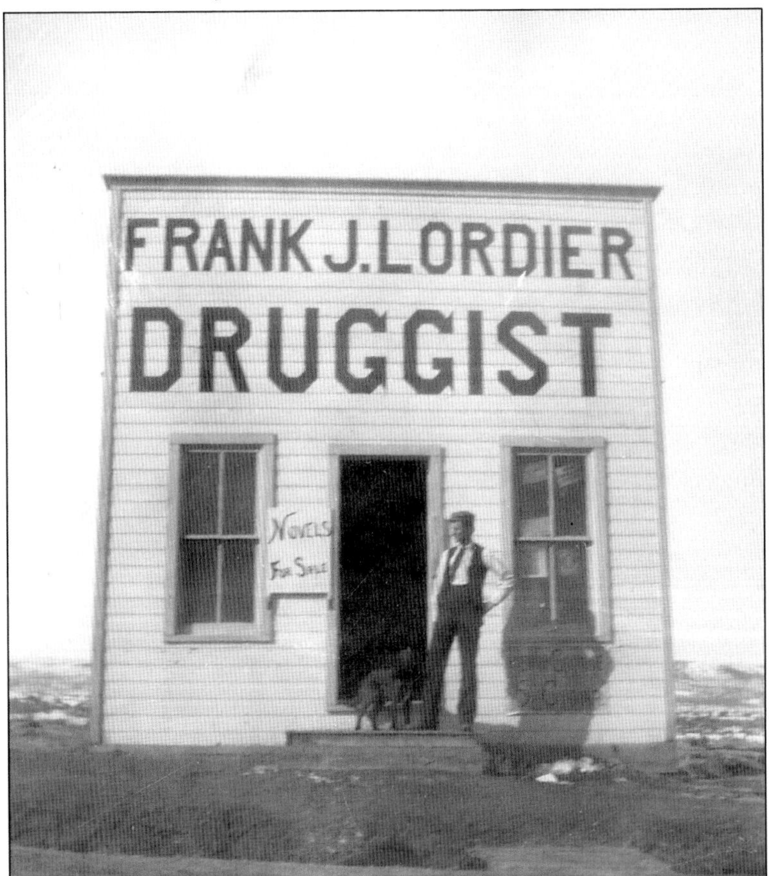

Frank Lordier operated an early drugstore in Grand Encampment. In the shadows is a Henry George 5¢ cigar advertisement. In the 1880s–1890s, Henry was a social philosopher who once ran for mayor of New York but was best known for his "Single Tax" or "Georgist" economics. His book *Progress and Poverty* made him one of the best-known philosophers of the time. The cigars were sold into the early 20th century. (Courtesy of Lora Nichols Collection.)

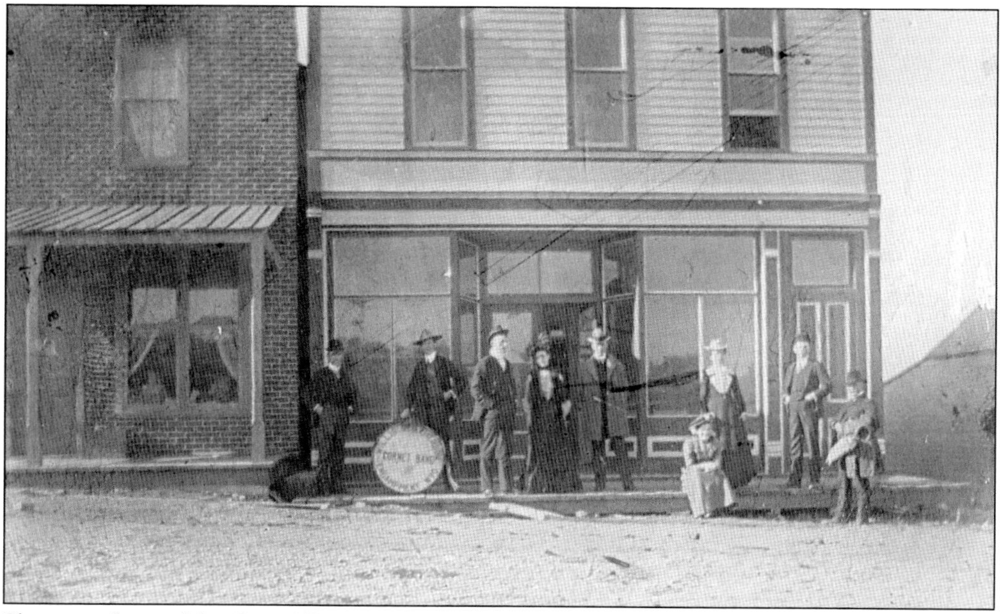

Shown in front of the Grand Encampment Herald building on Thanksgiving Day 1901 are, from left to right, A.E. Holt, Earle R. Clemens, W.C. Drury and wife, attorney Myers, Mary Root, Mrs. E.S. Drury, E.S. Drury, and Phil Rherndon. To the left is the Smith Photo Shop where Lora Nichols learned much of her photograph finishing skill. (Courtesy of GEM/Mrs. Earle Clemens.)

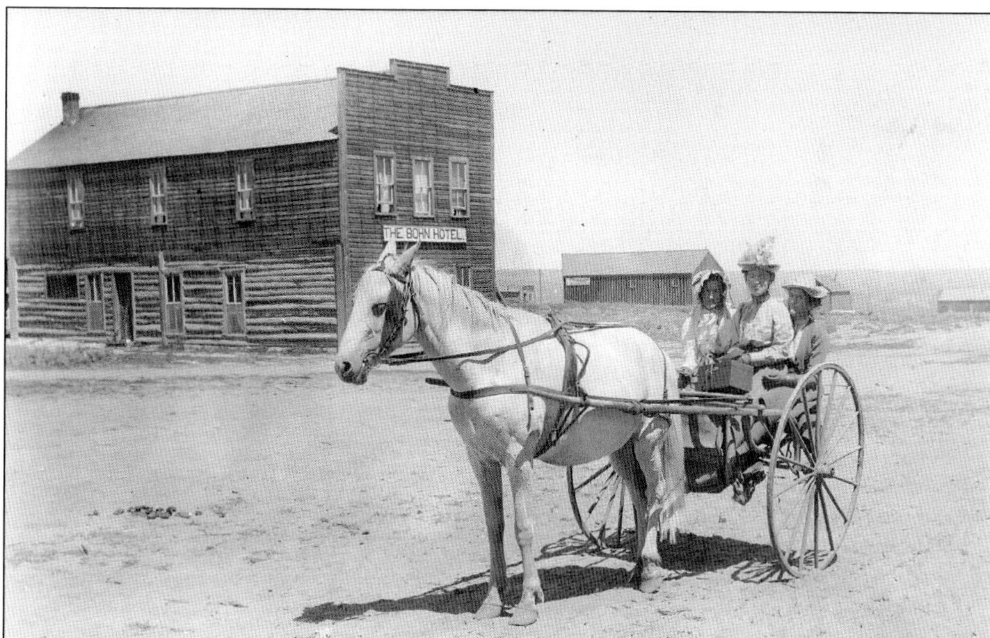

These three unidentified women appear cozy in their cart on Freeman Avenue in front of the Bohn Hotel. Their crowded state may mean they were seated only for the benefit of the photographer, not because they were traveling any great distance. Notable are the gloves worn by the woman at left. This photograph is by J.W. Fisher. (Courtesy of Candy Vyvey Moulton Collection.)

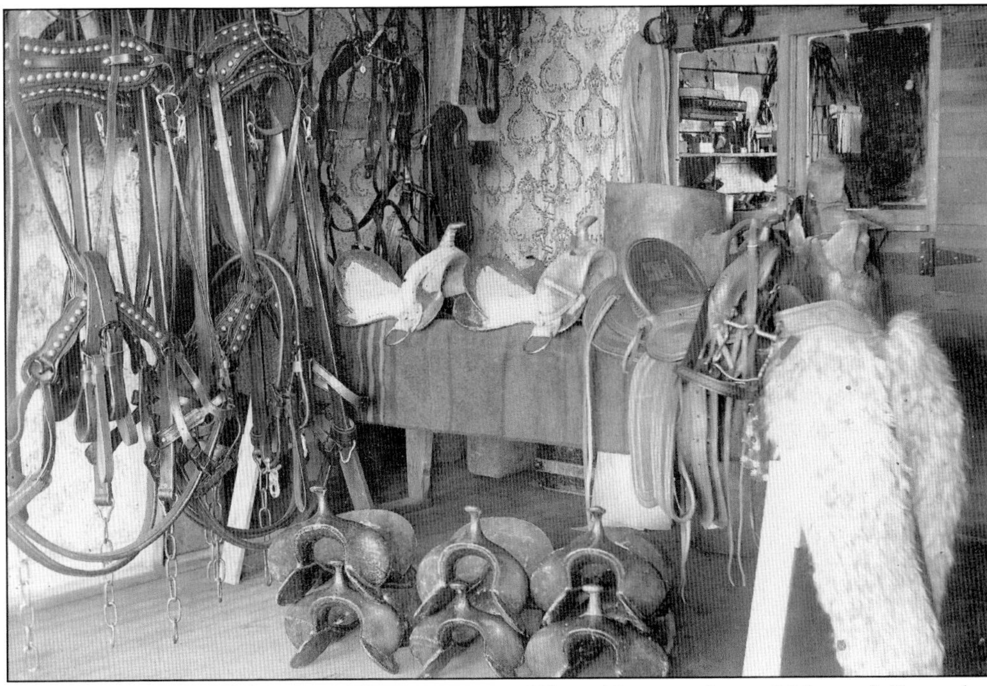

Jake Schmidt operated this Grand Encampment saddle and harness shop, which was fully stocked with saddles, harnesses, wooly chaps, and other tack and gear needed by cowboys and ranchmen. This photograph was taken in about 1911. (Courtesy of GEM.)

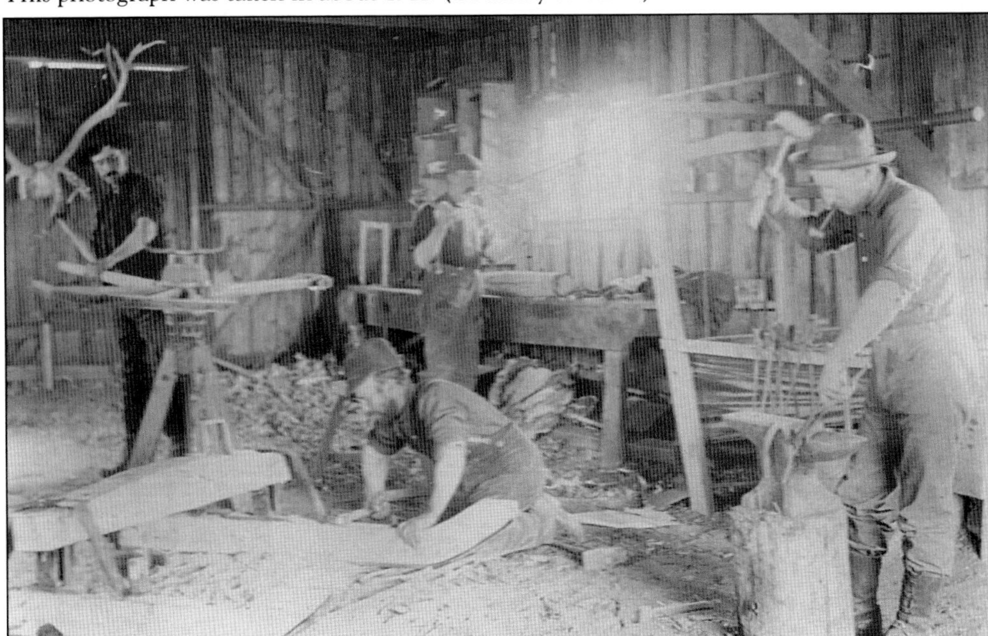

These four men are working in the Ferry and Tappan Blacksmith Shop. In the January 19, 1900, issue of the *Grand Encampment Herald*, A.J. Ferry announced the purchase of a lot on Rankin Avenue where he would build a blacksmith and general repair shop. He intended to "make or repair anything from a wagon to new home furniture." (Courtesy of GEM.)

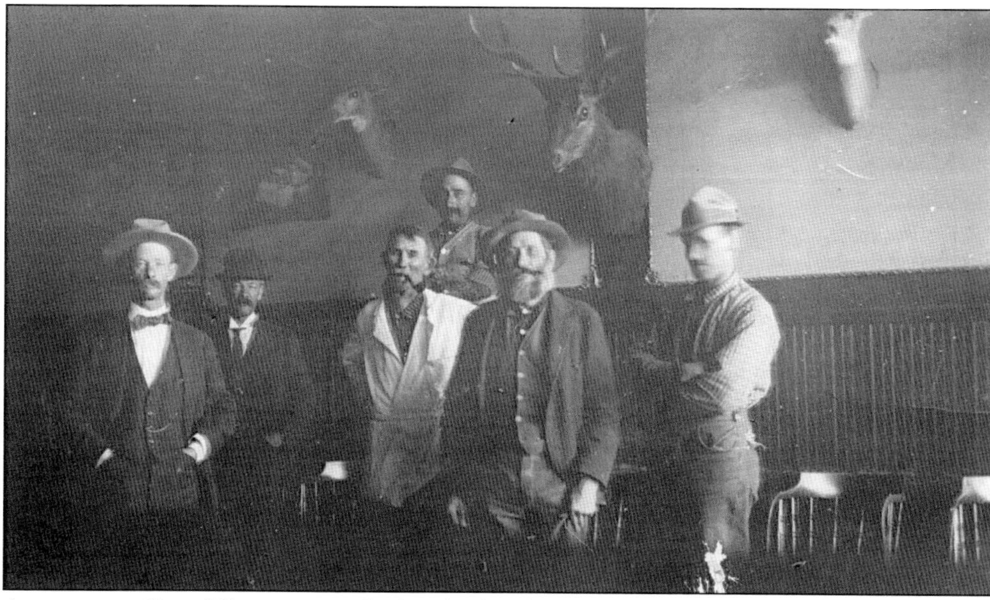

At one time, Grand Encampment had multiple saloons, including the Double O Bar owned by George Baker. From left to right are Pierce Culleton, H.P. "Doc" Culleton, Joe Green, Foster Kerns (in back), Emmett Fields, and unidentified. (Courtesy of GEM/Mamie Culleton Marshall.)

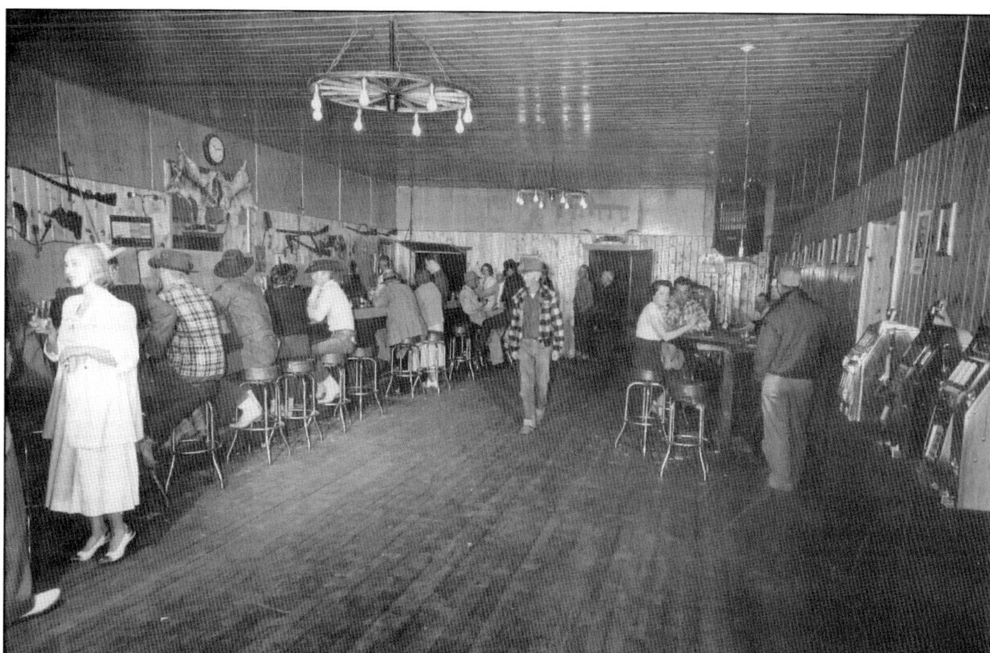

Fires tore through Encampment's business district more than once. Early conflagrations took out many of the saloons and other businesses. The Cowboy Bar remained a favorite watering hole into the 1960s. Shown at far left are Bill and Connie Sidley, Oday Nolde from A Bar A Ranch, Walt and Mrs. Eberhart, Marvin Reid, and John Marshall. The man walking in the center is Ellis Herring. The drinking and the dances in the Cowboy Bar ended when that building too burned one night, never to be replaced. (Courtesy of Candy Vyvey Moulton Collection.)

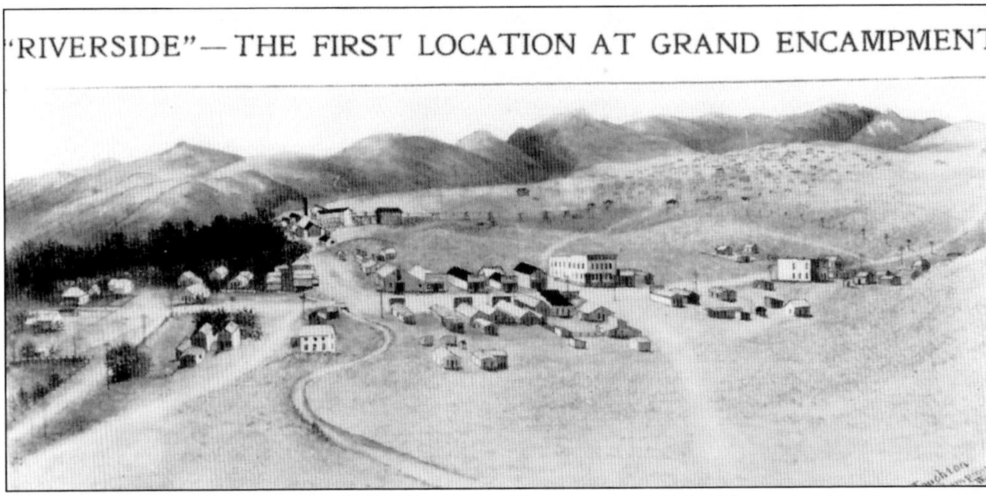

Merritt Dana Houghton prepared this drawing of Riverside in 1902. That town had begun more than a decade earlier and was named Doggett for Newton Doggett, although an early homestead that encompassed a portion of the townsite was filed on by Henry P. "Doc" Culleton. The towns appear linked because they are adjacent to each other, but Riverside and Encampment each have their own governing bodies. (Courtesy of GEM.)

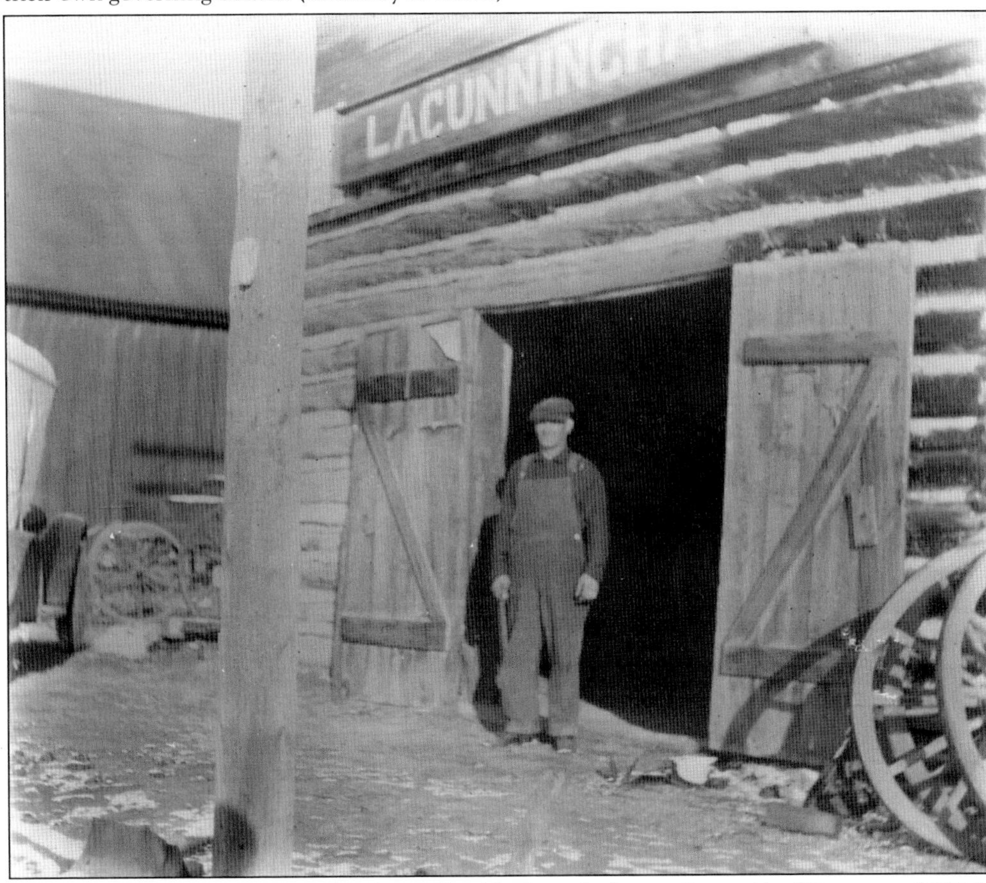

Louis Cunningham appears in the door of his blacksmith shop in Riverside. (Courtesy of GEM.)

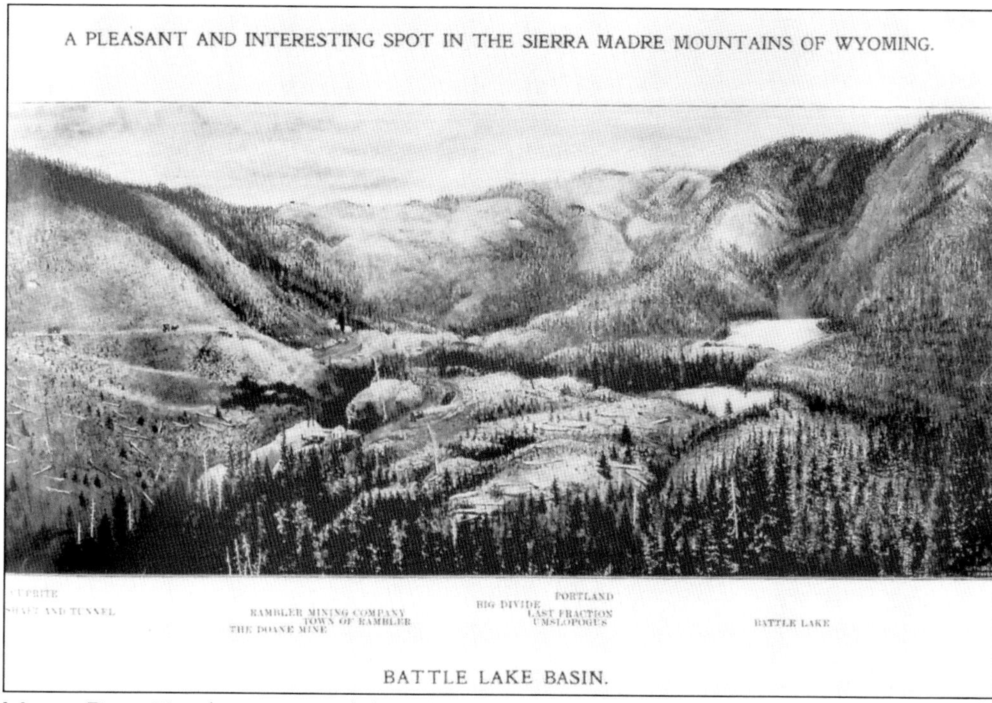

Merritt Dana Houghton prepared this illustration of the Battle Lake Basin, which shows, from left to right, Cuprite Shaft and Tunnel, Rambler Mining Company, the town of Rambler, the Doane Mine (Doane-Rambler), Big Divide, Last Fraction Mine, Portland Mine, and Battle Lake. This view is looking toward the east. (Courtesy of GEM.)

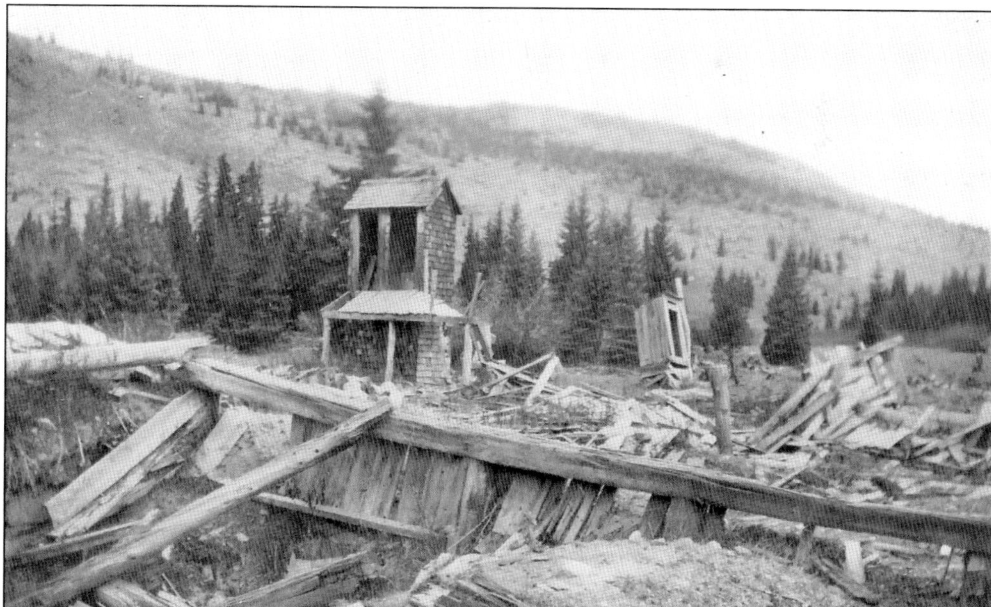

These are the ruins of the Hotel DeMorine at Battle. While Battle, located just east of the Continental Divide, is technically a ghost town because it has no official governing body, there are still cabins and homes in the area that are used seasonally. (Courtesy of GEM.)

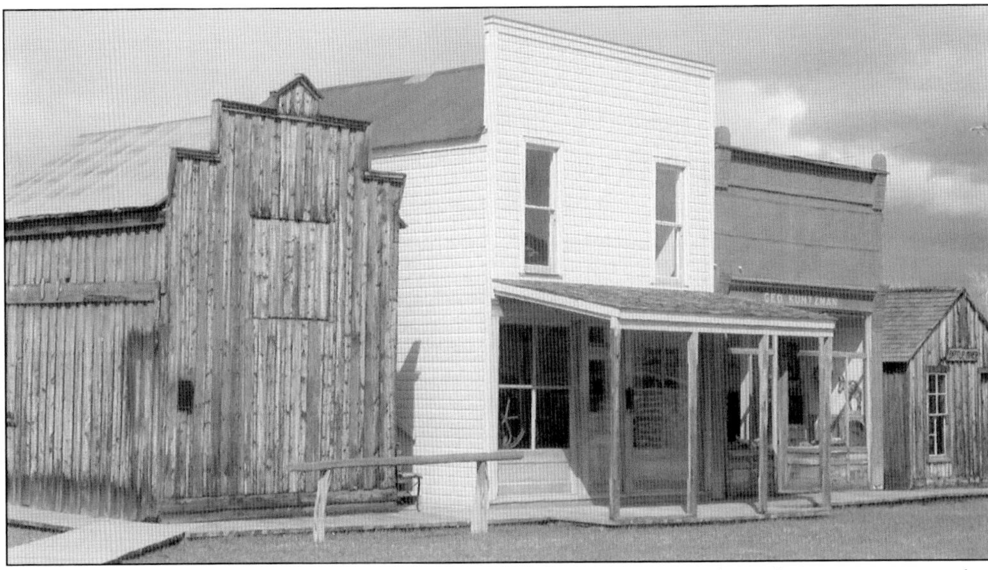

This image shows original buildings from Grand Encampment and nearby communities that form the town at the Grand Encampment Museum, which was started in 1964 by Vera and Bert Oldman and Hila Parkison. During the ensuing decades, additional historic structures have been placed at the museum, including a fire lookout tower, a stage station, and a cabin once used by tie hacks. (Courtesy of Candy Vyvey Moulton Collection.)

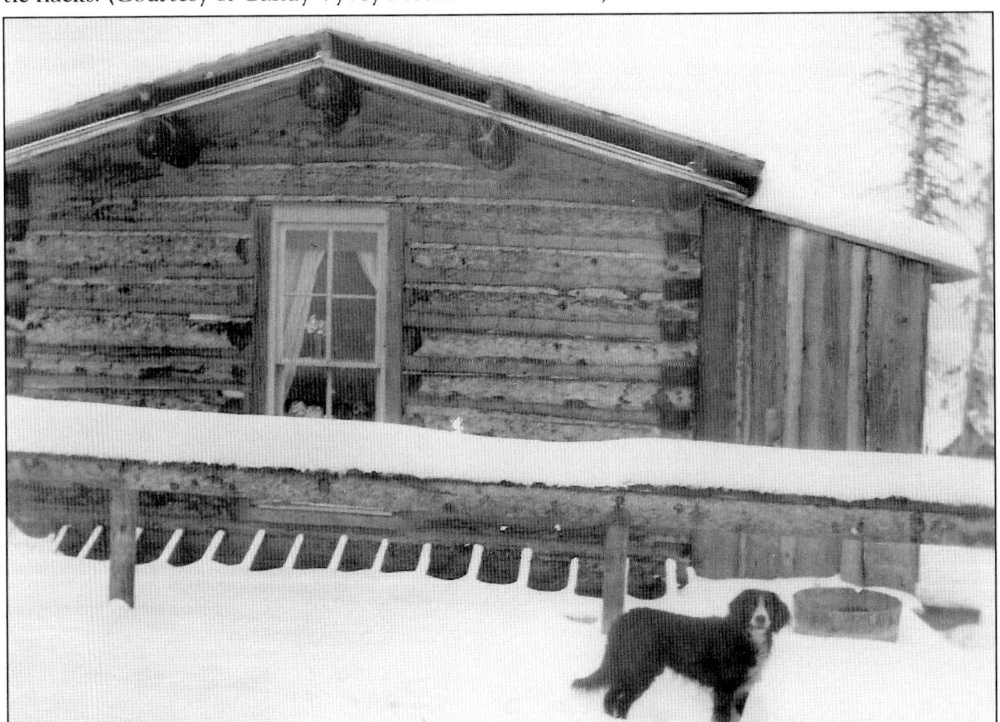

This is the Ledbetter cabin at Battle after a fresh falling of snow. This photograph would have been taken in early fall or late spring, given the depth of snow. This image includes Rex the dog and probably dates to about 1897. (Courtesy of GEM/Jack Ledbetter Collection.)

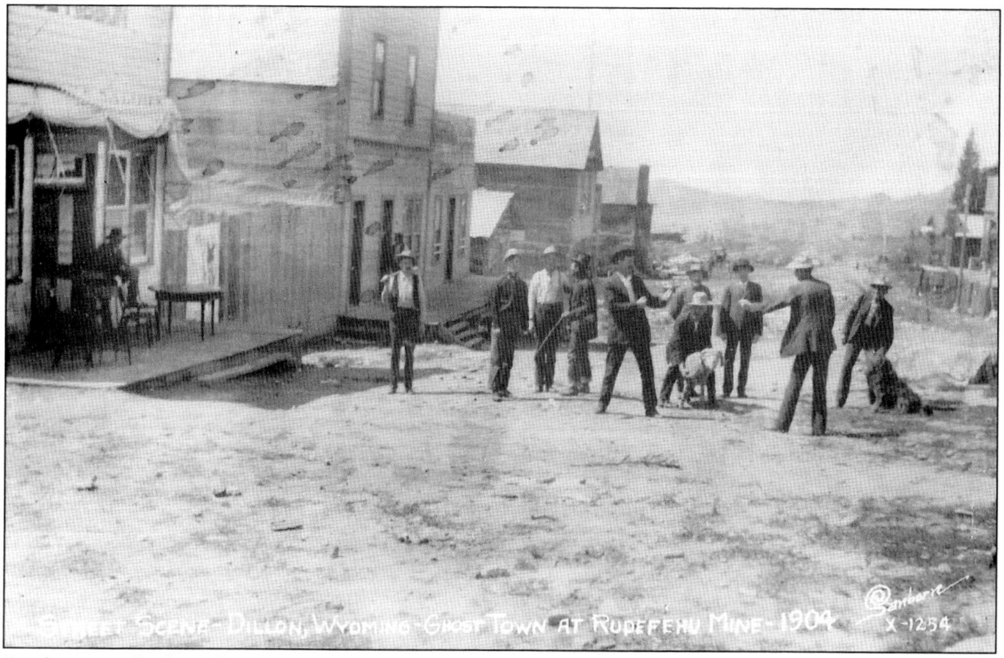

Sanborn took this photograph of the main street in Dillon in 1904. Named for Civil War and Indian War veteran Malachi Dillon who owned the boarding house and saloon, this town began when officials at Rudefeha declared that no liquor could be sold there, as it affected mining operations. Undaunted, the workers relocated to this site a mile downstream and began their new town. (Courtesy of GEM.)

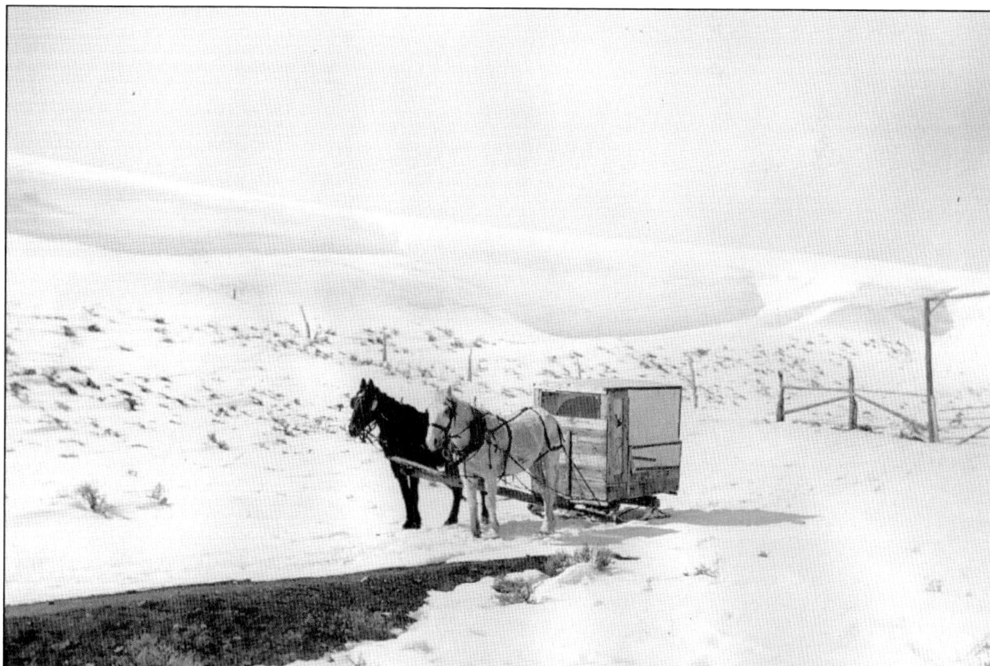

This was the sled used to transport the mail to Beaver Creek during the winter of 1929–1930. This photograph was taken near Bull Canyon. (Courtesy of GEM/Big Creek Ranch Album.)

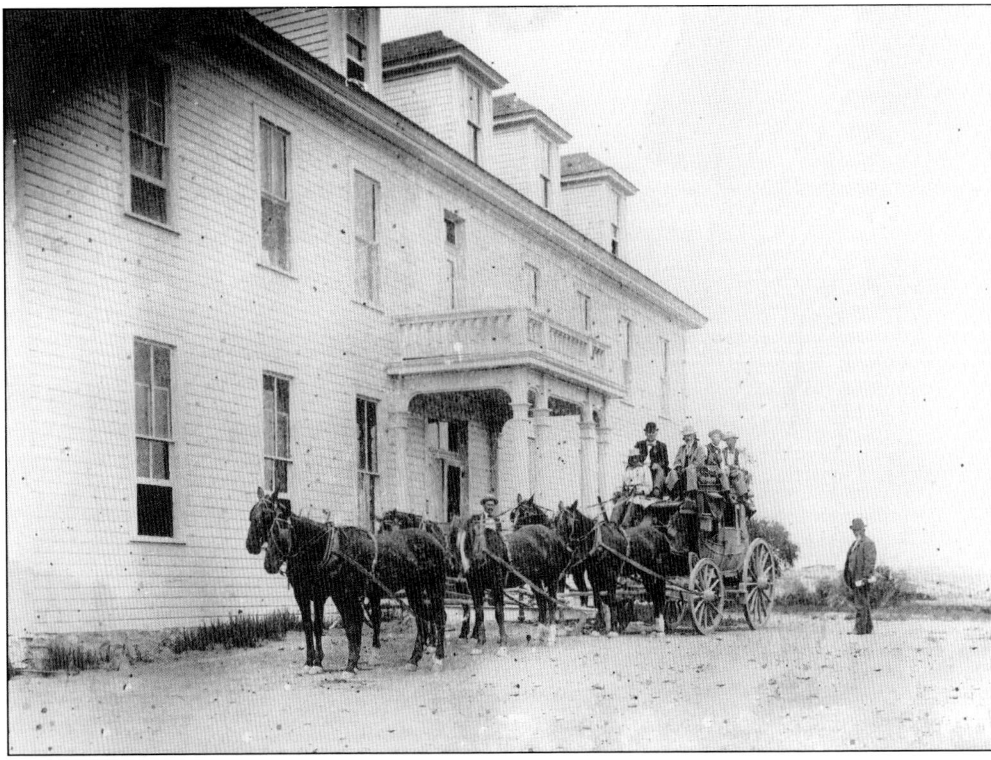

The Scribner Stage, which provided service between Walcott and Grand Encampment, makes a stop at the Caldwell Hotel (Hot Springs Hotel) in Saratoga. (Courtesy of GEM.)

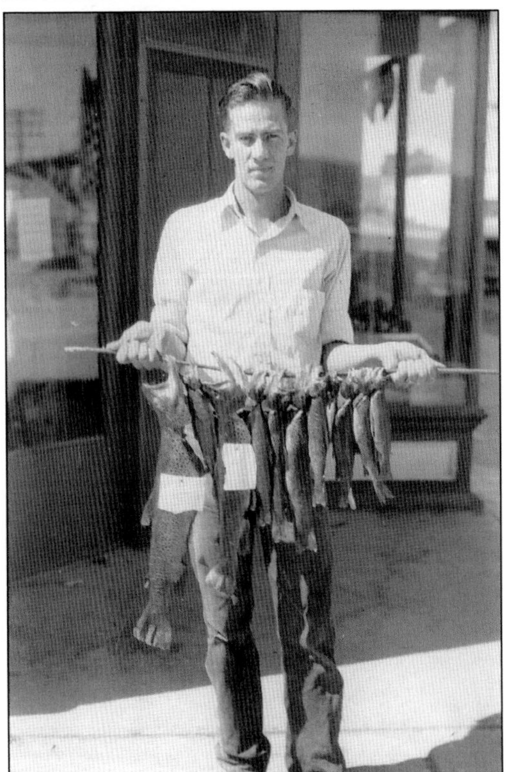

Eugene Herring, approximately age 17 in this c. 1939 image, holds a fine string of fish he caught in the pond behind the pipeline dam west of Encampment. This photograph was taken in front of Kuntzman's Cash Store, a business started by his in-laws and that he and his family operated for 70 years. (Courtesy of Candy Vyvey Moulton Collection.)

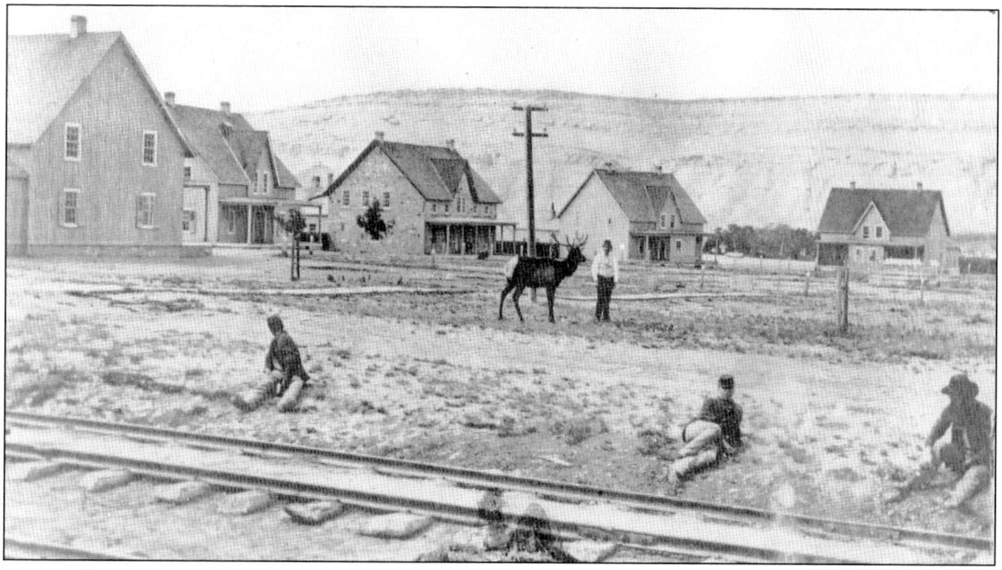

A pet elk of Tom Ryan's stands in front of the officers' quarters at Fort Fred Steele. Union Pacific Railroad tracks appear in the foreground. Fort Steele was established June 30, 1868, to protect Union Pacific tracklayers. It is named for Capt. Frederick Steele, 20th US Infantry, who died January 12, 1868, when he fell from a carriage. (Courtesy of GEM.)

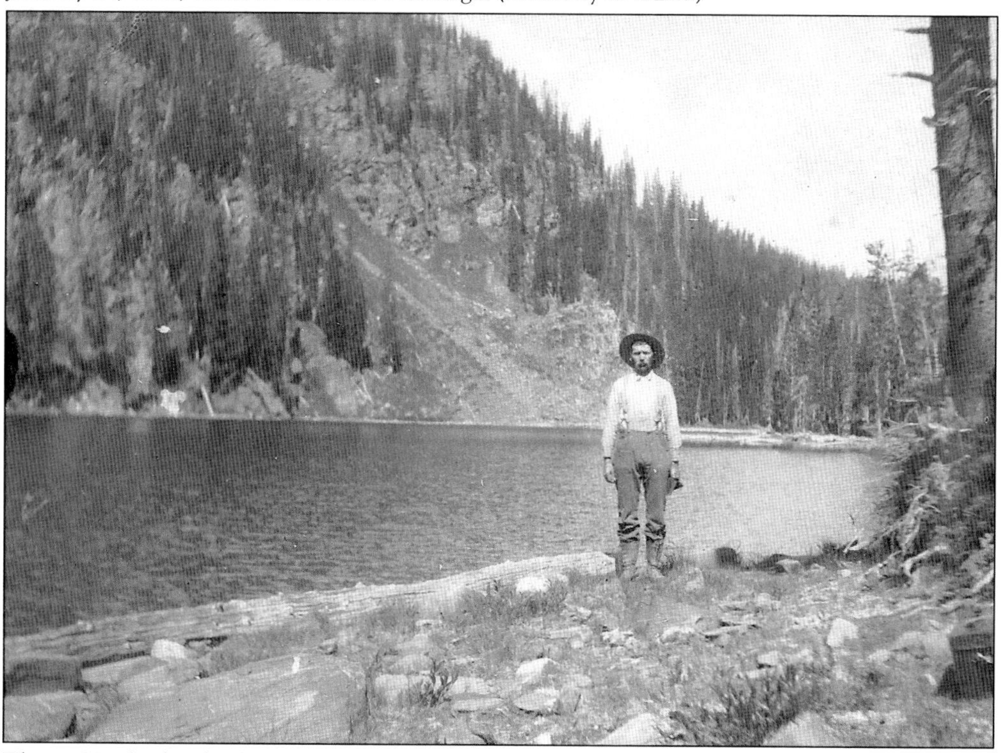

This is Hank Shank, the "scout" at Spring Creek Lake. The authors are sure that Hank would remind all reading this book that the fishing is good here, but when it is not, the fish stories are even better. In the words of Henry David Thoreau, "Many men go fishing all of their lives without knowing that it is not fish they are after." (Courtesy of GEM.)

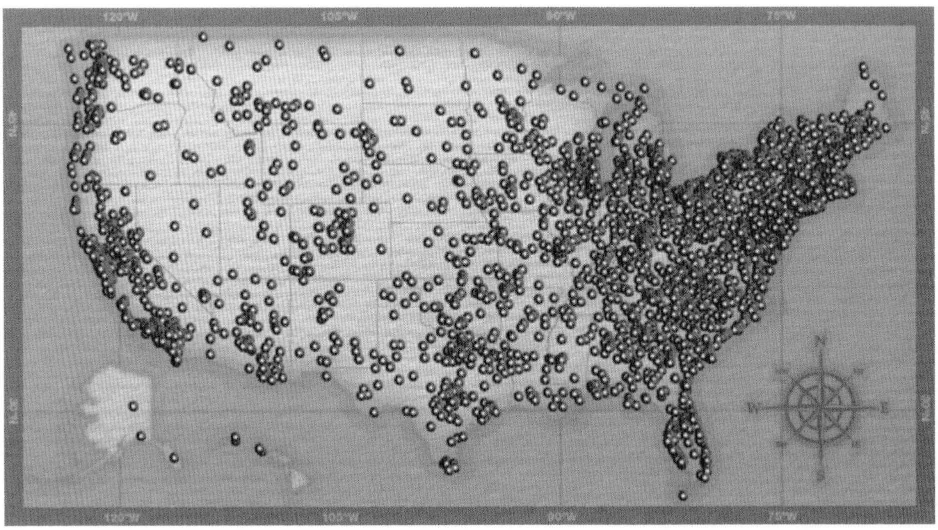

Consistent with our mission to preserve history on a local level, this book was printed in South Carolina on American-made paper and manufactured entirely in the United States. Products carrying the accredited Forest Stewardship Council (FSC) label are printed on 100 percent FSC-certified paper.